A Higher Law

The Life of Orson S. Murray

By

Tom Calarco

Published by Marcia Murray Holstrom

Pioneer Society Chair
Santa Clara County Historical & Genealogical Society
Copyright © 2023 by Tom Calarco

Cover and Book Design by Tom Calarco
All Photos Credited
All artwork from the Public Domain

ISBN: 978-0-9651922-8-6

This book is dedicated to Marcia Murray Holstrom, whose dedication to see a book about her ancestor Orson finally was realized.

Thanks are expressed to Brandon historian and history professor Kevin Thornton for help with information about Murray's life in Vermont, and to historians Karen Dinsmore and John Zimkus for help with information about Ohio.

Thanks go to my co-author of *Secret Lives of the Underground Railroad in New York City* and long-time colleague in researching the Underground Railroad, Don Papson and wife Vivian, who read through the manuscript and immensely improved its clarity.

The author made occasional revisions to quoted text—not affecting meaning or content—to facilitate clarity. Endnotes are appended after the Index and genealogical information.

Author Bio

Tom Calarco is the author / editor of eight books about the Underground Railroad (UGRR). They include The Underground Railroad and the Adirondack Region—for which he won the year 2008 Underground Railroad Free Press award for "Advancement of knowledge in UGRR studies—and Secret Lives of the Underground Railroad in New York City, which he co-authored with Don Papson, published in 2015. He has written for many publications during the last 30 years, including more than a decade as a stringer for antiques publications and as a classical music reviewer. For seven years he wrote the column, "Profiles in Perseverance," which highlighted the achievements of lawyers who overcame great personal obstacles, for the magazine, *Diversity and the Bar.*

Publisher Tribute

After many years of genealogical research and teaching genealogy classes I realized that writing a book about one of my significant ancestors was an important part of this family history process. Tom Calarco has published multiple books about The Underground Railroad and my third great grandfather was a key player in that effort. Fortunately, Tom agreed to tackle the project and working with Tom has been a fascinating process ending in an incredible comprehensive story about Orson Smith Murray. Thank you, Tom, for your professionalism in this process and for using your proven writing talent to bring Orson's story to all of his descendants and to those studying how we overcame a tragic part of our history by eliminating slavery in the United States. Marcia Murray Holstrom

Preface

Orson Murray was a complicated person, a rugged, virile man whose wild appearance made some apprehensive. But there was nothing to fear from this deeply intellectual individual whose golden rule was non-violence and turning the other cheek. Though he also could be rude and arrogant, it was always in the service of what he thought was right and beneficial to others. It is hoped that this work will lead others to explore his life and perhaps create their own interpretations.

Tom Calarco, Lebanon, Ohio, June 22, 2023

Table of Contents

Chapter 1   Beginnings

Chapter 2   Antislavery

Chapter 3   Antislavery Lecturer

Chapter 4   The Second Coming of Christ

Chapter 5   The Clarkson of Vermont

Chapter 6   Mobs, Riots, Tar and Feather

Chapter 7   Early Days of the Telegraph

Chapter 8   Pro-Slavery in Church and State

Chapter 9   The Intrepid Abolitionist

Chapter 10   God Owns His Work

Chapter 11   The Radical Messenger

Chapter 12   Cohorts and Collaborators

Chapter 13   Antislavery Is Our Religion

1

Chapter 14   A Trip, and A Terrible Conflagration

Chapter 15   Fugitive Slaves and God

Chapter 16   Death Under His Roof

Chapter 17   A Non-Government, Woman's Rights Man

Chapter 18   Murray Turns Away from the Church

Chapter 19   Signs of the Times

Chapter 20   The Inconvenient Truth

Chapter 21   The Beginning of the Regeneration

Chapter 22   The Perilous Journey to Ohio

Chapter 23   Coming to Ohio

Chapter 24   The Product of the Soil

Chapter 25   The Underground Railroad and Fruit Hills

Chapter 26   Free Paper for Free Thinkers

Chapter 27   Carlos Emerges

2

Chapter 28   Infamous Witness

Chapter 29   Dying of the Light

Chapter 30   The Grim Reaper

Chapter 31   Robert Cheyne Moves to Fruit Hills

Chapter 32   Here, Now, and Hereafter

Chapter 33   The Mysterious Manifestation: Carlos Speaks

Chapter 34   Extra! Extra! Read All About It!

Chapter 35   A Transition Period

Chapter 36   Murray's Garden

Chapter 37   The Struggle of the Hour

Chapter 38   The Reunion of the Abolitionists

Chapter 39   Grandpa Orson

Chapter 40   Deathbed Thoughts

Chapter 41   Ashes to Ashes, Dust to Dust

Chapter 1

Beginnings

Looking across Lake Champlain from Vermont at McNeil's Ferry

There must've been a comet hailing the birth of Orson Smith Murray on the night of September 23, 1806 in Orwell, Vermont. His father, Jonathan Murray, had recently moved there from Guilford, Connecticut with two uncles. His mother, Roselinda Bascom, had come during childhood with her family from Newport, New Hampshire. Her grandson Charles described her as "a woman of high intelligence, [who] possessed unusual powers of memory."[1]

Orwell was a farming village near Lake Champlain, a little south across the lake from Fort Ticonderoga, a picturesque place surrounded by small furry green mountains; "where earth and air and water give unmeasured recompense; where one feels not the featherweight of care, but luxuriates in the calm, rich gladness that stirs the boughs of the goodly trees, [that] sings in the low murmurs of the lake waves," as one contemporary described it.[2]

His parents were devout, orthodox New England Baptists. Of Scottish descent, Orson had extended family on both sides. His uncle, Eber, was the pioneer resident of Orwell when he came to the Vermont wilderness in 1783 and along with Ephraim and William Fisher founded the First Baptist Church in 1787.[3] Other Murrays followed him. By 1810, there were 16 Murray families in Vermont with nearly 100 total members.[4]

They were pioneers, young families with children. It was a time of great activity, of clearing land, erecting grist mills, sawmills, tanneries, of building roads, and having eleven children— Orson, the oldest. Nearly 70 percent of Vermont was under 26 in 1810, and more than 60 percent of those under 10.[5]

Mining ore, and products made from it, was a major industry.[6] The first blast furnace was constructed in Orwell in 1787 and twenty years later an "inexhaustible" source of iron ore was discovered in nearby Brandon.[7] Prior to the Civil War, there were an estimated 288 blast furnaces, forges, foundries, and kilns, making charcoal, iron, and other metal tools and products like tea kettles, pots, frying pans, bread pans, griddles, and stoves, the majority of them in the south-central region of Vermont where Murray grew up.[8]

Orwell was a prosperous location for farming. It was said at that time there were no poor people living there.[9] Its main crops were wheat, corn, potatoes, maple syrup, and wool.[10] As a youth, Orson was noted for his ability with an ax in chopping down trees. His son Charles wrote of him that "in later life he found pleasure, relief from mental fatigue, and recreation in swinging his axe. He was a rare artist in use of the axe."[11]

Descriptions of him said he was lean and muscular,[12] probably owing to years of physical labor up through his twenties working in the fields. While farm chores were likely a constant in his youth, he showed a great aptitude for "book learning." Silas Wright, the future governor of New York, then a young teacher living nearby, tutored him when he was seven and encouraged him.[13]

Perhaps it was the combination of his inborn intellectual energy and the spiritual Awakening[1] of his age, which gave birth to the reformer in him. Religious revivals were common in Vermont at this time and would be throughout his years living there. One accounting of revivals in the state from the years of 1815-1818 enumerated 45.[14]

Romanticized view of 19th century revival

We can only surmise how the fervor influenced him or such noted spiritual leaders like Joseph Smith, founder of Mormonism, born the year before Murray in Vermont, and William Miller who lived along the Vermont border and predicted the Second Coming of Christ would occur in 1843.

The Awakening was a passionate entreaty to make everything right with God, promising salvation to all who followed the son of God, Jesus Christ. As one of the great evangelists of the era, Charles Finney, proclaimed:

---

[1] There were two Great Awakenings of religious fervor in the U.S. The first led by Massachusetts preacher Jonathan Edwards occurred from 1730-1770; the second which was characterized by the camp meetings occurred from 1800-1830. Its leader was Lorenzo Dow.

Lorenzo Dow

Now the great business of the Church is to reform the world, to put away every kind of sin. The Church of Christ was . . . designed . . . to lift up her voice and put forth her energies against iniquity in high and low places—to reform individuals, communities. and governments, and never rest until . . . until every form of iniquity be driven from the earth[15]

Hundreds of circuit riders often on horseback scoured the nation's virgin countryside bringing the gospel to the formerly lost souls, and numerous religious tracts and periodicals soon were bringing God's word into the farthest reaches of the frontier, promising salvation to those who renounced sin and did good deeds. It proclaimed that they needed to get ready for the imminent Millennium, the second coming of Christ and that all would be judged, the wicked facing eternal damnation. This revival experience touched almost every rural hamlet springing up in America, and by the 1830's, almost every American village had a Sunday school and a chapter of a religious society. It created a great network of Christianity, whose goal was the annihilation of sin.[16] It spawned a moral revolution that would leave its mark for more than a century, inspiring the great reform movements of temperance, abolition, and women's rights and reformers.

Perhaps the greatest of all circuit riders, who made annual lecture tours in Vermont during Orson's formative period, was the legendary Lorenzo Dow.

"In his lifetime [Dow] traveled not less than two hundred thousand miles, preaching to more people than any other man . . . .

He went from New England to the extremities of the Union in the West repeatedly. Several times . . . to Canada, once to the West Indies . . . three times to England, everywhere drawing great crowds about him. Friend of the oppressed, he knew no path but that of duty . . . . Conversant with the Scriptures, intolerant of wrong, witty and brilliant, he assembled his hearers by the thousands."[17]

They often referred to him as Crazy Dow, but he was just all afire with awakening, at least that's how some described him, this man with shoulder-length hair and a flowing beard. What else would possess someone to travel constantly and spread the word about repentance in order to save souls? It wasn't money or pleasure that he sought, but probably it was fame, notoriety, the attention, like celebrities of our time.[18]

He was an inveterate promoter, continually advertising his sermons, pamphlets, and books in the newspapers of the day. "His dress is mean, his voice harsh, gesticulation and delivery ungraceful to the extreme," one contemporary description said, "and his whole appearance and manners calculated to excite the curiosity and wonder of his believers."[19]

Many stories were told about him. One often told was about the man who came before his lecture and asked if he could help in finding the man who stole his ax. Dow assured him he would and told the man to come that evening. Dow brought a large stone and put it on his pulpit. He said he had heard that someone had stolen one of their neighbor's axes. He told the audience that he knew who it was and that the man had better duck because – he paused and picked up the stone – because I'm going to hit him in the head with this stone. Dow made a motion as though to throw it and the man who stole the ax ducked.[20]

He was kind to his friends but harsh to those who opposed him much like the man Murray would become.

On May 13, 1820, a chunk of earth the size of five football fields near the Murray farm broke off and sunk into Lake Champlain.[21] Perhaps locals might've attributed some spiritual significance to it. Perhaps it influenced Orson who shortly after was baptized into the Freewill Baptist Church and developed aspirations for the ministry, and took up his first cause, Temperance, at the age of 17.[22]

Murray would remain temperate throughout his life not only in drink but in diet and while not a teetotaling vegetarian, close to it, subscribing to the diet principles of Sylvester Graham that "bad eating is as great an evil as bad drinking."[23]

He married his first wife, Catherine Higgins in 1827, putting his vocation on hold. During these years, he also attended Shoreham Academy and Castleton Seminary. Formal schooling had not been provided to him as a boy.[24] He and Catherine also welcomed two boys into their household: Carlos in 1828 and Marsena in 1829.

Licensed as a Baptist minister about 1830 (listed as living in Shoreham during the 1830 census), he only occasionally tended to his ministerial duties and instead expressed his views through contributions to the various periodicals of the time, his first published article in 1831 discussing Temperance.[25]

Chapter 2

Antislavery

Among all his many interests and convictions, antislavery would become his greatest passion. His mentor was William Lloyd Garrison and his early attacks on the Colonization movement, which were published in *The Liberator* and as a monograph, "Thoughts on Colonization."

The scheme of removing free blacks from America and sending them to Africa was the brainchild of the American Colonization Society, which was founded in 1816 by some of the most illustrious figures of the founding of the U.S., including Thomas Jefferson, James Madison, James Monroe, Chief Justice John Marshall, Senator Henry Clay, and Francis Scott Key. Its purpose was to send both free and enslaved blacks to Africa to form their own nation, which they named Liberia.[II]

While ostensibly benevolent, there were other motives. For instance, Jefferson had written that the "amalgamation [of blacks] with other colors produces a degradation to which no lover of this country, no lover of excellence in human character, can innocently consent."[26] That one of our greatest founding fathers, revered as a champion of liberty wrote something so blatantly racist shows the depth of racism that existed at the founding of our nation.

Fear undoubtedly was another factor. Continual slave insurrections, the first major revolt planned in 1800 by Gabriel Prosser, whose conspiracy involved thousands of Virginia and most recently the far bloodier insurrection led by Nat Turner in 1830

[II] The first colonists, free black Americans, were shipped to Liberia in 1822 (https://www.history.com/news/slavery-american-colonization-society-liberia).

brought even greater urgency to the plan. For this reason, not only were they reluctant to free the slaves, fearing retribution, but they looked for a plan of emigration.

Along with the prohibition of the international slave trade in 1807, the Colonization Society imagined itself to be another step on the road to gradual emancipation. In Africa, it alleged, blacks would have the freedom to form a life on their own terms without the legacy of slavery hindering them.

However, most blacks in the U.S. considered America their home. As early as 1817, 3,000 blacks met in Philadelphia to consider the idea of migrating to Africa.[27] Leading it was Bishop Richard Allen of the American Methodist Episcopal Zion (AMEZ) Church. The meeting house resounded with the word, no, when attendees were asked if they approved of the idea.[28] Black leaders later charged that the Colonization Society's propaganda served to increase racial discrimination because it stressed that the poverty and ignorance of free blacks in America was the result of their natural inferiority. Those opposed to Colonization also believed that sending free blacks from America to Africa would allow slavery to endure and pledged never to abandon their brothers in slavery.[III]

This wasn't readily apparent to whites because of the professed benevolence of the Colonization Society and its support from religious institutions. But more significant was racial segregation, which prevented whites from knowing the true wishes of blacks. In

---

[III] "Disclaiming, as we emphatically do, a wish or desire to interpose our opinions and feelings between the plan of Colonization and the judgment of those whose wisdom as far as exceeds ours as their situations are exalted above ours, we humbly, respectfully, and fervently entreat and beseech your disapprobation of the plan of Colonization now offered by the American Society for colonizing the free people of color of the United States . . ." (Louis Mellinger, "The Attitude of Free Negroes to Colonization," *Journal of Negro History*, 1916: 279).

fact, many who later embraced immediate emancipation were advocates of Colonization, among them the Tappans, Birney, Gerrit Smith, and William Lloyd Garrison.

Editor of the *Journal of the Times* in Bennington from 1828-1829, Garrison, like the majority who were white in Vermont,[IV] opposed slavery and supported gradual emancipation. Most Vermonters then believed that slavery was a state matter, which was the then traditional view of the matter, and only the slave states had the right to abolish it.

William Lloyd Garrison

Ironically, it was a pro-Colonization meeting that led Garrison to change his views. Pioneer antislavery editor, Benjamin Lundy, was there and he invited him to Baltimore to help with Lundy's *Genius of Emancipation*, and he accepted.

There Garrison immersed himself in the black community, attending the Sabbath in black churches, and saw firsthand the evils of slavery. Not only did it convince him that slavery needed immediate abolition, but that Colonization was a mistake.

Garrison returned to Boston and on January 1, 1831, launched his weekly newspaper, *The Liberator*. A year later he organized the New England Anti-Slavery Society and published "Thoughts on Colonization" in which he exposed the racist intent of the Colonization Society.

The Anti-Slavery Society summarized it in a resolution stating, "The plan of colonizing the blacks in Africa . . . is preposterous in the extreme, and every attempt to put its principles into operation is an unrighteous persecution, levelled against the free people of color, to secure and perpetuate slavery in our country."[29]

[IV] According to the 1830 U.S. census, there were 279,776 whites and 881 blacks living in the state.

Their annual report also noted the disapproval of the Colonization Society by twenty black communities, including those in Philadelphia, New York, Boston, Baltimore, and the District of Columbia.[30]

When Murray became aware of these sentiments about Colonization is uncertain. But at least as early as January 8, 1831, one week after launching *The Liberator*, Garrison published an anti-Colonization news item. More detailed information was published in the May 5, 1832 issue which reported the New England society's reasons for opposing the Colonization Society.[31]

The first we know of Murray's interest comes from the October 2, 1832 issue of the *Vermont Telegraph*, five years before he became its proprietor. In a letter to the editor, he complained that his comment, renouncing the pro-Colonization views in the *Rutland Herald* written by someone who signed off as CW, was rejected for publication. Murray had alleged that the writer's comments that the Colonization society was benevolent, that it would benefit slaves and free people of color, in both America and Africa, were untrue.

The *Telegraph* was not sympathetic, explaining that: "We thought that it was evident that he was inclined to adopt the enthusiastic and visionary views of the Boston Liberator; and it was our opinion that an exhibition of these views would prove less interesting and profitable, and less welcome to the great mass of our readers . . ."[32]

However, two weeks later, it published Orson's submission. In it, he compared how the number of slaves who were being sent to Africa and freedom by the society to how many more were being enslaved during the same period, showing clearly that the society was not contributing to gradual emancipation, that instead slavery was actually growing: "I call on C.W. or any man to correct me, that members of the society in slave-holding states actually seize and drag into bondage far more than they liberate, by a ten-fold proportion."[33]

It was the first of a series of attacks on Colonization that he wrote in the next two years for the *Telegraph* and history would support his contention. Only 13,000 colonists were sent from America to Liberia after by the time of the Civil War while the slave population doubled from two million to four million from the years 1830-to-1860.[34] In addition, an estimated 50,000 Africans were smuggled into the U.S. after the International Slave Trade was outlawed in 1808.[35]

Chapter 3

Antislavery Lecturer

Murray would soon become an infamous antislavery lecturer in Vermont. But he was not the first to test its abolition waters there. In May and June of 1832, the New England Anti-Slavery Society sent Peacham, Vermont native, Oliver Johnson on a lecture tour through

the state. Johnson had become friends with Garrison when he moved to Boston and began his own newspaper, *The Christian Soldier*, which debuted the same year as *The Liberator*. Their offices were adjoined for more than a year.[36]

Oliver Johnson

Four years younger than Garrison,[V] Johnson was already an admirer of him, having followed the latter's Bennington newspaper, *The Journal of the Times,* when Johnson was serving an apprenticeship at *The Watchman* in Montpelier. After his move to Boston, they became lifelong friends.[37]

Apparently, Johnson's lectures caused little stir at the time, but no societies had been formed. The state's first antislavery society wasn't founded until almost a year later in the village of Jamaica, Vermont where "[A resolution in favor of The Colonization Society] was the subject of spirited discussion for five or six [weeks]," but

---

[V] Murray was only a year younger than Garrison.

was voted down. Instead, the following was passed, "that the Colonization Society, instead of weakening the chains of slavery, has a direct tendency to strengthen them; therefore, is unworthy of our support."[38]

But the battle over public opinion was not over and the  Colonization society's continuous propaganda won over the majority.[39] While those in Vermont were from the earliest time opposed to slavery, they supported gradual emancipation at this time and had been persuaded by the arguments of the Society and its support from the religious denominations of its good intentions. Furthermore, animosity towards Garrison, whom Murray supported, was widespread because of what at that time was considered Garrison's bold and unpopular views. This was the situation Murray faced when hired in May 1833 to lecture for the New England Society for a three-month period, being paid $125 (about $4,000 today).[40]

Like the earlier circuit riders, he took his message on horseback through the rugged wilderness roads that connected the Vermont farming communities.[41] While circuit riders were usually welcomed as bringers of the good news, what Murray encountered was a series of threatening mobs. The following is Murray's description of one of his early confrontations in Middlebury:

During the discourse there was scraping of feet,

AGENCY IN VERMONT.

☞ We are authorised to announce, that Mr. Orson S. Murray of Shoreham, Addison Co., Vermont, has been appointed an Agent of the New-England Anti-Slavery Society in that State. He is recommended to the people of Vermont, as a man eminently worthy of their highest confidence and esteem.

The Liberator, May 4, 1833

frequent showering of corn over the room, and other disturbances designed to break up the meeting; but I succeeded in getting through. The next day I was informed that the disturbers were principally college students, friends of the Colonization Society, who went with corn in their pockets and canes in their hands, with a view to put down the fanaticism . . ."[42]

However, the *Middlebury Argus* was not sympathetic: "Mr. Murray's mission ought to be and in fact is denounced by every friend of his country as foolish and misguided . . . . New England has no business interfering with the property of the citizens of Virginia or attempt to control its municipal regulations in regard to that property. The acquirement or the relinquishment of it is a matter peculiarly their own and about which we have no right to dictate."[43]

Fortunately, a local clergyman prevented the mob in Middlebury from carrying out any violence against Murray.

Similar responses occurred at succeeding meetings in Rutland and Castleton, where "a gang of boys . . . talked, ran about the room, opened and shut the door, burnt powder on the stove" and continuously disturbed his lecture.[44]

Murray was undeterred. A month later, he took a 200-mile journey to Philadelphia as the only representative from Vermont to attend the formation of the American Anti-Slavery Society, which was the brainchild of Garrison.[45] He didn't write about it, but John Greenleaf Whittier did and expressed the anxiety that Orson must've felt on his journey and the level of fear they faced at this time.

I was unused to travelling; Whittier recalled. My life had been spent on a secluded farm; and the journey, mostly by stagecoach, at that time was really a formidable one. Moreover, the few abolitionists were everywhere spoken against, their persons threatened, and in some instances a price set on their heads by Southern legislators. Pennsylvania was on the borders of slavery, and it needed small effort of imagination to picture . . . the breaking up of the Convention and maltreatment of its members. This latter consideration I do not think weighed much with me, although I was better prepared for serious danger than for anything like personal indignity. I had read Governor Trumbull's description of the tarring and feathering of his hero MacFingal, when, after the application of the melted tar, the featherbed was ripped open and shaken over him[VI] . . . and I confess I was quite unwilling to undergo a martyrdom which my best friends could scarcely refrain from laughing at.[46]

Samuel May corroborated this in his memoir, writing that most newspapers at that time were not supportive of abolitionists and were encouraging their opponents, "who dealt in brickbats, rotten eggs, and tar and feathers." The police advised that they could not protect him in the evening, so their meetings had to be conducted during daylight. We were denounced, he wrote, as "fanatics, amalgamationists, disorganizers, disturbers of the peace, and dangerous enemies of the country."[47]

Whittier took the stage to Boston and met with Garrison with whom he traveled the rest of the way. Railroads were in their infancy then and travel was either by stagecoach or boat. To get to Philadelphia from New England meant going by coach all the way to New York City or taking a stage to Albany and a steamer to New York. Murray may have ridden by horseback to Albany, however.[48] From New York, another steamer would take them to New Jersey and from there a short stage ride to another steamer and Philadelphia, as Samuel May described in his account of his trip to the meeting.[49]

[VI] This refers to an 18th century poem that depicts a tar and feathering; in fact, two years later, William Lloyd Garrison was nearly tarred and feathered on the streets of Boston.

On the morning of the first day of the gathering, Beriah Green, president of the Oneida Institute, the manual labor college noted for its enrollment of black men, was chosen to preside. Green had been pastor of the Congregational Church in nearby Brandon when Murray was a teenager. Sixty-two delegates were in attendance.

Whittier provided this description:

Looking over the assembly, I noticed that it was mainly composed of comparatively young men, some in middle age, and a few beyond that period. They were nearly all plainly dressed, with a view to comfort rather than elegance. Many of the faces turned towards me wore a look of expectancy and suppressed enthusiasm; all had the earnestness which might be expected of men engaged in an enterprise beset with difficulty and perhaps with peril.[50]

Among the luminaries of abolitionist history there were Garrison, May, Whittier, Green, Elizur Wright, Dr. Bartholomew Fussell, James Miller McKim, Lewis Tappan, Robert Purvis, William Goodell, and Lucretia Mott, not a member but an observer because of her sex, and Orson S. Murray.[51]

A committee was appointed to compose the principles of the society, which deferred to Garrison, who drew them up overnight for presentation the next day. The committee recommended some minor revisions, and the basic principles of the society and the antislavery movement were established that continued until the Civil War.[52]

Its preamble began with these immortal words of abolitionist lore: Whereas the Most High God 'hath made of one blood all nations of men to dwell on all the face of the earth,' and hath commanded them to love their neighbors as themselves . . . . We believe we owe it to the oppressed, to our fellow citizens who hold slaves, to our whole country, to posterity, and to

God, to do all that is lawfully in our power to bring about the extinction of slavery.[53]

It advocated the use of persuasion or "moral suasion" as they called it, of using logic and moral common sense to show the slaveholders their errors. At the same it would never resort to force or violence in their effort to persuade. Slavery needed to be abolished in the District of Columbia and the new territories, and they called on Congress to carry it forward. They also demanded ending the domestic slave trade which allowed the auctioning on  stage of slaves like furniture to the highest bidder, some that were then being conducted within site of the White House, auctions that were sometimes used as a punishment to send a slave to the Deep South where the working conditions were exhausting and greatly shortened their lives. It condemned Colonization and affirmed the principle that "All men are created equal and endowed by their creator with certain inalienable rights," but scolded the Founding Fathers for their failure to end slavery.

It rejected the idea of compensation to the slaveholders because "slavery is a crime, and human beings are not objects for sale." But it recognized the right of each state to decide on the legality of slavery within its boundaries and in which Congress had no right to interfere. Consequently, they stressed the moral obligation of those in the Free states to use their words and influence to change the opinions of the southerners. But opposing those so heavily invested, financially and emotionally in the continuance of slavery, was not going to be easy.

They certainly tried, some fanatically, pledging to organize anti-slavery societies, circulate anti-slavery literature, enlist the clergy and the newspapers, send agents to spread their message, purify the churches, strongly discouraged the return of fugitive slaves but cautioned the slaves against insurrection. Its standards were high and support unanimous.[54]

Samuel May described the occasion as they prepared to sign their "Declaration of Sentiments":

> I cannot describe the holy enthusiasm which lighted up every face as we gathered around the table on which the Declaration lay, to put our names to that sacred instrument. It seemed to me that every man's heart was in his hand, — as if everyone felt that he was about to offer himself a living sacrifice in the cause of freedom, and to do it cheerfully. There are moments when heart touches heart, and souls flow into one another. That was such a moment. I was in them and they in me; we were all one.[55]

Murray was inspired, and with his spirit fortified, he arranged for a meeting in Bennington on his way back home. When he entered the meeting house, he found a group already assembled discussing whether to allow him to speak.

> The Colonization Society was spoken of with warm approbation, as being the best plan, having for its object not only the amelioration of the condition of the colored population, but also of spreading the gospel to the heathen of Africa and giving them the blessings of civilization. A zeal worthy of the importance of the subject pervaded the meeting and it was unanimously voted that they were not in favor of hearing the address, and Murray was invited to leave the house.[56]

He had better luck the next day speaking to a "full house" in nearby Factory Village, which gave him "good attention.[57] Riding horseback over snow-covered mountains, he made one last stop in the village of Rupert, 40 miles south of Orwell, and organized his first antislavery society, the fourth in Vermont, before returning home.

Chapter 4

The Second Coming of Christ

William Miller Farmhouse

"Behold the Judge is at the door. Soon, very soon, we will be attendants at the burial of nature." [58]

The signs of the times seemed to augur the Second Coming of Christ. And the man who recognized them lived less than a day's ride from Murray's Orwell, about 15 miles south in Low Hampton, N.Y.

William Miller had begun preaching his prophecy after fifteen years of intense study of the Bible. A devout Baptist, he had grown up in a pious family, one of sixteen children. His grandfather,

Elnathan Phelps, was the first pastor of the Orwell Baptist Church of which Orson's uncle, Eber Murray, was a founder.

Miller was a voracious reader as a boy, reading books by the fireplace of his family's farmhouse, and had a remarkable memory. After serving with distinction during the War of 1812, fighting in the victorious Battle of Plattsburgh, and rising to the rank of Captain, Miller went home to farming and his family, and became the local Justice of Peace. He also experienced a religious awakening that initiated his study of the Bible.[59]

Aided by his photographic memory, Miller became so versed in the Bible that he could "not only repeat almost any passage, but name the exact place, book, chapter verse where it can be found."[60] During that period there was much conjecture about the Second Coming of Christ. For instance, the Shaker religion which arose during the close of the First Great Awakening was based on preparation for the Second Coming, and others. But how the ideas then circulating influenced Miller is not known. He focused his study on the prophecies and believed he had discovered the time of the "Second Coming," using a complex system based on prophecies in the books of *Daniel* and *Revelation* to arrive at a generalized date when the Apocalypse would occur.[61] While he insisted he did not know the exact date, he believed it to be sometime in 1843.

He discussed his prediction privately with others for 13 years until finally in 1831, he felt the obligation to make it public when he was invited to speak at the Baptist Church in Dresden, NY. It was an empowering experience.

"As soon as I commenced speaking," he later wrote, "all my diffidence and embarrassment were gone, and I felt impressed only with the greatness of the subject, which, by the providence of God, I was enabled to present."[62]

Surprisingly, his message was enthusiastically received, and he was asked to return. "They flocked in from neighboring towns," and "a revival commenced . . . . From thence I went to . . . other towns

. . . . Churches were thrown open everywhere, and I lectured to crowded houses through the western part of Vermont, the northern part of New York, and in Canada East [Quebec] . . ."[63]

The next year he began a series of columns that year and in 1833 in the *Telegraph*, explaining how he had used the prophecies in the Bible to calculate the time of the Second Coming, signing them W.M. This was three years before Murray became its publisher: "At the earnest solicitation of some of your readers, I have consented to give my views of the personal reign of Christ, through the medium of the Telegraph," he wrote.[64] He followed with another lengthier commentary in the next issue, beginning, "I shall begin by showing that his coming is the first great event, to which the church is directed to look for her deliverance."[65]

In the March 12, 1833 issue, he referenced the eleventh chapter of Revelations, verses 11-19, to illustrate his theory.

Verse 15: " 'And the seventh angel sounded; and there were great voices in heaven, saying. The kingdoms of this world are become the kingdoms of our Lord and his Christ, and he shall reign forever and ever.' This will soon be fulfilled.

"Many servants of God, who wait upon the altar, and observe the signs of the times, do believe and publish, that Christ is near at hand," he wrote, "and that the kingdoms of this world, will soon become the kingdom of our Lord . . . 'and the time of the dead, that they should be judged' . . . shows us what is shortly coming to pass." [66]

These columns were enough to impress an itinerant preacher, Henry Jones, to begin spreading Miller's message on his own. Adding to the surprising turn of events was a momentous astronomical occurrence on November 13, 1833. Miller saw it as a prophetic confirmation of his theory. A celestial event, perhaps like no other in recorded history splashed across the night skies of North

America.[VII] It was seen throughout the northeast and as far west as Indiana and as far south as Alabama. Hundreds of thousands of meteors rained down in less than an hour in a shocking and dazzling display. It started around 5 a.m. eastern time so many missed the fire of stars that occurred just before the morning call of the rooster. Those fortunate enough to see left eyewitness accounts.

From Baltimore, "the stars, or some other bodies presenting a fiery appearance, were descending in torrents as rapid and numerous as ever I saw flakes of snow or drops of rain in the midst of a storm" . . . .[67] From New York, "The zenith, the north, and the west also showed the falling stars in the very image of one thing and of only one I ever heard of—and we felt in our hearts that it was the sign of the last days. For truly the stars of Heaven fall onto the earth, even as a fig tree casteth her untimely figs when she is shaken by a mighty wind"[68] . . . . From

---

[VII] Professor Denison Olmstead, of Yale College, wrote in 1843: "Those who were so fortunate as to witness the exhibition of shooting stars on the morning of November 13, 1833, probably saw the greatest display of celestial fireworks that has ever been seen since the creation of the world, or at least within the annals covered by the pages of history" ("Last Day Tokens" 1843). And to this day, astronomers agree it was perhaps the most magnificent display of shooting stars in recorded history.

Connecticut, "We pronounce the raining of fire which we saw on Wednesday morning last . . . a sure forerunner—a merciful sign of the great and dreadful day which the inhabitants of the earth will witness when the Sixth Seal shall be opened. The time is just at hand described, not only in the New Testament, but in the Old."[69] From Vermont, "Ten thousand fireballs of shooting stars, were incessantly coursing down . . . . The largest of these balls appeared of the breadth of 2 or 3 inches, moving with great celerity, and throwing off a very white light. The trains, which for a few moments some of them left visible, had the appearance of the beams or trails . . ."[70]

Such references to Biblical prophecy were common, [VIII] so it is not surprising that this astonishing starburst from the heavens would cause Miller to conclude that they presaged Christ's Second Coming. It compelled Miller to write an exuberant letter to a friend about it, which read in part:

> [The Bible] is past, present, and to come; it discourses the first great cause of all effects, and the effects of all causes; it speaks of life, death, and judgment, body, soul, and spirit, heaven, earth, and hell; it makes use of all nature as figures, to sum up the value of the gospel; and declares itself to be the word of God. And your friend and brother believe it.[71]

Coincidentally, that month, Miller published his book detailing how he had calculated the date of the Second Coming and what would come to pass. It was entitled, *Evidences from Scripture and History of the Second Coming of Christ about the year 1843 . . .*

Miller cautioned that it was time for people to cleanse their souls and purge all sin and to have their reckoning with God. While some clergy discounted Miller's prediction of the time of the Second Coming, they supported his efforts which attracted many converts

---

[VIII] A reference to *Revelation 6: 16*

to their churches. And gradually he began to capture the imagination of more adherents.

During the spring of 1835, Miller made an extended tour through the Champlain region of New York. Forty-three Baptist ministers from towns where he lectured signed an affidavit attesting that Miller's views were "worthy to be read and known of all men." That fall he toured the St. Lawrence Valley in New York promoting his message and book. Other preachers also began to spread his message. The following year, he sparked a revival at the Baptist Church in Lansingburgh, New York, sixty miles south of Low Hampton.[72]

Chapter 5

The Clarkson of Vermont

The courage Murray displayed is beyond question, but his labors for the cause also took great energy. He was then a young man not yet 30 and hardened physically by farm work. Riding horseback over mountain paths and dirt roads, to get to the next village, even during winter when it is notoriously cold and snowy there, surely took great determination.

Murray was not one to temper his arguments, and his boldness made a difficult situation worse. The hatred for abolitionists was growing and a mob mentality had developed.

"I was out about four weeks," he wrote, "spent most of the time in Windsor County—delivered sixteen lectures— was prevented from four others by violence—formed a Society in Hancock of about twenty members; in Granville, later Kingston, of about thirty; and in Rochester of about sixty, including some of the most valuable men in these towns . . . . In other towns, meetings were respectfully and, in some instances, quite fully attended. *The Vermont Chronicle* is very extensively read in the region which I visited, but great numbers are renouncing its heresies on this subject; and hundreds are joining our ranks. The principal opposition appeared in Randolph, Woodstock, Windsor, and Charlotte."[73]

An ex-U.S. Senator had spread the word in Randolph that Murray must not be allowed to speak before his arrival. At the appointed time of the lecture, men and boys armed with eggs and other projectiles met Murray at the meeting house. But the house was closed and under advisement, he left town.

In Woodstock, on a snowy bitter cold evening, Murray reported that the meeting house supposed to have been opened by a Judge Hutchinson, was closed. A person waiting at the house warned him of a mob coming. But then the Judge showed up and brought him to the courthouse. "Murray has the right to speak," the Judge told the gathering crowd, and the courthouse was opened.[74]

Murray waited on the stage for people to take their seats, but it seemed most remained standing in the back. When it appeared that the crowd was settled in, Murray began to speak but almost simultaneously with his first word, the foot stomping began.

It got louder and louder. The Judge jumped up and shouted at them to stop but they refused to listen. Nevertheless, Murray tried to speak when suddenly a flurry of snowballs assaulted him. As he hurried off the stage and out of the courthouse, escorted by the Judge and his two sons, the mob howled: "Over with him, over with him!"

Murray later wrote that he feared that "the howling pro-slavery horde were bent on lassoing me in the street."[75]

The following day a schoolroom was found for a lecture in South Woodstock, four miles away. But again he was interrupted, this time by protesters with horns and drums, parading through the village streets. Four of them showed up at his place of lodging, threatening him. The proprietor, a Mr. Slayton, told them to leave, and offered the use of his hotel for the lecture. While a mob did show, they were turned away – one old sea captain having to be forcibly dragged out— and Murray was able to complete his lecture.

Two days later, he went to Windsor and learned that both the Baptist and Congregational churches were closed to him. He applied for access to the courthouse and was given permission to speak on Monday and Tuesday. Meanwhile, he went to Hartland and gave a lecture on Sunday.

On Monday before the appointed meeting in Windsor, he spoke with residents. They said they were opposed to the anti-slavery society and that they supported the Colonization Society. He also had a confrontation with Ebenezer Carter Tracy, better known as

31

E.C. Tracy, the editor of the *Vermont Chronicle*, a religious publication of the Congregational Church, who opposed immediate emancipation and supported the Colonization Society. There were about 100 attendees, most of them standing by the doorway, as they did in Woodstock. After he stepped on stage and attempted to speak, the crowd began stamping, whooping, and yelling beyond anything "[he] could have imagined," and then began throwing all sorts of things at him. He quickly departed.[76]

In Charlotte, while speaking, four men rushed the stage and carried Murray out, one at each arm and leg.[77]

"They attempt by violence, to hinder my speaking," he wrote to *The Liberator*, "because I oppose the Colonization Society. And do they expect to convince the enlightened people of our State that they are right and I am wrong, by thrusting their hands into their own ears, and stopping my mouth . . . . What does it argue for the merits of any institution that it shrinks from investigation and defends itself with brute force and facts and arguments?"[78]

Nevertheless, he had personally organized four anti-slavery societies (in Rupert, Hancock, Granville, and Rochester), for which Garrison wrote: "In zeal, in boldness, in untiring perseverance, in generous philanthropy, and in personal suffering, Mr. Murray is the CLARKSON of Vermont,"[79]

Thomas Clarkson, the influential British abolitionist and author of the *History of the Abolition of the Slave Trade,* played perhaps the greatest role of anyone in ending Slavery in the British Empire. High praise for young Murray, who was not yet 30 years old.

While many in Vermont opposed Murray and immediate emancipation, his supporters gradually grew, and on April 30, 1834, Vermont formed the nation's first state antislavery society with 100 delegates from 30 towns and villages.[80]

Appointed as Corresponding Secretary, Murray was chosen to write its resolutions. Among them: "That in the language of the

Declaration of Independence 'we hold these truths to be self-evident, that all men are created equal . . .

[That] Therefore . . . Slavery is a direct violation, both of the law of God and the plainest principles of republican freedom.

That as men, Christians & Americans we owe opposition to a system which makes war upon the rights of men.

That . . . no scheme for the abolition of Slavery in the United States . . . offers any prospect of success . . . but that of immediate emancipation. That by Immediate Emancipation we mean, the immediate enactment on the part of the slaveholding States of such laws as shall restore to the black man his "inalienable rights" and place him in the enjoyment of civil liberty."

VERMONT ANTI-SLAVERY CONVENTION.

In pursuance of public notice, the delegates to this Convention met at the Court House in Middlebury, on the 30th day of April, 1834.

The meeting was opened with prayer by the Rev. James Milligan, of Ryegate.

Col. JONATHAN P. MILLER, of Montpelier, was elected President, pro. tem., and EDWARD D. BARBER, Esq. of Middlebury, was chosen Secretary pro. tem.

On motion, it was

Resolved, That all persons, who are friendly to the doctrine of Immediate Emancipation, be invited to seats in this Convention.

On motion, Messrs. Edward D. Barber, Isaac Wescott, Oliver J. Eells, Ithamar Smith, and O. S. Murray, were appointed a Committee to report a list of Officers of the Convention; and on their nomination, the following gentlemen were appointed:

PRESIDENT.

JOHN IDE, of Waterbury.

VICE-PRESIDENTS.

JONA. P. MILLER, of Montpelier.
ELISHA BASCOM, of Shoreham.
JAMES MILLIGAN, of Ryegate.
R. T. ROBINSON, of Ferrisburgh.

O. S. MURRAY, of Orwell, } *Secretaries.*
C. L. KNAPP, of Montpelier, }

A singular resolution also was offered, thanking O.S. Murray, "for his labors and sacrifices . . . in behalf of the Anti-Slavery cause in this State . . ."[81]

Among his supporters and a vice-president of the new society was his great uncle, Elisha Bascom, the brother of his mother's father.

While abolitionists met with some success, their supporters were overwhelmingly in the minority and violence against them increased. The anger they encountered was heightened with the arrival of British abolitionist orator George Thompson in the fall of 1834. He had come at the invitation of Garrison when he had visited England. Thompson spoke frequently throughout the North, and his meetings were well publicized. Considered one of the great orators of that time, he not only gained many adherents, but his eloquence also grated against southern sensibilities.

Nevertheless, the abolitionists had no intention of giving up. They seized on a new tactic in 1835, sending abolitionist literature in the mail. The South reacted and 152 anti-abolition meetings were held that year.[82] Among violent reactions were a $20,000 reward placed on the head of Arthur Tappan, President of the American

Anti-Slavery Society, and the ransacking of the post office in Charleston, South Carolina, and burning of abolitionist mail. This led to the suppression of abolitionist mail in the South. In another well-known incident that year former Lane Rebel, Amos Dresser, was whipped publicly in Nashville, TN, for having anti-slavery literature in his possession. Dresser later became an antislavery agent in Vermont.

It was in such a climate that Murray continued his antislavery outreach, organizing five more antislavery societies in 1835: in hometown Orwell, nearby Shoreham, Hancock, Rochester, and Granville.[83] Despite the establishment of the state society and of local societies where he earlier had been mobbed in Middlebury, Bennington, Rutland, and Castleton,[84] angry opposition continued unabated. From July to October 1835, 35 riots against abolitionists and 11 against people of color occurred in the U.S.[85] One of them included the dismantling of the Noyes Academy in Canaan, New Hampshire that admitted young black men, or colored as they were referenced, by a mob of more than 300 men with 190 oxen pulling the building off its foundation.[86]

COLORED SCHOOLS BROKEN UP, IN THE FREE STATES.

Chapter 6

Mobs, Riots, Tar and Feather

On October 1, 1835, Murray published his first issue of the *Vermont Telegraph*. Considering his views on antislavery and the threat of violence against abolitionists, it was a daring if not hazardous undertaking. Three weeks later, on the weekend of October 23, a serendipitous intersection of mob violence against the abolitionists occurred in Boston, Montpelier, and Utica, New York.

The first occurred in Vermont at a lecture given in Montpelier by Rev. Samuel May, who would be one of the abolitionist movement's foremost leaders. He had been giving a series of lectures there under the sponsorship of the American Anti-Slavery Society that were not well received. The last was at the invitation of Vermont Antislavery Society.

"Everywhere," May said, "I met with insult. I was mobbed five times."[87]

His last meeting was in Montpelier. Because many of the state legislators were abolitionists, he was given permission to speak at the state legislative building. The crowd overflowed and spilled outside. A few eggs and stones were thrown through the windows but not enough to deter the proceedings.

The next night, upon request, May spoke at the First Presbyterian Church. Signs were posted that morning urging people not to attend, and if necessary, force would be used to prevent him from speaking. At noon, he received a letter signed by seven prominent citizens requesting him to leave "without any further attempt to hold forth the absurd doctrine of antislavery and save them the trouble of using any other measures to that effect."[88]

May ignored the threat. At the appointed hour, he rose to give his speech when he was immediately confronted. May asked for what reasons he should not be allowed to speak. The audience quieted but when May resumed, cries of anger filled the church hall: "Down with him!" "Throw him over!" "Choke him!"[89]

May was determined to continue but suddenly the crowd rushed the pulpit. Only by the force of the personality and strength of local hero and politician, Colonel Jonathan P. Miller, who had fought in the Greek War of Independence, was the mob stopped and May allowed to leave unharmed. Little did he know that the violence was even worse in Boston and upstate New York.[90]

A larger and more aggressive mob occupied the courthouse in Utica where the organizational meeting of New York State Anti-Slavery Society was scheduled, awaiting the arrival of 1,000 delegates who were coming to organize a state society to coordinate the increasing number of anti-slavery societies in the state.[91] But the abolitionists learning of the opposition's plans moved the meeting to a local church. Alvan Stewart, president of the Utica Anti-Slavery Society, made an inspirational opening speech, recalling the legacy of the Founding Fathers, urging the delegates to remain steadfast in the face of opposition.[92]

After Stewart's speech, a constitution forming the New York State Anti-Slavery Society was passed. Lewis Tappan was reading a declaration of sentiments when a committee representing the mob at the courthouse barged in and demanded to speak.[93] Their leader, Judge Chester Hayden, read a series of statements that condemned

the abolitionists. The protesters also demanded an apology for disrupting their community.[94]

Drunken screams from outside were heard and banging on the walls. A motion was made to end the meeting, but instead a tall man of distinction rose. All eyes fixed on him. It was Gerrit Smith.

"I am not an abolitionist, but I support their right to be heard, and I invite you all to my estate tomorrow to resume the meeting."[95]

The meeting was concluded as the racket outside grew louder. As the delegates departed, they met the angry mob armed with ropes and ladders and fire hooks, which suggested they were going to tear down the building. But the departure of the abolitionists stopped them, and they simply hurled obscenities. So, they moved to the offices of the *Utica Standard and Democrat* to take out their wrath, breaking into its office and throwing their press into the street.[96]

The next day 590 delegates met without incident at Gerrit Smith's estate in Peterboro and completed the organization of the New York State Antislavery Society.[97]

In Boston, the mob lawlessness had reached a crescendo. The animosity for Thompson who was lecturing in New England at the time had boiled over. Word got out that he had told students at Andover Seminary that slaves should slit the throats of their masters, something he later vehemently denied.[98] But the comment was accepted as truth by the anti-abolitionists. Everywhere he went became the occasion for a mob, and it was reported that he had recently escaped a lynch mob in Concord, New Hampshire.[99]

On that climactic October weekend, it was rumored Thompson had been invited to speak at a meeting of the Boston Female Anti-Slavery Society, He was supposed to have spoken a week earlier but the meeting was cancelled. Having escaped a lynch mob in Concord, New Hampshire, he had gone into hiding. The meeting was rescheduled for the next week and though Thompson was not coming, a huge crowd of angry men had gathered outside its meeting hall, which was in the same building as the offices of *The Liberator*.

More than a 1000, perhaps as many as 3,000—accounts differ— were gathered outside (numbers comparable to the recent January 6 Insurrection), some spilling up the stairs to the entrance of the meeting. Inside, 25 female abolitionists, 10 of color, were in discussion. The mob outside howled and screamed. They did not know that Thompson was not there and would not be coming.

Site of *The Liberator* offices

Fortunately, before things got out of hand, Mayor Theodore Lyman arrived. He ordered the meeting closed and the mob to disperse. He told them Thompson was not there, which outraged them. Suddenly, they turned their wrath on Garrison, who was in his office next door, and who had earlier passed in view to talk to the ladies in the meeting.[100] "We must have Garrison! Out with him! Lynch him!"[101]

They demanded that the ladies' antislavery signboard be removed, and the mayor consented. As the crowd focused on the sign, the mayor slipped into Garrison's office and told him to climb out the back window. By the time the sign was torn to pieces, Garrison had jumped down to some overhanging roof and into a lane where a carpenter he knew had a shop. But he was seen entering by one of the rioters. They forced their way in and found Garrison hiding upstairs. They seized him and at first thought of throwing him out the window but decided against this. Instead, they tied a rope round him and let him out the window and down by a ladder. Seized by several men, he was dragged along and beaten by rioters who tore off his clothes. The mayor came on the scene but was pushed aside. It was only by the grace of a posse of police officers that they were able to prevent him from being taken to the tar kettle.[IX] Half-naked, Garrison was taken to the mayor's office. They got him clothing and committed him to the city jail for protection. A carriage was sent as a decoy in case the mob was

[IX] It is believed the rioters were planning to tar and feather Garrison.

still watching, followed by a second carriage that took him to the city jail. On the way, however, the ruse was discovered by some of the rioters who rushed the carriage and tried to drag him out. They clung to the wheels, dashed open the doors, seized hold of the horses and tried to upset the carriage. But the driver plied his whip on the horses and on the rioters, and by some miracle Garrison was deposited safely at the jail and locked up. He was released the next day and advised to leave Boston for a few days. Even so, when he returned, he had to change his residence. A lesser man might've packed up and left town.[102]

Amidst this chaos, Murray stepped even more boldly into the fray.

Chapter 7

Early Days of the Telegraph

VERMONT TELEGR

MURRAY, EDITOR AND PUBLISHER   "I AM SET FOR THE DEFENCE OF THE GOSPEL."

1 E. VIII.   BRANDON, OCTOBER 1, 1835.

Whoever could, at the present time, enter upon the duties of managing a religious press, without a deep and lively sense of accountability to God, to the church, and to his country, would truly be chargeable with rashness and presumptuousness ...[103]

So, in this time of ferment, Orson S. Murray introduced himself as new publisher and editor of the *Vermont Telegraph*, the paper of the Baptist Church in Vermont, launching his first issue on October 1, 1835. He was then a devout Baptist who believed in God with his whole soul. Murray also was taking a hiatus from antislavery lecturing, signing one of the reports in another publication during this period as the "Late agent of the Vt. A.S.S."[104]

According to one profile of Murray, he had been helped in acquiring the *Telegraph* by evangelical Baptist preacher, Rev. William Arthur,[105] the father of future President Chester Arthur. Arthur had several pastorates in Vermont from 1831-1835. Ten years older than Orson, he was a fire and brimstone preacher who alienated people everywhere he went, moving  from congregation to congregation because of his uncompromising and fiercely independent ideas. In addition, he was a classical scholar,

Rev. Wm. Arthur

who knew Greek and Latin, very learned in the history of antiquity and an assortment of topics. Their mutual intellectual bent and their agreement about the evil of slavery apparently sparked a friendship.[106]

That summer after arranging the purchase of the *Telegraph*, Murray moved from Orwell to Brandon and Arthur moved to New York.[X] [107] Apparently, Murray was able to negotiate bargain prices as the *Telegraph's* investors were losing money and sold their shares for 50-to-75 percent of their investment. Nearly all of them sold out to him on the condition that the paper remain as the voice of the state's Baptists.[108]

While he had been a contract lecturer with the New England Anti-Slavery Society for about two years at $500 annually ($16,000 today), and continued to farm, he also needed loans to complete the transaction, which were endorsed by the town's leading citizen, John Conant.[109]

A local government official, the richest man in the region with holdings in grist mills, furnaces, and the local bank, but more

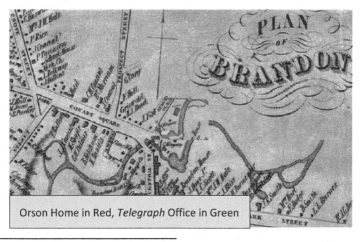

Orson Home in Red, *Telegraph* Office in Green

[X] An April 23, 1835 meeting of the Vermont Anti-Slavery Society shows Orson listing his residence as Orwell; an announcement of his purchase of the *Telegraph* made in July shows his residence as Brandon.

importantly the most prominent elder in the Brandon Baptist Church, Conant likely arranged for Murray and his family to reside at the Baptist parsonage.[110] In 1838, Murray purchased a lot from Nathan T. Sprague, the town's real estate mogul, and a loan from Conant to purchase a 16-acre plot of land from the Baptist Church. The Sprague mortgage was secured by his uncle, Asahel Murray, and his brothers-in-law, Horace Higgins, the brother of his wife, and Lorrain Cutts, the husband of his oldest sister, Emeline.[111]

Thereafter, he probably built his house, which still stands in Brandon. In 1839, he purchased another property from Carlton Parker. Local historian Kevin Thornton's best guess from reading the deeds is that this 16-acres was adjacent to his other properties, which sat along the banks of the Neshobe River.

Murray's evangelical roots were in evidence on the front page of his first issue, publishing a lecture to promote revivals by Charles Finney, whose opening words proclaimed, "Break up your fallow ground for it is to seek the Lord, till he come and rain consciousness upon you." *Hosea x 12.*

Murray home in Brandon, courtesy Kevin Thornton

On the second page was a lecture by Dr. Lyman Beecher, Harriet Beecher Stowe's father, "The Absurdities of Atheism."

But while religion generally occupied the front page, antislavery was usually inside. One of the state's leading abolitionists, Murray had put himself in a favorable position for spreading his gospel as owner of the *Telegraph*. Accounts of antislavery societies, meetings, and editorials were a constant presence.

Commenting on the mobbing in Utica and Montpelier, and the near lynching of Garrison, Murray wrote:

> What has produced the present state of things in our country— that violence reigns, laws are disregarded, constitutional rights trampled down, and human life made as the life of brute beasts, so that blood cries to God from the ground—that out government totters on its foundation, and the people are given to drink of the cup of the mourning and woe? What is the cause of all this?—that's the question—tremendous question, too; for somebody must give account of this matter in the day of reckoning.
>
> Plain, faithful teaching of plain truths—truths that expose sins, especially popular songs—sins of the church, or of the world, or both—has always been the occasion of disturbance and alarm among those whose consciences have been awakened, or whose selfishness has been attacked. The history of all great reformations furnishes abundant testimony to this point. It was so in the days of the patriarchs and prophets—it was so in the time of our Savior and his Apostles—it has been so ever since—it is so now. It is in the nature of things that it should be so. The lovers of unrighteousness are sure to take fire at the faithful preaching of gospel truth. Powder is not surer to explode at the approach of this spark.[112]

One of the first antislavery meetings reported in Murray's *Telegraph* was the November 19 report of the formation of the Washington County (NY) Antislavery Society by fellow Baptist

Erastus Culver of nearby Union Village, N.Y., entitled quite appropriately: "Spirit of the Times: More Mobbing."[113]

An attorney and a dedicated abolitionist, Culver would later be elected to Congress and eventually move to New York City where his law firm became renowned for defending fugitive slaves. One of its attorneys was future President Chester Arthur, son of Rev. Arthur, who became pastor of Union Village's Bottskill Baptist Church from 1839-1844, succeeding the influential Baptist abolitionist, Rev. Nathaniel Colver, who moved to Boston and the Tremont Temple, site of many abolitionist activities. The young Arthur would be the lead attorney in the Culver firm's most famous case involving the Lemmon fugitive slaves in 1855.[xi]

When the committee of arrangements arrived in the morning at the church where the meeting was to be held later that evening, Culver reported, they found that "the church had been entered by some ruffians, the doors fastened, and the windows nailed down. An effigy was suspended at the door, representing a Negro, on which was fastened a slip of paper, signed 'Judge Lynch' . . . . warning abolitionists of their danger from this judge."[114] The delegates were able, however, to get in through a window, and after making the necessary preparations for the meeting, they retired for dinner at local public house.

When they returned, a drunken mob of about 20 men greeted them. "[They] had barred the door, bracing iron bars and rails against

---

[xi] Chester Arthur successfully defended a family of eight slaves who sought their freedom after being brought into New York by their owner from Virginia. It was the first of a series of civil rights cases involving free blacks and fugitive slaves that Culver's law firm would successfully represent. In this case, the slaveholder Jonathan Lemmon, enroute by boat to Texas, had taken his slaves off the boat to a boarding house in New York. A free black man had discovered this and petitioned one of the Justices of the Superior Court of New York for their freedom then sought the legal services of Culver, who also had become a New York City Judge.

it; had fastened down the windows, while the church rung with the savage shouts of those within."[115] The abolitionists demanded entry but were threatened by the mob, which followed them when they returned to the public house to hold their meeting.

"[Two] entered the convention . . . [and] broke in upon the proceedings," reported Culver. "The landlord immediately asked them to civilly go out. They refused, with an oath. He then promptly seized the largest one by the shoulder . . . [who] soon found . . . his face in close contact with the rough ground. He [the disrupter] gathered up and made for the house, at the landlord. Assistance was called for, and he was bound with a rope."[116]

The mob meanwhile stood by and did nothing. But soon their cause was given support by a "well-dressed, fair looking citizen of Argyle," driving a stylish horse and buggy, who "drove several times through the street with an image representing a large Negro with arms extended and fastened to the hind end of the wagon. Finding that this did not disturb the convention, he soon drove round to the North side of the house, and backed his wagon and image up directly into the window of the room where the convention was sitting, and there remained till the meeting was through, the mob in the streets raising shouts of triumph . . ."[117]

Nevertheless, the meeting concluded successfully. "Slavery must and will be abolished," Culver wrote . . . "The frowning tyrant at the South, his cringing echo at the North, the cowardly minister, the fawning politician and the mob-encouraging press are preparing for the condemnation that awaits them . . ."[118]

Fortuitous words. But the mainstream press echoed public opposition. The *Boston Mercantile Journal* editorialized: "a meeting of the Abolitionists is but the signal for the assemblage of a mob. This being the case, it becomes the duty of those, in whose hands the public authorities of a city or town are vested, to prevent such meetings by the strong arm of the law."[119]

Chapter 8

Pro-Slavery in Church and State

Disapproval of abolition reverberated as well in both halls of State and Church. The January 7, 1836 issue of the *Telegraph* included a letter condemning the Baptist General Tract Society for "forbidding their agents to interfere 'with the agitating question of slavery,'" and "requiring of them 'a pledge that they will in no way, intermeddle with that question while in the commission of that Society.'" [120] It was a manifestation of the war brewing between pro-slavery and anti-slavery clerics in nearly every major denomination but Catholicism.[121] Nathaniel Colver, who participated in the Underground Railroad[122] in Erastus' Culver's Union Village, was among the leading northern Baptists leading the charge against the southern Baptists.

Though still a minority in the North, the abolitionist Baptists now had a powerful ally in Murray, and he seemed to relish the battle.

"It is time for the people to awake," he wrote. "If they know and regard what belongs to their peace and safety, let them at once open their eyes and watch the movements of the foul spirit of aristocracy and slavery, everywhere lurking in their midst, and now showing itself in high place, in this, so called, *republic.*[123]

Murray was criticizing a recent statement made by Governor Macy of New York, who accused the abolitionists of desiring war with the slave-holding states, stating:

I can conceive no other object that the abolitionists can have . . . but to embark . . . in a crusade against the slave holding states, for the purpose of forcing abolition upon them by violence and bloodshed."[124] The moment the people are ready to do the bidding of such creatures . . . the days of liberty, in this land, are numbered and finished. But the people are not ready. They are not prepared for suicide or self-enslavement. They already begin to see that the contest is now a life and death struggle between liberty and slavery, not only as it concerns two million and a half already in chains, but as it concerns themselves, the people of the United States.

Has it come to this, that, in the sixtieth year of Independence—the Liberty—of these United States, the Governor of the State of New York wages war upon the right of opinion! But while liberty's noblest institutions are being torn down to make place for the towers of aristocracy—while human rights are ruthlessly trampled on by cloven feet—while all freedom is so furiously outraged, to withhold or restrain our voice, feeble as it is, would be moral treason.[125]

But another setback to abolitionism occurred on February 8. Congressman Henry Pinckney of South Carolina proposed his infamous Gag resolution stating that the House of Representatives had no constitutional right to interfere with slavery. It proposed a "Gag Rule" on Congress in relation to discussion of slavery, stating that "all petitions, memorials, resolutions, propositions, or papers, relating in any way, or to any extent whatever, to the subject of slavery, or the abolition of slavery, shall, without being either printed or referred, be laid upon the table, and that *no further action whatever shall be had* thereon."[126]

Pinckney's proposal was a measure to blunt the American Anti-Slavery's petition drive, which the *Telegraph* had reported sent 176 petitions in 1835 to Congress protesting the continuation of slavery.[127]

Murray's report of the second annual meeting of the Starksboro and Lincoln Anti-Slavery Society, in March of 1836, occupied nearly a full page of the *Telegraph,* focusing on the Gag Rule.

"Whereas, various attempts have recently been made, both at the South and the North to muzzle the press, and prevent discussion on the subject of slavery" the Society resolved, "we regard every such attempt, as being totally repugnant to the spirit of our free institutions, and a base infringement of the right of citizens . . ."

There were other such resolutions by antislavery societies, but on May 26, 1836, by an overwhelming majority of 117-68,[128] Congress passed the Pinckney Resolutions, effectively removing criticism of slavery from Congress and suspending a basic right provided in the Constitution.

Murray ignored this. Instead, he reprinted an inspiring account of George Thompson's reception in England after fleeing the United States following several rumored lynching attempts in New England.

Thompson recounted his experiences at the reception in the Bristol Street chapel in England. More than 2,000 spectators crowded in, with many others turned away. Applause and cheers greeted him as he stepped onto the stage and sat down behind the pulpit. He expressed joy at the sight of so many enthusiastic supporters. He assured them that his devotion to the cause of freedom remained "undiminished." Referring to England's success in ending slavery, he said he was confident that they could "[slay] the monster on our own borders." He believed that they would not have to resort to violence but could win the war "by opinion operating on opinion; by merely enlisting the pulpit, the press, and the platform, in the work of that reformation" like it was done in England, or so he had hoped.

The following week Murray reported on the New England Anti-Slavery Convention, which he attended as one of its corresponding secretaries. A highlight he wrote was the reading of a "thrilling letter" from George Thompson. A resolution by English abolitionist Charles Stuart, a former mentor of Theodore Weld, seconded by Murray, was passed during the convention:

> Resolved, That when the church becomes so corrupt as to use
> its influence to delay and prevent the fulfillment of the will of
> Christ respecting righteousness, peace, purity, and

temperance, it becomes necessary for those who live and reverence the gospel, to associate themselves anew for the support of these its fundamental principles, and that such associations are the true and only church of Christ.

On July 12, 1836, came another assault on the Constitution and First Amendment. Without warning at midnight, a band of men in Cincinnati broke into the offices of James Birney's anti-slavery newspaper, *The Philanthropist*, destroyed the week's issue, and carried away the press. A former South Carolina slaveholder, Birney had become an abolitionist and moved to the North. Undaunted, he purchased a new press and resumed printing. On the night of July 30,

James Birney

a second mob broke into the office, tossed the press into the street, and were about to set the building on fire when the mayor interceded. Nevertheless, the mob hauled away the press and cast it into the Ohio River. They then proceeded to the home of Birney, who was out of town delivering a lecture. Frustrated, the mob wrecked some havoc on buildings in the black community before city officials finally forced them to disperse.[129]

Tensions in the North were heated enough, but after the Lane Debates, a public discussion of slavery and the merits of Colonization at Cincinnati's Lane Theological Institute drew national attention, it was a veritable inferno.

The *Telegraph* lamented:

Now that it has become an everyday occurrence for the most sacred right of American citizens to be invaded by prowling, murderous mobs, it is high time that each member of community find where he stands and on which side he is casting his influence. Our soul has long ago been so sickened with every day's report of wrong and outrage with which earth is filled that for some time past we have omitted reports of ordinary riots, tumults and commotions. It now again becomes our painful duty to record recent acts of most deliberate, high-handed villainy. [130]

In St. Louis, tensions over the question of slavery also escalated when a mob broke into the office of the *St. Louis Observer*, a religious publication like Murray's. The editor, Elijah Lovejoy first came to St. Louis in 1827 where he taught school and worked for a newspaper, *The Times*. After attending a revival in February of 1832 given by Dr. David Nelson,[XII] he decided to study for the ministry, and returned east to attend Princeton Theological School. He returned to St. Louis in 1833 where he started the *Observer*, in November of that year. Although he condemned slavery, he alleged he was not an abolitionist but supported gradual emancipation. [131]

However, during the summer of 1835, while Lovejoy was away at a conference, two abolitionists were discovered aiding fugitive slaves and whipped by a mob. When he returned, he was confronted with an angry demand by some of the city's leading citizens that he stop all discussion of slavery. At the same time, a package of bibles that he mailed was discovered to have included a copy of the *Emancipator*, the official publication of the American Anti-Slavery Society. Despite the pressure, Lovejoy refused to agree to stop speaking out about whatever he believed to be wrong and insisted on his constitutional right of free speech.

Finally, hell broke loose. On April 28, 1836, while Lovejoy was out of town at a Presbyterian convention in Pittsburgh, a black man was burned alive.

Francis McIntosh, a black cook on a riverboat, had intervened during a fight on the St. Louis wharf between two friends and two

---

[XII] A notorious Underground Railroad agent

police officers. His friends got away but not him. As the officers took him into custody, he asked how long he might be in jail. When they said five years, he broke loose and pulled out a knife. He stabbed one officer who fell away, and then slit the throat of the other, killing him. Shortly after, McIntosh was apprehended and put in the local jail.

A crowd gathered around the dead officer's body, and despite pleas from the Sheriff and another local citizen, the infuriated mob broke into the jail. "Some seized him by the hair, some by the arms and legs; and in this way he was carried to a large locust tree . . . not far from the jail. He was then chained to the tree with his back against its trunk."[132]

It was said that thousands had gathered to gawk at the hideous affair and "all was silent as death while the executioners were piling the wood around the victim. He said not a word till he felt that the flames had seized him. He then uttered an awful howl, attempting to sing and pray, then hung his head and suffered in silence. After the flames had surrounded their prey—his eyes burned out of his head, and his mouth apparently parched to a cinder—someone in the crowd . . . proposed to end his misery by shooting him. But it was replied that he was already out of his pain.

"No, no," cried the [victim], "I am suffering as much as ever. Shoot me! Shoot me!"

"No," exclaimed one of the fiends, "no, he shall not be shot. I would sooner slack the fire if that would increase his misery!"[133]

Some months later, after the leaders of the mob were exonerated, an outraged Lovejoy condemned the Judge who coincidentally was named Lawless:

Burning of McIntosh at St. Louis, in April, 1836.

We covet not the loss of property, nor the honors of martyrdom; but better, far better, that the office of the *Observer* should be scattered in fragments to the four winds of heaven; yea, better that editor, printer, and publishers should be chained to the same tree as Mcintosh, and share his fate, than that the doctrines promulgated by Judge Lawless, from the bench, should become prevalent in this community. For they are subversive of all law, and at once open the door for the perpetration, by a congregated mob, calling themselves the people, of every species of violence, and that, too, with perfect impunity . . . .

And the ignorance and prejudice which could lead to such an expression of opinion, however censurable in the Judge, is still more pitiable in the man.[134]

After this editorial, a mob broke into Lovejoy's office and destroyed his printing press. This forced him to move 20 miles north to the city of Alton in the free state of Illinois.

Chapter 9

The Intrepid Abolitionist

Despite opposition almost everywhere, the abolitionists remained resolute. Fortified by the uncompromising Garrison, fearless journalists like Birney and Lovejoy, and intrepid spokesmen like Murray, they would not back down. And, in the forefront, was the courageous and gifted antislavery lecturer, Theodore Weld.

Like evangelicals Lorenzo Dow and mentor Charles Finney,

Weld was a spellbinding speaker. His ability may have even surpassed Finney, judging by contemporary accounts.[135]

After a mysterious illness left Weld temporarily blind as a teen, he found he had a natural gift for eloquence, and undertook a three-year journey from New York through Ohio,

Theodore Weld

then back across Pennsylvania and Maryland to Washington, DC, supporting himself by lecturing on mnemonics, the art of memorizing—an incredible undertaking when one considers the wilderness that was the nation at the time. A few years later, a chance introduction to Finney led him on his life's path. It was Finney who referred him to Arthur Tappan.

The nation's first benefactor of moral reform, Tappan sent Weld on a tour into the South promoting one of his moral reform projects: manual labor schools to improve the education of the poor, many of whom were free blacks. Just to get an idea how inexhaustible Weld's energy was at that time, consider his description from his 120-page report on his mission to promote Manual Labor Schools, which he made for Tappan prior to enrolling in Lane Seminary. Serialized in ten issues of the *Telegraph*, it covered a year's long journey during 1832-1833 for which Weld estimated that he had travelled 4,575 miles, had given 236 public addresses, and written 282 letters.[136]

Weld, who had already been introduced to antislavery, grew convinced of it during this mission into the South. One of Weld's objectives was to look for a potential school that might adopt Tappan's Manual Labor School idea. The school he identified was Lane Seminary in Cincinnati, and after his mission was completed, he enrolled there.

However, the school's president Lyman Beecher was a "colonizationist," like many who opposed slavery but didn't comprehend the realities of what it meant for African Americans, whether free or slave, to be sent away from their homeland to a primitive jungle as Africa was at that time. After stirring up the student body, Weld organized a series of debates with the Lane faculty arguing the merits of immediate emancipation versus those of Colonization. The sessions combined lecture, prayer, public confession, and strong appeals. They were held for eighteen nights, the first nine devoted to the wisdom of immediate emancipation and the next nine devoted to a consideration of African colonization. It was basically the student body who were for immediate emancipation against the faculty who were for Colonization.

Fittingly called the Lane Rebels, the students numbered 51 and set up a school for Cincinnati's black community, as well as participated in the Underground Railroad. After the students refused to stop their abolitionist activity, they were expelled. Many matriculated to Oberlin College while others became anti-slavery lecturers and influential figures in the abolitionist movement.[XIII]

After leaving Lane, Weld joined the ranks of the early American Anti-Slavery lecturers who included Murray, William Goodell, Samuel May, Oliver Johnson, and Henry B. Stanton. His first antislavery mission was to abolitionize Ohio.

No one faced down mobs as fearlessly or successfully as Weld, who withstood eggs, sticks, stones, and bricks.

In March of 1835, he visited Zanesville, which had been selected for a meeting to organize a state society. It was chosen because of its centralized location but while there were anti-slavery supporters in the area, there also were strong anti-abolitionist feelings.

His first lecture was greeted by a mob, which "broke the windows, tore off the gate, and attacked [him] with stones and clubs." He was undeterred. Finally, "on the sixteenth night," he wrote, "hundreds pledged themselves for immediatism. The way for the state convention was prepared."[137]

In 1836, Weld began abolitionizing upstate New York. Murray published this glowing report, following Weld's journey of 400 miles to Ithaca:

> What! Another convention for the formation of a State Anti-Slavery Society! — Massachusetts, Vermont, Maine, New Hampshire, Kentucky, Ohio, New York, and now Rhode Island! Let us sing unto the Lord, for he hath triumphed gloriously. Be His alone the praise! The toil, the peril, the suffering of shame, the spoiling of goods, the loss of all things,

---

[XIII] They included Weld; Henry B. Stanton, noted antislavery lecturer and husband of Elizabeth Cady Stanton; George Clark, "the Liberty Singer"; Amos Dresser, American Antislavery agent; George Whipple, secretary of the American Missionary Society; Hiram Wilson, the fugitive slave missionary; and Marius Robinson, editor of the Anti-Slavery Bugle.

be this our lot and joy, and this our song, in the house of our pilgrimage . . .

Success to a good cause is God's endorsement . . . . Woe unto us if our zeal and faith do not keep pace with our responsibilities . . . . If every new accession to our cause, girds us anew buoys up to higher aims, gives us a fresher baptism, a holier unction, and a firmer anchorage on God, then shall our light break forth as the morning, and thick darkness become noonday.[138]

About this time, Weld and Stanton were asked by Lewis Tappan and other leaders of the American Anti-Slavery Society to begin recruiting antislavery lecturers during their travels.[139]

Weld made several trips across the North into Ohio and Pennsylvania and back through upstate New York before finally arriving at the agency convention in New York City in mid-November. One notable report he sent from Troy, N.Y., to *The Liberator* captured the indomitable spirit that pushed him on:

Twice a rush was made up the aisles to drag me from the pulpit. Stones, pieces of bricks, eggs, cents, sticks . . . were thrown at me while speaking.

As I came out of the house . . . I was a target for all sorts of missiles, was hit by two stones though not hurt seriously. The mob made desperate efforts to get me into their clutches, but were kept at bay by our friends, though often with extreme difficulty . . . .

Anti-Abolition fury . . . is breaking out anew and with deadlier hate than ever. Let every abolitionist debate the matter, once for all, and settle it with himself, whether he is an abolitionist from impulse or principle—whether he can lie upon the rack— and clasp the faggot— and tread with steady step the

57

scaffold—whether he can stand at the post of duty and having done all, and suffered all . . . fall and die a martyr . . .[140]

Finally in mid-November, Weld arrived at the American Anti-slavery Society office in New York City to lead the agency convention and provide two weeks of instruction for both old and newly recruited lecturers. Murray was invited but declined.

At least 32 in all attended and possibly more. They included: Garrison, Stanton, Dresser, Lewis Tappan, Beriah Green, Rev. Nathaniel Colver, J. Miller McKim, the Burleigh brothers, Rev. John Cross, Henry C. Wright, Jonathan Blanchard, Elizur Wright, Samuel Cornish, and Weld's future wife, Angelina Grimke.[141]

Topics discussed at the Weld training session included what is slavery; what is immediate emancipation and what is gradual emancipation; why not lecture in the South; would the emancipated slaves overrun the North; the consequences in the South of emancipation; compensation to slaveholders for emancipation; treatment of free "Colored" in the North; Hebrew slavery; Colonization; and prejudice. Some days Weld lectured more than eight hours, and William Lloyd Garrison said of the event that he had no time to eat, write, or see his wife and added, "it seemed we were just entering upon the threshold of the great question of slavery—so exhaustless is the theme, so vast the relations involved in the well-being and freedom of [humanity]."[142]

In Murray's second-to-last issue in 1836, he was joyful and optimistic about the prospect of antislavery as reflected in this buoyant report of the organization of an antislavery society in Burlington where he had been mobbed two years before, in which he mocked his attackers.

Where were the ferocious mobites . . . who broke up . . . the first anti-slavery meeting held in Burlington, trampling on the Constitution of Vermont . . . and the rights of their fellow citizens? Where were they [when] their fellow townsmen were

58

permitted . . . to utter sentiments dictated by Revelation and common sense?[143]

Murray did have one complaint, however, and it was about a resolution that commended the alleged success of those American blacks who were sent to Africa by the Colonization Society. Nevertheless, the founding of an anti-slavery society committed to immediate emancipation in a city where in the past he had been threatened with violence was an encouraging sign. He added: "We would only warn abolitionists against any . . . doctrine and influences that will retard their progress—No compromising . . . . Cry, immediate repentance—immediate emancipation—or be silent."[144]

Chapter 10

God Owns His Work

As Whitney Cross wrote in *The Burned-Over District*, his epic study of the Second Great Awakening, the epoch was characterized by an obsession with one idea or moral problem, what Charles Finney called "religious ultraism." This described Murray's obsession with reform and the antislavery movement. It also was characterized by visions, premonitions, and visitations by God (or what would be described today as "Born Again" experiences), which one might ascribe to Miller's obsession with the Bible and the Second Coming.

Rev. John Rankin, the noted Underground Railroad agent, wrote, "A revival helps the anti-slavery cause. The more religion, the more benevolence, and of course more pity for the poor slave."[145]

These revivals had established a routine that included multiple days or even weeks. They called this practice, "protracted meetings." They also included multiple denominations and invited an evangelist from outside the community to lead the revival.[146]

"Whatever our missionary and evangelizing orators intended, [wrote abolitionist editor, William Goodell], whatever they were thinking of, they were God's instruments for putting into the minds of others 'thoughts that burned,' for the emancipation of the enslaved . . . . Revivals of religion, [demanded] 'immediate and unconditional repentance' of all sin, as the only condition of forgiveness and salvation."[147]

A fitting example was the three-week revival held in Union Village (Greenwich), Washington County, NY, in February of 1837, which was described in detail in the *Telegraph*. The report was written by fellow Baptist abolitionist, Erastus Culver.

60

The revival was called at the request of the pastor of the

Bottskill Baptist Church, Rev. Nathaniel Colver. It was co-sponsored by the village's Congregational Church which was in turmoil over the issue of slavery. As was customary, an evangelist, Elder William Grant of Moriah in neighboring Essex County was invited to lead the revival.

Rev. Nathaniel Colver

Colver described the scene: The concourse of people that thronged the house of God, day and night was immense, ranging from 700-1500 .... The meeting continued twenty-one days, and seemingly with unabated interest up to the last. The work evinced the power of the Holy Ghost. Rum drinkers, Universalists, Infidels, Mobocrats, and backsliders were indiscriminately mowed down before it. There was mourning, and sighing, and weeping, and confessing .... [148]

Culver reported at least 250 conversions as well as the formation of a new Congregational Church founded on the principles of no tolerance with slavery or any church which continued to tolerate it. He added:

The works of reform do not kill revivals. A fact here: On Monday evening of the second week of our meeting, was the monthly concert for the abolition of slavery. The meeting was not crowded out and put by for fear of killing the revival. The occasion was met – and, in a vast concourse, many a fervent prayer was put up for the poor slave; and, we believe, many a hearty amen was responded by those who had just been emancipated from the bondage of sin. The revival did not stop – but increased. God owned the work. [149]

61

Later that year, Murray echoed Culver's faith in God when he assessed his two years publishing the *Telegraph*.

> I was led to the undertaking by a desire to employ, in the most efficient way, whatever powers God had given and would give me, to assist in the overthrow of Satan's Kingdom . . . . The consequence of doing right, when it would displease men was altogether a greater restraint than the consequence of doing wrong and displeasing God . . . Intemperance and Licentiousness, War and Slavery had entrenched and fortified themselves within the pale of the church . . . . The faithful, who maintained their standing upon the broken walls, lifting up the voice of warning and rebuke, were few and far between.
>
> It was at such a time, under such circumstances, and against such fearful odds, that I undertook to make the *Telegraph* speak out against all sin. [150]

Despite Murray's good intentions, he was being threatened with prosecution. Some insisted that he stop opposing war, meddling with slavery, and discussing licentiousness and intemperance. Some threatened to withhold their support which he needed to continue publication of the paper. Murray, however, was defiant.

> God's command came, he wrote. Lift up thy voice like a trumpet and show my people their transgression . . . . My colors were hoisted and nailed to the mast, proclaiming eternal war against sin—in and out of the church, sin locally and nationwide, committed in person or indirectly, in all places. I have only done my duty . . . . to stand on guard by day, and on sentry by night. [151]

He admitted he had involved himself in controversy, but added so had Christ and the Apostles, as well as the founders of the church.

The *Telegraph* will continue to be what it has been, for two years past . . . . While it will be devoted primarily to Religion and Morals, it will look assiduously after all the great interests of mankind. Literature—chaste and profitable miscellany— important news of the day, including a synopsis of the doings of government, state and national—and last, though not least, agriculture shall have due attention.[152]

During the remainder of 1837 Murray continued his war with slaveholding clerics and those who tolerated them. Nearly an entire issue of the paper was devoted to defending an attack on Garrison by five clerics who claimed to be abolitionists. They alleged that he had falsely accused two of their southern colleagues of being slaveholders. They also defended the right to prevent the discussion of slavery in church and insisted that pastors had the right to prevent the discussion of slavery in their churches.

Garrison's rebuttal was fierce and lengthy. One of the clerics in question, he said, believed that slavery was sanctioned by God and consistent with Christianity. Another was a family member of a slaveholder. Furthermore, he charged, if pastors prevented the discussion of slavery, it was a violation of their mission to eliminate all sin and would seriously impede the ending of slavery.[153]

A later report from the New York abolitionist paper, *Friend of Man*, gave full support to Garrison:

> The truth is, Jesus Christ never commissioned his pastors to have dominion over men's faith and lord it over his own heritage. They should feed the people with knowledge, and not forbid them to gain all the knowledge they can . . . . Abolitionism has survived mob-law—It has transformed the threat of legislative gag-law into a low bow for abolition votes. But in contact with the claim of pastoral supremacy, its wheels grind heavily: the car almost ceases, for the time being, to move forward.[154]

There was a war being waged against pro-slavery religion and Murray was one of its foot soldiers.

Chapter 11

The Radical Messenger

Murray was an "ultraist," the term used then for an iconoclast, and with which he identified. He envisioned an ideal society which pursued perfection, an idealist in the fiercest sense of the word. Not only that, but he was uncompromising in his opinions and would almost never admit he was wrong.

He was equivocal, however, about William Miller.

While Miller had attracted many followers, there were nevertheless many clergy who were skeptical of his prediction and some had thought he may have changed the time. He addressed it in an October 1837 issue of the *Telegraph*: "This is to give notice to my friends," he wrote, "and all who may feel interested . . . that I have not changed my views for more than eighteen years; neither have I seen, heard, or read any particle of evidence, which has staggered my faith in believing that Christ will make his appearance the second time on or before A.D. 1843."[155]

Though skeptical, Murray remained open to the possibility. It reveals the depth of his faith at that time:

Whether the scriptures warrant mortals in undertaking to fix on the time when the Son of Man shall come again "in power and great glory," is with me a question, Murray wrote. But this view of the matter [does not lessen] the motives to diligence in making preparations for such an event—for, as the Bible is from God, and as Christianity is everlasting truth, such an event will come, sooner or later; and if the precise time be hidden from us . . . "as a thief in the night," is the strongest possible reason why we should be in preparation for it, every hour and every moment.[156]

In the *Telegraph*'s final issue of 1837, Murray published the first of a series of criticisms of Miller's theory by Orwell Baptist minister, Aaron Angier. It was not the first such critique of Miller. Rev. K. Haven, pastor of the Shoreham Baptist Church had written one a year earlier in Montpelier's *Universalist Watchman*. Haven's commentary ran in three separate issues and pointed out the discrepancies and inconsistencies in the calculations made by Miller in arriving at the time of the Coming. "This is however all guessing," he wrote, "which is scarcely allowable in fixing important data."[157]

Angier's comments were more personal and challenging.

"Much of your historical proof or what you suppose is the accomplishment of certain prophecies by their corresponding events, needs examining," concluded Aaron Angier. "Still, I may be deceived. Discussion, in the right spirit, will do no harm."[158]

In succeeding columns, Angier questioned the logical conclusions of Miller's theories about the literal and figurative meaning of times and numbers in scriptural prophecy and how they suggested or identified various historical events, which had enabled him to fix an approximate date for the Second Coming.

Miller's response was hostile. He said that Angier had intentionally misrepresented and misstated the facts to deceive others.

Angier denied that he had tried to misstate the facts and said that Miller simply had refused to answer his questions or acknowledge any errors that Angier had exposed.[159]

But Murray sided with Angier, writing in part:

"The spirit which he [Miller] manifests throughout is totally unbecoming any follower of Christ—more especially of one who professes to be instantly waiting his coming. His personal attack on the motives and Christian character of his opponent, are such as ought not be indulged in, under such circumstances by a Christian—I will say, by any civilized man . . ."[160]

66

Nevertheless, Murray continued to publish news about Miller, in keeping with regular reporting of revivals that were occurring throughout the Northeast.

Among the many other topics about which Murray had a continual and strong interest was the ethical justification of war.

"We deprecate the whole business of war at all times and under all circumstances. It is anti-Christian—It is inhuman—It is brutish. Christians at war?" Murray stated in an early issue of the *Telegraph*, using the Christian ethic as his rationale.[161]

This was clearly enunciated in his first "Peace Department" column nine months later, the first of a series of columns that he published periodically for two years in which he detailed his opposition to war.

"Ye have heard that it hath been said, an eye for an eye, and a tooth for a tooth; but I say unto you, that ye resist not evil: but whosoever shall smite Thee on thy right cheek, turn to him the other also."

> Self-defense . . . is the first law of nature; but it is of nature only, it belongs solely to the animal life; and the brute creation knowing no further, act up to the perfection of their nature. Had man, like them, no higher privilege than mortal existence, he might be right in following their example: but man is a rational creature and has an immortal soul to guard from every taint of guilt, and disobedience to his Maker's will: consequently, if duty to his God call for it, he is to give up all, even his natural life. He that loses his life for my sake, shall find it," saith the Savior. Thus, the martyrs yielded their backs to the scourge, their breasts to the sword of the executioner, and their bodies to the flames, without resistance or a murmur: even praying for their murderers.[162]

It marked the beginning of a ten-part series: "The Lawfulness of War for Christians, Examined."

"It is not expected that all will yet subscribe to the sentiments now appearing in our peace department," he added separately on page two about his new column which almost always appeared on page 4. "But we hope that Christians will at least give them a candid, prayerful examination, and compare them with the teaching of the New Testament."[163]

His views were on the extreme end of anti-war even today because he believed war was not justified even in self-defense. This position caused him to clash with the American Peace Society which had formed in New York in 1828, and a peace society in Brandon, which published its intention in the *Telegraph* to form an organization based on the national society in February of 1837.[164] In the week preceding, Murray published an article from the December issue of the *American Advocate for Peace*, part of which he republished the following week:

> The Peace Society requires no pledge from its members. For aught that appears in its constitution, the greatest warrior of the age might become one of its members and contributors. No pledge is required to individual conduct, no creed or subscription to any class of sentiments. Its members may believe in the necessity, or even utility, in certain cases, of war . . . . If it be conceded that some wars are just and necessary, it cannot, on the other hand be denied, that even these wars are in many respects fraught with suffering and distress; while of those which are necessary and unjust, nothing flows but unmixed evil.[165]

Murray added: "No pledge required with respect to individual conduct! . . . . Today he may join a Society whose object is the suppression and removal of an enormous sin: tomorrow he may be the leader in the practice of that very sin and all the while retain his standing as a good and efficient member of the Society!"[166]

Nevertheless, a state auxiliary to the national peace society was formed later that year, which Murray helped organize and which resulted in a debate about the issue of justifying war in self-defense, which he chronicled in the paper. Murray was among the minority of participants who declined membership because they insisted that the society should prohibit the membership of those who sanctioned war in self-defense. Instead, the constitution stated: "Any person may become a member of this Society, by signing its constitution, conforming to [the principle that all war is contrary to the spirit of the gospel] . . ."[167]

Murray suggested that this allowed those who participated in war or justified it to become members. He was not the only participant to express such views, which he published in the *Telegraph*, including a lengthy statement by Rowland T. Robinson.

Among other complaints, Robinson voiced his disappointment that the Vermont Peace Society refused to adopt an article into their Constitution that renounced all preparations for war such as "military academies, fortifications, arsenals, military trainings," and every activity that fostered the waging of war.[168]

Also weighing in was William Lloyd Garrison, who condemned the anti-Christian role of government officials: "What is a peace man? Surely, not . . . he who fills the station of commander-in-chief of all the military forces . . . . Nor he who delights to celebrate the deeds of Bunker Hill, of Saratoga, and of Monmouth . . ."[169]

These views, which even today would be considered radical, were representative of the ultraism that Murray consistently expressed not only in Vermont but throughout his life.

While peace was on the mind of Murray, a war was brewing along the Canadian border. A "Patriot Movement" had arisen among a small group of Canadians which had been joined by Americans who wanted to convert Canada into a Republican government like the U.S. Murray did not dwell on the political aspects of the war and simply reported the facts as best he could. However, he did provide one editorial that showed consistency with his opinion about war.

> . . . whatever intelligence is given in the *Telegraph*, in regard to existing war, in Canada and elsewhere, is given merely as intelligence—with no sympathy or countenance, on my own part, for the violent movements on either side—I am dependent on other papers for intelligence on the subject[XIV] . . . . Let it be distinctly understood that I take no responsibility for any partiality any of them betray. My object is to learn and communicate the facts as they are, as near as I can obtain them.[170]

Josiah Henson

Ironically, while the Patriot War was alleged to be a war fighting for greater freedom by the rebels, it was opposed by black Canadians, most of whom were fugitives from slavery. Many of them had signed up to fight against the rebellion, fearing that a change of government would jeopardize their freedom. They included noted fugitive slave, Josiah Henson. Though Underground Railroad conductor Rev J.W. Loguen, was asked to lead a company of black soldiers, he did not accept the offer. However, he said, "The colored population [in Canada] at that time were almost-to-a-man, fugitives from the States. They could not, therefore, be passive when the success of the invaders would break the only arms interposed for their security and destroy the only asylum for African freedom in North America."[171]

Murray's disagreement with the peace societies and its sanction of war in self-defense caused him to turn his interest toward non-

---

[XIV] It is interesting to note that only a brief notice of the Alamo appeared in the *Telegraph* with no details aside from it being blown up by the Mexican army – *Vermont Telegraph*, August 4, 1836, page 3.

resistance, which followed an ethic like his personal resistance to any violence. But they went further, refusing to support any governmental activity with which they in good conscience could not accept.

By the fall of 1838, Murray made that very clear. Writing in response to an editorial in the *New York Observer*, which cast doubt on the future of the New England Non-Resistance Society and suggested that only "thorough-going Roger Williams Baptists" would support it, he wrote:

> Why, instead of vying with each other in heaping calumny upon the Non-Resistance Society, do they not show the discordance of its doctrines with the precepts and practices of the Prince of Peace? The Editor of the Watchman is informed that there is at least one Baptist who is a member of the Society. The Editor of the Observer is the more informed of the two. He is right in supposing that "thorough-going Roger Williams Baptists" will be among the first to embrace the doctrine of "Peace on earth, good will towards men." Consistency requires it of them. I may be permitted here to say altho' I call no man master on earth next to the name of Christian, let me be called a "thorough-going Roger Williams Baptist." There are thousands of them among the Green-Mountains of Vermont, who love the unadulterated truth, as they love the pure waters that gush from our hills. They love to follow in the path which Jesus trod. They love to listen to the still, small voice" which whispers, "this is the way, walk ye in it." How fast they will embrace the doctrine of perfect peace and love, it does not become me to predict. As a matter of intelligence, however . . . their attention is invited to the following resolution, adopted at the recent session of the Vermont Association: Resolved, That all war and fighting are sinful, that to keep in preparation for war is not the way to prevent war; and therefore that it is the duty of all Christians to

refrain from bearing arms, and in every way to withhold their influence from the anti-Christian system.[172]

Murray's "Peace" column was renamed "Non-Resistance," through which he continued to articulate his position on non-violence. In a series of debates with Rev. Harvey Curtis, pastor of the Brandon Congregational Church, who believed violence was justified in self-defense, Murray continued to argue in favor of non-resistance and was in complete agreement with this declaration of the Boston Peace Society:

> We believe that the penal code of the old covenant, AN EYE FOR AN EYE, AND A TOOTH FOR A TOOTH, has been abrogated by JESUS CHRIST; and that under the new covenant, the forgiveness, instead of the punishment of enemies, has been enjoined upon all his disciples, in all cases whatsoever. To extort money from enemies, or set them upon a pillory, or cast them into prison, or hang them upon a gallows, is obviously not to forgive, but to take retribution. VENGEANCE IS MINE —I WILL REPAY, SAITH THE LORD.

Chapter 12

Cohorts and Collaborators

Though Murray was known from his earliest years as cantankerous and arrogant, someone who fought, though only verbally, even with friends, he still needed support. There were a few who contributed to his efforts more than most.

Murray's closest ally during the *Telegraph* years was probably Jedidiah Holcomb. A Brandon blacksmith, he initiated his association with the *Telegraph* with a bizarre advertisement of his business, with the headline, "Left-Handed Notice." He wrote, "Now, as I am left-handed, I shall go the other way."

Before long, Holcomb became a regular contributor to the *Telegraph*. His first cause was Temperance, but like Murray, his focus shifted to antislavery, and as early as 1838 was on the executive committee of the Vermont Anti-Slavery Society.[173] He also joined Murray on temperance and other reform societies, and in 1839 was a Vermont delegate with Murray at the annual meeting of the American Anti-Slavery Society. They remained friends after Murray left and moved to Ohio. His first editorial publication discussed the issues of slavery and women's rights. They included the following:

> I therefore wish every professed Christian, and everyone else, who desires the universal prevalence of freedom, to examine [the issue of slavery] thoroughly and candidly, and see on which side they are. If the principles laid down by said Constitution are not correct—if they are not in accordance with those taught by the Savior, I certainly have a desire that someone would furnish a plan that is right.[174]

For the most part, in 1837, Holcomb confined himself to stirring arguments against "rum-sellers" and the vice of alcohol, as well as occasional ads about things like horse sales:[175]

His temperance lecture on July 4, 1837 took up a good portion of two issues of the *Telegraph*:

This is the day on which thousands of our fellow countrymen meet, to celebrate the declaration of the Independence . . . .

We have met for the purpose of rehearsing some of the deeds of an enemy far more detrimental to our country, than was the *stamp* and *other* acts of the British government previous to the revolutionary war—an enemy who, *at this time*, possesses more power in the world than ever did the combined powers of Europe, *called the Holy Alliance*. We will also contemplate some of the means which may be used in destroying the *power* of the monster—The enemy we speak of, is *alcohol . . .*[176]

HORSE FOR SALE.

The subscriber has a valuable bay Horse which he wishes to exchange for cash down, or a good cash obligation, payable in three months. He will sell the horse for 150 dollars provided he is offered that price soon.

J. HOLCOMB.

Brandon, April 10, 1837.   29.tf

He concluded with an impassioned call to scripture:

If there be joy in heaven over one sinner that repenteth, how much more joy must there be, when this enemy shall have been conquered. The voice of a great multitude on earth will be heard, saying Alleluia! Then, both saints and angels in heaven, and saints on earth will give God the glory, saying, Amen, Alleluia! For in and through Him was the Beast conquered.[177]

Such religious fervor reflected the intense passion of the Awakening which was still very much alive.

In 1838, Holcomb wrote a strong appeal in the *Telegraph* for the support of immediate emancipation, joining with Murray in his feud with E.C. Tracy:

> There are probably more people in the non-slave-holding States who agree that slavery as it exists in the United States, is a sin—an evil that ought to be done away with, than there are that agree on the mode of doing it away, and the time to be employed in accomplishing the object. The evil has been standing so long, and is of such magnitude, that many people suppose the word immediate ought not to be applied, while speaking of removing it. The Editors of the *Vermont Chronicle* admitted (last spring while answering questions put to them by a correspondent of theirs) that the sin of slavery ought to be repented of immediately—(Here I would ask what the sin is?]—still contending that it was not necessarily sin to hold the legal relation of master to slave . . .[178]

Later in 1838, Holcomb launched another attack on the *Chronicle* when it reprinted an article that suggested the abolitionists in the North were alienating southern ministers and those in the Colonization movement who opposed slavery but did not support immediate emancipation, and that if the abolitionists were less acrimonious, then an accommodation would be possible.[179]

In a brief Christmas appeal to the readership for support, Murray praised Holcomb, writing, "Allow me to call the attention of Baptist brethren to what a Congregational brother has done for the *Telegraph* during the past year—and at the same time in this manner to express my grateful acknowledgments to the latter. The full amount of his patronage is still more than is here credited . . ."[180]

However, they also developed differences. Perhaps their first such disagreement, while cordial, occurred over the concept of non-violence as explained in Scripture. While Holcomb contended that some means of violence was permitted in self-defense, Murray apparently had moved to a position that contended, violence even in self-defense was not sanctioned by Scripture.[181] Holcomb would remain a supporter of Murray despite their differences and in 1843 after Murray announced his intention of leaving Vermont, he and Murray's brother, David, began publishing the abolitionist newspaper, *The Voice of Freedom*.

Another important Murray cohort was Brandon's leading citizen and entrepreneur, John Conant. Not only did he lend financial assistance as earlier described but he also was a committed abolitionist and president of the Brandon Anti-Slavery Society. In 1837, he wrote an editorial for the *Telegraph*, explaining why he was an abolitionist. This was the first paragraph:

> The question is often asked, why are you an abolitionist? The answer is ready:—Because, politically speaking, the cause of freedom is the cause of truth; humanly speaking, it is the cause of humanity; but more conclusively and religiously speaking, it is the cause of God, which latter reason includes both the former.[182]

Conant was the inventor of the Conant Stove, first produced in 1819. Casting was obtained from the Pittsford Iron Works, which had a ready supply of the region's vast quantity of hematite ore, and which had recently erected a blast furnace. It supplied the iron necessary for stove making. The stove proved to be a great success and was sold as far west as Ohio and largely responsible for the town's prosperity.[183]

Ruins of Vermont blast furnace

The ad below from the *Telegraph* is signed by Conant's sons.

Much like the Tappans, Conant participated in many reform and religious organizations, but on a smaller stage. Hemenway's *Gazetteer* had this to say about him:

> No man's name has been more intimately associated with the town of Brandon for the last half century than John Conant; not, however, on account of the public positions he has held, but from the nature, extent, and successful prosecution of his business operations for a long series of years, which gave employment to a large number of persons.
>
> In all public measures for the improvement of the place, or for the advancement of literary or religious objects, he took an active part; and where money was required to carry forward such measures, or for such objects, his zeal was most prominently exhibited in his liberal contributions.[184]

Murray probably never could've published the *Telegraph* as long as he did, especially with his personality, without Conant's imprimatur. Yet as early as 1839, they already had their first, though minor, disagreement about Murray's criticism of Hamilton College in central New York.[185]

Rowland T. Robinson, of nearby Ferrisburgh, and Murray were natural allies with their zealous anti-slavery. A close friend of Oliver Johnson, Garrison's right-hand man, Robinson quickly took a leading role in Vermont's anti-slavery movement, and became the state's most heralded Underground Railroad participant, who was twice documented in the *Telegraph* by Murray as his collaborator in aiding fugitive slaves,[186] though his activity declined both in helping fugitive slaves and involvement in the antislavery movement after 1850.

Their relationship is also illustrated in the hiring for a time of Robinson's son to apprentice as a printer at the Telegraph though short-lived.[187]

Murray had an easy affinity with Quakers like Robinson because in addition to their antislavery beliefs, they both were strong advocates of women's rights and non-violence. Murray had an affection for Robinson that lasted throughout his life, writing a personal heartfelt letter to him from Ohio in 1875.

"One week ago, I had a visit from our good friend, John Orvis. Among my first and particular inquiries, as to his knowledge of existing persons and things in Vermont, was to know if our old and excellent Brother and patron, Rowland T. Robinson, is still living. He said you were living, six months ago; and thought it would have come to his knowledge if you had since died – unless quite recently. So, I write to let you know, if living, that I am also living, and that I hold in grateful remembrance the experience I had in making your acquaintance and enjoying your society. The remembrance of those experiences of long years ago, and of your many loving kindnesses, will be cherished while I live and retain power of memory.[188]

Chapter 13

Antislavery Is Our Religion

Beneath the veneer of religion, the *Telegraph* was about much, much more. Subtly, Murray put the coverage of religion on the front page, leaving pages two and three, sometimes even page four to write about antislavery and other societal reforms, at least in the early years.

However, when confronted with this by a reader who wanted more emphasis on religion, he snapped with a long-winded retaliation filled with the biting sarcasm for which he was infamous.

It is to be presumed that the following forbearing, kind, decent, gentlemanly piece, was intended for our private benefit, and not for the public eye. We feel under no special obligation, however, to suppress it, or to correct its diction, orthography, or punctuation, and therefore give it, verbatim et literatim et punctuatim, with an appendage of two or three notes.

The reader's letter was then printed with its many spelling and grammatical errors.

Murray followed by answering each of the reader's complaints then challenged their anti-slavery beliefs:

Show us in what your anti-slavery consists. Our anti-slavery is a part of our religion. If yours is less, it is greatly deficient; and if you are professedly a religious man, either your anti-slavery or your religion is spurious, or both. For every true follower of Jesus Christ will remember them that are in bonds as bound with them—will warn oppressors of their sin, their folly and their danger—and he will do this as a religious duty, because

79

God requires it. He will not, like the hypocritical Priest and Levite, turn away and pass by on the other side.[189]

Interestingly, Murray claimed that only a minor part of the *Telegraph* discussed slavery, saying usually only a sixth and sometimes a tenth of the paper dealt with abolition. A brief review of the issues of the *Telegraph*, however, shows otherwise.

Murray was right about one thing—slavery was a religious issue, a matter of right and wrong, and the true believer could not possibly support slavery. The Bible against slavery was a common topic throughout his tenure at the *Telegraph*, along with continual diatribes against southern churches who allowed not only its members but its clergy to own slaves.

Abolitionists like Murray were merely following their consciences, James Birney wrote, and persevering "amidst menace and insult, in bearing their testimony against wrong, in giving utterance to their deep convictions—such men . . . have rendered freedom a more essential service than anybody . . . among us. The defenders of freedom are not those who claim and exercise rights which no one assails . . . . They are those who stand up for rights which mobs, conspiracies, or single tyrants put in jeopardy, who contend for liberty to that particular form, which is threatened at the moment by the many or the few—To the abolitionists belong this honor."[190]

While opposition against them continued, the tide began to turn in Vermont for the abolitionists. On November 16, 1836, the Vermont General Assembly had resolved that Congress has the power to abolish slavery and the slave trade in DC.[191] A reader of the *Telegraph* offered a long commentary on the use of products made from slave labor: "May they not reasonably suspect our motives, when they perceive our [necessity] to abstain from the luxuries of their soil . . . luxuries so destructive to the lives of those engaged in procuring them, as to be emphatically 'the price of blood' . . . ."

Using these products, the contributor insisted, made the user an accomplice to its sin. "Be not 'partakers of other men's sins.' " [192]

Among other items in the *Telegraph* that stoked the fires of abolition included a prophetic warning from the *Richmond Whig* by Virginia Governor McDuffie that the abolitionists' "interference with Southern rights would be just cause of war in the case of a foreign nation, and is just cause for separation . . ."

Another, reprinted from *The Liberator* was a report of the Ladies Anti-Slavery Fair in Boston where they sold such items as "free labor" cakes, quilts woven with anti-slavery poems, boxes and bookmarks with abolitionist slogans.

Also, in the news was continued coverage of the Gag Rule by Congress, reporting that former President and Congressman John Quincy Adams had attempted to offer a petition from 150 ladies in Massachusetts calling for the end of slavery. That such petitions were not considered at that time because of the Gag Rule underscored the southern dominance of the federal government. In fact, the slave states were overrepresented in the Presidency, the Supreme Court, and key positions in the federal government.[193] This led to the passage of such autocratic measures like the Fugitive Slave Law of 1850 that required all citizens to be slavecatchers.[xv]

The Gag Rule was also among the chief concerns of the Ferrisburgh Anti-Slavery Society. It sent a petition to Congress drafted by Rowland T. Robinson lamenting "the moral desolation resulting from the system of slavery legally tolerated in our country, in which the master as well as the slave is involved; and for the best interests of both, we desire its speedy and peaceful termination."[194]

[xv] Those who refused to aid the authorities in the apprehension of a fugitive slave were subject to the same penalties for those who actively assisted them: six months in jail or $1,000 fine for each fugitive assisted.

The third annual meeting of the Vermont Anti-Slavery Society was held in Brandon. A strong statement in opposition to slavery was presented:

Slavery is inconsistent with the general education of the people—its influence is to widen the distance between the rich and the poor, and to keep the latter in ignorance and degradation. If the sovereignty is to be and to remain in the hands of the people, the people must be enlightened and endowed with wisdom. Education, intellectual and moral, must extend to all . . . . Slavery is in its nature opposed to such a state of things. Where it exists, there must and will be laws to prevent the education of the poor, and these laws will be vigilantly enforced by guards by day and patrols by night.[XVI]

Again, the Gag Rule was of great concern.

The policy of the North is freedom of discussion and universal education. The policy of the South is the restriction of both. Those antagonist principles are now putting forth their legitimate and mutually hostile action—action that must, in the nature of the case, increase in power and effect until the one or other prevails.[195]

Two months later, on May 9, the fourth annual meeting of the American Anti-Slavery Society was held, and the state society was well represented with 60 delegates from 12 counties, one of whom was Murray.

[XVI] Laws that prohibited the teaching of reading to slaves were in place and nightly slave patrols had been established throughout the South after the Nat Turner Rebellion in 1830. The inability to read was a great impediment to their organizing rebellions as well as taking flight to the North.

It reported that 483 new antislavery societies had joined the national society during the previous year, bringing the total in the nation to 1006.[196] Forming these societies were seventy antislavery lecturers and society representatives in the field bringing the abolition message. A report of emancipated slaves who had become farmers in Ohio was given. While the Society did not seek to organize a political party devoted to ending slavery, it did encourage political action by influencing those in Congress. It commended the efforts of the Grimke sisters and George Thompson, and voiced opposition to the annexation of Texas or any new slave state.[197]

A resolution offered by James Birney condemned gradual emancipation: "Those who talk of ameliorating slavery, or of removing the evils of slavery and retaining slavery, are the defenders of perpetual bondage . . ." Immediate emancipation forced the slaveholder to confront their moral principles, he said, to bring them to the "law of God and press [them] to do justice and show mercy," today, not tomorrow.[198]

The idea of gradual emancipation favored by the South originated, Birney explained, after the failed slave rebellion led by Gabriel Prosser in Virginia 35 years earlier. Various plans had been discussed to move blacks to other territories in North America. This led to the creation of the American Colonization Society and its mission to return blacks to Africa, an idea presented as benevolent and supported by most churches but wholly at odds with the wishes of free blacks. During the 20 years of its existence, the Colonization Society had sent only 4,000 slaves to Africa while the slave population had increased by one million and was continuing to increase by 75,000 each year. Colonization was favored by the South, Birney emphasized, because it did not end slavery.

"If it is wrong to hold men in slavery, it is wrong to hold any in slavery. If it is wrong to hold them in slavery forever, it is wrong to hold them at all . . . Had I the power to do it in a word. I would not wait till I have finished these remarks, before I had sounded throughout the land, IMMEDIATE EMANCIPATION—ALL AT ONCE.[199]

Presbyterian minister, Rev. Charles Gardner followed with the following resolution: "That sufficient evidence has been given to the world to convince the enlightened public, that the immediate emancipation of the colored people is morally right and politically safe."[200]

Gardner reported several stories of emancipated slaves in Ohio, who had become successful farmers, including a gifted slave preacher in Kentucky, Shadrach Green. He added free blacks had been steadfast against Colonization since the beginning and concluded with fire and brimstone: "And the mountain shook, and the lightning flashed, and the thunder rolled, and the clouds appeared, portending that God was about to give law to men. And what is the law? 'Lay up these my words in your heart and in your soul, and bind them for a sign upon your hand, that they maybe as frontless between your eyes . . . . And thou shalt write them upon the door posts of thy house, and upon thy gates . . . . I say then that immediate abolition is both morally right and politically safe."[201]

Methodist minister, Rev Orange Scott followed with this resolution: "That the doctrines and precepts of our holy religion abundantly sustain our nation's declaration, 'that all men are created equal, that they are endowed with certain inalienable rights, among which are life, liberty, and the pursuit of happiness,' and therefore the condemnation of American slavery is equally demanded by our professions as republicans and Christians . . . .[202]

As this resolution suggested, there was a great deal of rancor between abolitionists and clergy during this time, and many clergy were beginning to join the sides of the abolitionists because of the obvious immorality of slavery. It was a total contradiction of Christ's teachings to possess slaves or even allow slavery. Nevertheless, southern clergy took offense at this and tried to justify slavery by showing that it existed in the Bible. Others said that it was their right to refuse to read antislavery notices in their churches. Some even said that they agreed that slavery was wrong but disapproved of attacking clergy who owned slaves. They warned that these attacks prevented support for immediate emancipation.[203]

In fact, abolitionism had become like a religion for some during this time, and numerous church groups and synods formed their own churches on account of this belief. These churches were called "come-outers."[204]

Orthodox Congregational Free Church, Union Village

One of these come-outer churches was in Union Village, near the New York border with Vermont, and which was organized in 1837 when radical abolitionist Baptist preacher, Nathaniel Colver, was then pastor of the neighboring Bottskill Baptist Church. It had formed out of a schism in the Dutch Reformed Church. It involved only 13 members in the beginning, renowned physician Dr. Hiram Corliss and William H. Mowry, son of wealthy village forefather William, its organizers. Named The Orthodox Congregational Church, it was from its start called the "Free Church." Its *Manual* stated that it was formed because the "practical love of mankind" had been forsaken in much of the Christian world by the "tolerance and even endorsement with . . . huge evils like intemperance, slavery, and war."[205]

One of the church's first major meetings, held in conjunction with the Bottskill Church, expressed outrage at the problems facing Elijah Lovejoy.

It was now more than a year since Lovejoy had moved and had resumed publishing his newspaper under the sponsorship of the Presbyterian Church in Alton, Illinois, 20 miles upriver, renaming it the *Alton Observer*. It had not been without great difficulty, because the printing press he had salvaged when his office was ransacked was destroyed by a mob while it was being shipped to Alton.

While not abolitionists, the people of Alton for the most part did not support slavery, and Illinois was after all, a free state. However, they believed that they had no right to interfere with states where it was legal. Lovejoy assured them that he was not an abolitionist and they helped him restore his press. But as time passed, Lovejoy's support for immediate emancipation grew and his views had clearly become those of a dedicated abolitionist. It was a bit puzzling because he continually insisted that he wasn't an abolitionist despite printing opinions strongly in support of immediate emancipation. Things came to a head when he published an editorial in the June 29, 1837 issue that included the following:

> We need not add a word touching the vast importance of [slavery]. With slavery in the several States we have nothing to do, except in the way of argument and persuasion; but let every free man in this republic remember that so long as slavery exists in the District of Columbia, he is himself a slaveholder, and a licenser of the horrid traffic in slaves, carried on under the very shadow of the capitol's walls. *We have a right to interfere there* [author's italics], and that right brings with it a solemn duty, which we may not innocently neglect.[206]

The following week, Lovejoy went further proposing the formation of a state anti-slavery society and explaining in detail the tenets of abolitionism, concluding with these words: "Abolitionists believe that as all men are born free, so all who are now held as slaves in this country were BORN FREE, and that they are slaves now is the sin, not of those who introduced the race into this country, but of those, and those alone, who now hold them, and have held them in slavery from their birth."[207]

These editorials ignited a fiery response. Some charged Lovejoy with reneging on his word to avoid discussion of Abolition though he had never promised to do so. The local newspaper, *Missouri Republican*, attacked Lovejoy: "The editor of the *Observer* has merited the full measure of community's indignation . . . . He has by his adhesion to the odious doctrines of Abolitionism . . . forfeited all claims to the protection of that or any other community."[208]

Nevertheless, Lovejoy continued his antislavery activities, organizing the Madison County Anti-Slavery Society at the Presbyterian Church and calling for the organization of a state anti-slavery society. What might've infuriated anti-abolitionists even more, however, was the publication of a letter charging Illinois citizens with holding hundreds of individuals in slavery.[209]

The *Republican* responded even more boldly, calling for the removal of Lovejoy and his newspaper:

"We perceive that an Anti-Slavery Society has been formed at Upper-Alton, and many others, doubtless, will shortly spring up in different parts of the State. We had hoped that our neighbors would have ejected from amongst them that minister of mischief, the Observer, or at least corrected its course.

"Something must be done in this matter, and that speedily. The good people of Illinois must either put a stop to the efforts of these fanatics or expel them from their community . . . . It is to this we appeal, and hope that the appeal will not be unheeded."[210]

Four days later, enemies of Lovejoy spotted him while in town to obtain medicine for his wife. A mob soon gathered around him and threatened to tar and feather him. Lovejoy asked that the medicine he had come to get would be brought to his wife and that she not be harmed. They agreed. Lovejoy then made an appeal to God, saying "I am in your hands, and you must do with me whatever God permits you to do." This made them hesitate and they let him go unharmed.[211]

But an hour later, they went after his press and broke into the *Observer* office and destroyed it.

Lovejoy offered his resignation as editor of the paper to the church, but it was refused, so he soldiered on and with support from outside sources Lovejoy purchased yet another press. Remarkably, however, shortly after its arrival, it was destroyed when the warehouse where it was being stored overnight was broken into.[212]

In the meantime, Lovejoy took his family to visit his wife's mother in St. Charles, Missouri, a town northeast of St. Louis, about 25 miles from Alton. At the invitation of Rev. William Campbell, the local Presbyterian minister and an old friend, he preached the Sabbath service. At the close of evening services, a stranger passed a note of warning to him. Out of concern, Rev. Campbell went with him to his mother-in-law's house.

After an hour of socializing with Campbell, they were accosted by a mob, some of whom forced their way inside the house and tried to drag Lovejoy out, but due to the efforts of Rev. Campbell, they retreated. Apparently, neighbors friendly to the family gathered and though the mob returned, they remained outside, hooting and jeering, demanding that Lovejoy leave town. Finally, a note was delivered to the mob that Lovejoy would be leaving on the next stage in the morning. This seemed to pacify them enough for him to sneak out to a friend's house where he was given a horse so that he could leave that night.[213]

Lovejoy remained undaunted, and he announced that he would resume publication once again as soon as another press arrived. Some friends counseled him to move north to Quincy, a town with a strong abolitionist population, and he said he would consider this. However, he insisted that he would remain in Alton if in fact the Church wished it.

In the meantime, he had drawn support from a group of citizens in Alton. While the mayor advised them that they had the legal right to protect his property with the use of arms, if necessary, he wouldn't commit to offering protection.

In October, the state anti-slavery society met in Alton to organize. But anti-abolitionists disrupted the meeting, and the delegates were forced to move it to a private home. A week later, a town meeting was held to discuss the *Observer's* continued publication. On November 3, a large and angry group demanded that Lovejoy leave Alton.

> Resolved, That the discussion of the doctrines of immediate Abolitionism, as they have been discussed in the columns of the ' Alton Observer,' would be destructive of the peace and harmony of the citizens of Alton, and that, therefore, we cannot recommend the re-establishment of that paper, or any other of a similar character, and conducted with a like spirit.[214]

Lovejoy refused to acquiesce. It was said he was calm but firm.

"If I leave here and go elsewhere, violence may overtake me in my retreat, and I have no more claim upon the protection of any other community than I have upon this; and I have concluded after consultation with my friends, and earnestly seeking counsel of God, to remain in Alton . . . . If the civil authorities refuse to protect me, I must look to God; and if I die, I have determined to make my grave in Alton."[215]

When the new press arrived on the night of November 5, 1837, it was placed in a building owned by Winthrop Gilman, which was composed of two connected stores connected to each other within. A group of armed supporters were stationed to protect it. Word spread of the press's arrival, but no serious action was taken by Lovejoy's opponents at first, and most of the armed supporters withdrew. However, rumors of an attack were brewing, and they returned. Among the guards were Lovejoy's younger brothers, Owen and Daniel, who had moved from Maine to support him. They assembled at the warehouse along with Elijah and Gilman. Not long after, on the night of November 7, a mob surrounded the building. Gilman attempted to reason with them and warned that anyone who tried to enter would be shot. Suddenly, there came a hail of stones and other objects.

Alton Riot -- Colorized Version, Credit NYPL

A group of armed supporters were stationed to protect it. Word spread of the press's arrival, but no serious action was taken by Lovejoy's opponents at first, and most of the armed supporters withdrew. However, rumors of an attack were brewing, and they returned, assembling at the warehouse along with Elijah and Gilman.

Not long after, on the night of November 7, a mob surrounded the building. Gilman attempted to reason with them and warned that anyone who tried to enter would be shot. Suddenly, there came a hail of stones and other objects, followed by bullets. Lovejoy, Gilman, and some others returned the fire, and killed a man named Bishop. It was said that it was a bullet from Lovejoy's gun that killed him.

There was a halt to the hostilities, and at this point the mayor intervened. Under a flag of truce, he entered the building. He asked Lovejoy to give up the press and that while he supported their right to protect themselves, there was nothing he could do to help them against the mob. But Lovejoy refused. When the mayor left, the mob set up a ladder to torch the building. As they mounted it, several of Elijah's supporters stormed outside and fired at the incendiaries. When they dispersed, Elijah and Royal Weller went outside to survey the scene. Several members of the mob were hiding behind a pile of lumber. One of them had a double-barreled shotgun and riddled Elijah with bullets, five of them striking him. Elijah turned and staggered into the warehouse up a flight of stairs, holding his chest, crying out, "Oh, God, I have been shot." He fell to the floor.[216]

His brother Owen, who later became a prominent abolitionist Congressman during the years leading up to and through the Civil War, kneeled over him. Watching his brother expire, Owen experienced an epiphany: "While I was beside the prostrate body of my murdered brother, Elijah, with fresh blood oozing from his perforated breast, on my knees, alone with the dead, I vowed never to forsake the cause for which his blood was sprinkled."[217]

The incident led another who would become a much more famous abolitionist, to experience an epiphany in Hudson, Ohio. During a church service commemorating Lovejoy, a young John Brown vowed to sacrifice his life to end slavery: "Here, before God, in the presence of these witnesses, from this time, I consecrate my life to the destruction of slavery!"[218] Murray was supportive:

The patriots of 76 had not a whit more to contend for than Lovejoy. He has fallen in the very palladium of human liberty—defense of the most precious rights of man; and his resistance was not made until these rights had been, in his own person, repeatedly and most monstrously invaded. He was sustained in his course by the constitution and the laws of this country, which recognizes his slayers as murderers, and requires their blood for atonement.

But how much better to have died, as Christ, the apostles, and the martyrs did passively; [XVII]or to have lived persecuted and outraged. 'Blessed are they which are persecuted for righteous sake.'[219]

[XVII] As shown in Chapter Nine, Murray was a non-resistant and did not believe in violence, even in self-defense.

Chapter 14

A Trip, and A Terrible Conflagration

Murray was never a wealthy man. "Mine is much the situation of the one who prayed to have neither poverty nor riches . . ." he wrote. "The wealth of knowledge is more valuable than all other wealth. It needs no insurance against fire or flood. It exempts from the taxation and torment . . . from doctors, lawyers, and priests."[220]

However, by 1838, Orson had five kids to support: Carlos, 10; Marsena, 9; Harriet, 5; Catherine 2 1/2, and Charles, who was then not yet a year old. In 1839, he purchased a second tract of land, probably to farm. As another of his bios states that he was a farmer throughout his life "to obtain his bread."[221]

Despite continual requests in the paper to delinquent subscribers, some even clergy,[222] it apparently supported him well enough, either with income or credit, to go on periodic trips for antislavery meetings, as well as journey throughout the state and northeastern New York to collect outstanding bills for the paper and recruit subscribers.

His most significant journeys were his yearly visit to attend the annual meeting of the American Anti-Slavery Society. He gave a full report in the *Telegraph* in 1838.[223]

He had a rocky start that year, he wrote, the only passenger to board the stage in Sudbury, about five miles from his home. It was near midnight and the plank road was so severe, he wrote, that it caused him to vomit during the ten-mile ride to Castleton. Some passengers joined him then, but the nausea continued, and he was forced to take a seat outside with the driver which gave him some relief. At a stopover in Granville, N.Y., he took a walk to see a former acquaintance. This settled his stomach, and he was able to eat a little bread and milk, his "favorite meal."[224]

In the evening, they reached Albany, only to miss the night boat to New York and forcing him to stay overnight at Safford's Temperance House. There he found sixteen Methodist ministers and many Methodist laymen on their way to a convention in Utica to discuss the denomination's position on slavery. One of the ministers told him it was the intention of the denomination, when founded by John Wesley, to abolish slavery among its members. But since some of its ministers had become slaveholders, they were facing resistance.

"The Lord spare and arouse them," Murray praised the ministers in the report of his journey, "and bless the Convention that now undertakes to bring back this people to obedience to His word. Other denominations, and the Baptists among the rest, need as much purifying, perhaps, from this flagrant sin as the Methodists."[225]

The next afternoon, Murray left for New York in the steamer, The Swallow, seen below.

On board he met with Gerrit Smith who was then 41, and Beriah Green, then 43. Orson was ten years younger. They had an interesting and uncomfortable encounter with a Baptist minister on the boat who opposed abolitionists. Uncharitable, bitter, quarreling with the Colonization Society and its good intentions to help "niggers," he raged. "You're fools." Even if he agreed with them, he added, which he didn't, he was on his way South to visit some congregations, and he surely wasn't going to interfere with slaveholders who had every right to own slaves.[226]

The next day, after some difficulty finding a room, Murray attended a Peace Convention at the Fourth Free Church, where he found congenial company and in the afternoon the business meeting of the American Anti-Slavery Society at the Broadway Tabernacle.

"A mighty host of choice spirits are assembled and assembling from all quarters, and great and glorious for will be done for the present, and for future generations," he wrote, "for time, and for eternity. Glory to god in the highest, for the auspices and the prospects!"[227]

The next morning, Murray described going with Henry B. Stanton to the New York City harbor to view a new steamship, the "Great Western," which arrived from England.

"It is a most magnificent thing. There is nothing brilliant in its outward appearance; but its inside finishing is splendid to extravagance and waste. The strength and massiveness of its machinery is without a parallel in anything I have seen."[228]

Murray had a toothache, so he was late to the business meeting and missed part of the debate between William Jay and Alvan Stewart. The issue was whether Congress has power over slavery in the states. It was important for the society because their constitution acknowledged that the states had priority over its legality and not Congress. The key point in Stewart's argument for Congress was that: "no person shall be deprived of life liberty or property without due process of law," which gave Congress not the states the power to legitimize slavery.

Wendell Phillips and Birney were against the change; Gerrit Smith for it, stating that, "Congress has what he would style the war power recognized in that clause of the constitution which gives to Congress the power to provide for the general welfare which is competent to the abolishment of slavery, in a war emergency which would make it necessary to arm the slaves for the defense of the country."

However, when a vote was held on changing the society's position, it was rejected. Though a majority of 43 for and 33 against, it was not enough for a 2/3 majority. Murray voted in the negative, explaining, "I most sincerely wish that clause had never been in the constitution. But as it has, thus far, imposed no hindrance . . . to our enterprise, and can impose none that I can conceive . . . and my opinion is that it had better remain . . ."[229]

Of course, in the future, all abolitionists would oppose the state's power to allow slavery, and this is what led to the Civil War.

On Saturday evening, six days after leaving home, he attended a lecture by Methodist minister, Rev. Orange Scott, who gave an account of denomination's meeting regarding slavery, noting that in three years, antislavery among the clergy had increased from 5 to "upwards of 2,000" with as many as 50,000 Methodists becoming abolitionists.

On Sunday he attended Lewis Tappan's Sabbath school in the lecture room of the Broadway Tabernacle. Upwards of 150 children and adults of all colors attended, he wrote. One case he mentioned was that of a former slave and mother who had lost her right hand, who was a washerwoman. She had been totally illiterate and was now reading the Bible. Tappan's daughters were among the teachers, and the school was open throughout the day and into the late evening.

On Monday, May 7th, the business meeting of the antislavery society resumed, and Tuesday was the anniversary of the American Anti-Slavery Society. That morning the crowd spilled from the Broadway Tabernacle into the street. Society President Arthur Tappan presided. Speakers included Henry B. Stanton, James Birney, James McCune Smith, Gerrit Smith, Lewis Tappan, and Alvan Stewart.

Among the resolutions: "That in our efforts to abolish slavery, we meet each other, not as members of any religious or political party; but as abolitionists, on the broad ground of common brotherhood and humanity, as moral and accountable beings, entitled to equal rights and privileges.

". . . that men who differ widely from each other on political and theological subjects, can labor harmoniously together, for its promotion, and that no political party or religious denomination, which is not in itself corrupt, has anything to fear from is progress or final triumph."

". . . that we observe with feelings of horror and execration, an export slave trade, commenced and prosecuted between the United States and Texas; and earnestly call on every patriot, and especially on members of Congress, to instant, persevering, and effectual exertions to put a stop to this nefarious traffic.

". . . that any person who aids in restoring the fugitive to his master and reimposing the chains of slavery upon a fellow-being, whether acting as a public officer or otherwise, is guilty of a crime against freedom, humanity and religion and should be regarded as the abettor of a base and cruel despotism.

"... that we recommend to abolitionists especially in the cities and larger villages and towns, to appoint committees of vigilance, whose duty it shall be to assist fugitives from slavery in making their escape, or in a legal vindication of their rights.[230]

That night Murray returned on the Swallow. Items were stolen from passengers while they slept; Murray said he lost $5, equivalent to over $100 today.

"The noise and confusion on board a steamboat are so constant and so great as to render a sleeping passenger an easy prey for prowling loafers," he said, explaining that the money was taken out of the pockets of his pants which had been set aside. The next morning, he took a boat to Troy, a packet up the Champlain Canal

 to Whitehall, and the steamboat Burlington to Orwell, arriving at 3 pm. "The Burlington is altogether the finest boat I ever saw," he wrote. "It is quite sufficiently elegant in its finishing, with comparatively very little of the extravagance of the Great Western."

At Orwell he met ten-year-old son Carlos driving their buggy and horses, a five-mile ride back to Brandon. [231]

A week or so later, Murray reported frantically in the *Telegraph*:

I stop the press and remove other matter to announce the horrifying fact that the peaceable and quiet city of Philadelphia has just now—at this late day in the history of American pro-slavery atrocities—been brought under the terrific reign of Lynch-Law. It may not be known to the readers of the *Telegraph* generally, that the abolitionists of Philadelphia have recently been erecting a spacious Hall in the city consecrated to the sacred cause of emancipation."[232]

Credit: Library Company of Philadelphia

A temple of Liberty, its construction had been inspired by the ideals of justice and equality and had been built through the sale of 2,000 shares of stock worth $20 each.[XVIII] Constructed of marble in the Greek-Revival style, it was 62 feet wide, 100 feet deep, and 42 feet high. The first floor housed the new offices of the Pennsylvania Anti-Slavery Society and its organ, the *Pennsylvania Freeman*; a free produce store, an antislavery reading room, several meeting rooms, and two large lecture rooms. Three stairways led to the second floor,

---

[XVIII] About $1.2 million in today's currency: https://www.in2013dollars.com/

which housed the auditorium, known as the "Grand Saloon," which could accommodate 3,000 persons.[233]

The building was ventilated through the roof and lighted with gas, a recent innovation, and over the speakers' platform was engraved in large gold letters," Virtue, Liberty, and Independence."[234]

This new marvel of Philadelphia was built to be a meeting place for reformers and those seeking human betterment, a shrine to the spirit of free discussion in ancient Greece. Abolitionists from around the nation were invited to the grand opening, which was to be followed by a series of reform meetings and events that week. Among those who came and spoke were William Lloyd Garrison, Alvan Stewart, Thomas Morris, Charles Burleigh, Lucretia Mott, Abby Kelley, Angelina Grimke Weld, and John Greenleaf Whittier, who had written a poem for the event:

> We dedicate our fair and lofty Hall,
> Pillar and arch, entablature and wall,
> As Virtue's shrine, as Liberty's abode,
> Sacred to Freedom, and to Freedom's God!

The grand opening on May 14, 1838 filled the auditorium of the Parthenon of Philadelphia with "one of the largest audiences ever assembled" in Philadelphia up to that time. The keynoter, David Brown, complimented the efforts of the abolitionists but because of his advocacy of gradual emancipation became the source of controversy.

The fireworks began the next day after a talk about the mistreatment of the Indians by Charles Burleigh, a friend of Murray who had given many antislavery lectures in Vermont. There were cries for Garrison, who had voiced his unhappiness with Brown, to speak.

First, Garrison criticized the building's managers because "not a single, colored brother has occupied a seat upon your platform." Then he attacked Brown. Slavery would not be ended without "a most tremendous excitement," he insisted. [235]

That night notices were posted around the city calling attention to the abolitionist meetings in Pennsylvania Hall, calling on citizens to rally the next morning in support of the right to own persons as property as guaranteed by the Constitution and demand that the antislavery meetings stop. It was suspected they had been posted by a southerner who had come to disrupt the proceedings.[236]

On the third day, as anti-abolition protesters gathered outside and hall managers called for police protection, an estimated 3,000 persons filled the auditorium. Garrison was to speak again as well as members of the Female Anti-Slavery Society, including Lucretia Mott and Angelina Grimke, who had recently married her more famous abolitionist husband, Theodore Weld. The sight of blacks and whites, some arm-in-arm, entering the hall infuriated the mob and Grimke's words enraged them even more:

> Those voices without tell us that the spirit of slavery is here and has been roused to wrath by our abolition speeches and conventions: for surely liberty would not foam and tear herself with rage . . . . This opposition shows that slavery has done its deadliest work in the hearts of our citizens . . . . cast out first the spirit of slavery from your own hearts and then lend your aid to convert the South . . . . The great men of this country will not do this work; the church will never do it. A desire to please the world, to keep the favor or all parties and of all conditions, makes them dumb on this and every other unpopular subject. They have become worldly-wise, and therefore God, in his wisdom, employs them not to carry on his plans of reformation and salvation. He hath chosen the foolish things of the world to confound the wise, and the weak to overcome the mighty.[237]

The mob began throwing rocks and brickbats at the windows. The shutters inside the windows protected those inside, but when the meeting ended, some blacks were assaulted.

Despite this, meetings planned for the next day were held, one of them, the American Convention of Women, which was to be the last one held in the Hall. The mob had gathered again and still there was no police protection. The rowdiness grew and the situation became tense. Finally, Mayor John Swift came to intercede.

After the women and others in attendance bravely left the building, pushing through the crowd, the mayor requested that the Hall be closed. He then spoke to the mob, asking them to disperse.

"There will be no meeting here this evening," he promised . . . "The managers had the right to hold their meeting, but as good citizens, they have, at my request, suspended their meeting for this evening. We never call out the military here! We do not need such measures. Indeed, I would, fellow citizens, look upon you as my police . . . . I trust you will abide by the laws and keep order. I now bid you farewell for the night."

After locking up the Hall, the mayor left amid the cry, "Three cheers for the mayor!"[238]

But the rioters betrayed the mayor and did not leave. Using crowbars, they burst open the door, and using axes tore up the seats and piled them in the center of the building. Opening the gas pipes, they applied torches to ignite a conflagration.[239]

The fire department came but instead of trying to stop the fire they only contained it so that it didn't spread. It was estimated that as many as 15,000 persons witnessed the scene, and it wasn't long before Philadelphia's Parthenon of liberty was burnt to ashes.[240]

Almost forgotten was the attempt to burn down the newly-built shelter for "colored" orphans, which the Good Will Fire Department saved.[241] Also, the home of abolitionist Lucretia Mott, which was targeted, was spared thanks to a diversion of the mob by a friend.[242]

The next day, Whittier wrote, "In the heart of this city a flame has gone up to Heaven. It will be seen from Maine to Georgia."[243]

Both the Mayor and Governor Joseph Ritner offered rewards of $2,000 and $500 respectively for information identifying the arsonists.[244] Two men were charged the following week, Samuel Yaeger and Edgar Kimmey.[245]

It was reported that Yaeger, the father of five children and a man of "considerable property" was released on bail. Kimmey, unable to make bail, was committed to jail; however, no information about a conviction was found.[246] Ironically, some years later an ad indicated Kimmey may have been a local fireman.[247]

Credit: Library Company of Philadelphia

Murray considered the conflagration to be a confirmation of abolition's success, writing of its opponents:

Short sighted indeed they must be, not to see that they defeat their own ends," Murray wrote, "that they add fuel to the fire which is consuming prejudice, caste and oppression—which is rapidly and effectually burning out from human society all the infernal abominations which their own nefarious doings are designed to perpetuate and promote. He who sitteth in the heavens will laugh at their folly . . . . Let this be the consolation of every philanthropist, and let not one effort be abated, until the truth goes forth as the morning and every work of the devil be brought to naught.[248]

Chapter 15

Fugitive Slaves and God

Orson's deep moral integrity naturally compelled him to take an interest in fugitive slaves. Items about fugitive slaves were regularly reported in the *Telegraph*. This interest was not merely journalistic. As son Charles wrote, "During the period of the perilous efforts of negroes in escaping from slavery conditions and seeking refuge in Canada, my father and mother rendered them aid abundantly at their home in Vermont."[249]

> A FUGITIVE from southern soul-driving passed through this village last week, on his way, and fleeing for life, to "Her Majesty's dominions!" He could not be persuaded that the evergreen hills of free Vermont could afford him a hiding-place for the sole of his foot, where he should be safe from the clutches of the kidnapper!
>
> I took names, dates, and other facts from him, for the purpose of giving some extended account; but, on more reflection, have thought best, for the safety of his benefactor at least, to suppress, at present, most of the names of persons and places.

The above account published in the April 11, 1838 issue of the *Telegraph* not only confirms Murray's role in the Underground Railroad but also implicates some of his collaborators. His account continues:

Suffice it, then, to give some very brief and general statements. He was helped away by the son of his master. His master had been drinking too much and had sold him to a "soul-driver,"

105

[the name given to those who bought and sold slaves for a living] for a more southern market. The son—with whom it would seem that this slave was a favorite—on learning the fact that he was sold, and that he was soon to be taken off, told him to go to a certain woods and wait until dark. He went, and at dark his benefactor came with a powerful horse, took him on behind and carried him north until half past 3 in the morning. He then left him, giving him advice and directions.

He had shown him the North Star and told him to travel nights and lie by during the day, for the first three days. He also gave him two different passes and a letter. The first pass was to be used until he reached a place mentioned and then to be destroyed and another used until he reached another place mentioned. After this he was to travel in a given direction, a given length of time, and then enquire for "Quakertown" in Pennsylvania. When he had reached Quakertown, he was to look for a man with a broad-brimmed hat, and a broad-tailed coat," to whom he was to give the letter. All this, it seems he succeeded in performing, with admirable success.

On reaching Quakertown, he found several men answering the description. So he selected the one who appeared to have the broadest-brimmed hat, to whom he gave the letter, and by whom he was hospitably received and entertained for the night, and directed onward in the morning. After travelling incessantly, and swimming one or two rivers which yet contained floating pieces of ice, he reached this place four weeks and six days from the time he started.

He is 23 years of age— has a strong physical constitution— sound common sense—a large share of intelligence for a slave— he is modest, amiable, and pious. His whole deportment convinces one of the truth of his story.

He summed up the advice which he received from his "young master," as he called his benefactor, on their final separation. He told me, said he, to drink no liquor, keep no bad company, and be obedient to the laws.

I asked him whether he had ever heard of the anti-slavery movements in the North, while he was in slavery. Yes, he had heard something of it through his young master who was in favor of it! He was confident that if by any means his old master's slaves should ever fall into the hands of his young master, he would remove them all to a free State and emancipate them!

The friends of the cause here labored to persuade him that, in the present state of things in Canada [the Patriot War], it would be better for him to remain in Vermont. We thought he would be safe here. But he thought otherwise. He enjoyed himself, he said, when in the society of sympathizing friends here, but when alone he was in constant fear. It was heart-breaking to witness the eagerness with which he panted to place his feet on land from which he might not be dragged into merciless bondage. While on his way hither, he had, in his travels on the side of a mountain, seen some deer that ran swiftly away at his approach. Raising his eyes and hands towards heaven, he exclaimed, "O my God! thought I, if I could run like these deer, how soon I would be free!"

We put him on board the stage--I gave him such waymarks towards Canada as our Allens, Barbers, Robinsons, Sabins, etc., and he had gone to a government of crowns and scepter, in pursuit of the precious boon of liberty, which no one had the power to extend to him in this boasted Republic.[250]

THE FUGITIVE SAFE.—The slave, who went through this town, recently, has sent a letter back to J. W. Hale of this village, in which he says, "I am in Canada, where there is *liberty!*" He was, at the time the letter was written, only a mile from the line—said he did not feel perfectly safe yet—should go further. He wished to know whether anything had ~~been heard~~ of his ~~pursuers.~~

Three weeks later, the *Telegraph* reported that the fugitive had arrived safely in Canada.[251]

These revelations in the *Telegraph* occurred the year after the first documented instance of aid to fugitive slaves in Vermont. XIX In a letter to Rowland T. Robinson at Rokeby, Oliver Johnson wrote, [Simon] had "intended going to Canada in the spring," Johnson wrote, "but says he would prefer to stay in the US if he could be safe . . . . I could not help thinking he would be a good man for you to hire . . ."[252]

Johnson, who was in western Pennsylvania on business for the American Anti-Slavery Society, also had written a letter to Robinson

---

XIX It is likely that fugitive slaves were being helped in Vermont much earlier. One legendary case involves Vermont Supreme Court Judge Theophilus Harrington of Clarendon who refused to honor a slaveholder's bill of sale for a fugitive slave in 1804, saying that he would only honor "a bill of sale from Almighty God" (Jacob Ullery, *Men of Vermont*, Brattleboro, VT: Transcript Publishing Company, 1894: 178).

two years earlier about a "colored boy named William who he wanted to place with Chauncey Knapp, the state's secretary of state and a leading member of the state anti-slavery society, which suggested he was a fugitive slave.[253]

RT Robinson home at Rokeby

Tying Murray close to the Robinson family in the Underground network is his hiring Robinson's son to apprentice as a printer for the *Telegraph*, in addition to their frequent contact through antislavery and temperance societies, and pretty much their full agreement on matters of morals and politics.

Another Vermont resident who wrote about aid to fugitive slaves there sent the following to *Friend of Man* in 1838:

> The cause is advancing nobly in this state. Indeed, it can hardly be otherwise, as its principles are better understood by the people of the Green Mountain state, so long noted for their ardent attachment to the fundamental principles of liberty, on which it is based . . . . I saw a few days since, a noble looking intelligent Virginian fleeing in pursuit of liberty, "to the land of kings where men are free." The people in several places in Vermont, in the exercise if their characteristic hospitality, invited him to remain with them; but he feared to remain with them . . . believing that no soil short of Canada could afford him an abode secure from the southern man-stealer.

The writer signed off as "AB (likely Austin Beecher), and this information was part of a report about the Chittenden County Anti-Slavery Society.[254]

The Underground Railroad was often a family matter. Family members and friends became natural associates in the humanitarian effort.

Jedidiah Holcomb was another collaborator. In 1841, he reported fugitive slave traffic in Brandon to the *National Anti-Slavery Standard*, the sister publication of *The Liberator*.

> I lately saw an advertisement, copied from a paper in the District of Columbia, offering a reward for a runaway female slave, her two brothers . . . I am pretty confident I saw the woman, on her way to Canada; and her owner, as he calls himself, may as well give up the chase. She acknowledged that she had a good master, but, nevertheless, wanted her liberty. She and her husband, who belonged to another man, set their wits to work, and contrived to slip away, separately. They met again in Pennsylvania, and, together, followed "the North star."

Holcomb added, "There are several individuals here, who gladly give a helping to all such wayfarers; and we not unfrequently have it in our power to do so."[255]

An insight to the clandestine network that was active in Vermont were reports of the heroic Fugitive Slave Missionary, Hiram Wilson.

In his Christmas issue for 1839, Murray published the Wilson account and appeal for assistance. The following is an excerpt from it:

> This work of justice and charity towards the outraged and afflicted poor has been moving forward silently for three years past. This mission has suffered much from want of laborers,

and still more from want of comfortable support for the few who have volunteered their services and labored with uncommon zeal and fidelity in this important harvest-field.

During the last winter, fifteen teachers [eleven from Oberlin, seven of them females] were employed in different parts of Upper Canada (Ontario), who evinced a spirit of self-denial and untiring devotion that would have done credit to any missionaries on the face of the earth.

[They] are located in settlements and places where the colored people are numerous, with specific instructions from the superintendent of the mission to labor specially for the welfare, temporal and eternal of the colored population .... Most of them are prosecuting their studies preparatory for the ministry and missions, and need a reasonable compensation for their time . . . For myself and family, we have received nothing for more than 18 months past, but a scanty subsistence, and have suffered much, and blessed be God are willing to suffer yet more, if relief should not come, rather than abandon the work.[256]

Wilson continued, criticizing the American Anti-Slavery Society for failing to supply the promised support. Only the New York State Anti-Slavery Society had contributed a small donation of $50 ($1600 in 2022), he said, and he had traveled 10,000 miles in the previous 18 months, 3,000 by foot, at a cost of $250. He needed more assistance.

"Much of the time I have toiled and struggled through wintry storms and piercing cold, in nightly silence, while a selfish, cold-hearted world was wrapped in slumbers around me. Of this I do not complain but rather rejoice and count it a precious privilege to do and dare and suffer, if needs be, in such a worthy cause as that of

111

our blessed Savior and his cast out and afflicted poor . . . . Will not some of the noble-hearted Green Mountaineers lend a helping hand?"[257]

The next year, Holcomb proposed a drive to collect clothing for Wilson in an article in the *Telegraph*. He followed it up some months later with a list of the items that he collected and sent to Wilson. There was one bed quilt, 25 pairs of socks, 5 coats, 5 shirts, 5 pairs of pants, 4 pairs of shoes. 2 mittens, 2 hats, a skirt, and a pair of boots, as well as an assortment of cotton and woolen cloth and yarn.[258]

In 1842, in a discussion in the *Telegraph* about what a fugitive slave might expropriate from their owners to aid their escape, Holcomb wrote: "I think I have had much enjoyment in feeding and lodging the fugitive, and I trust I shall ever be ready to aid in a similar way."[259]

That year, Murray also confessed that his aid to fugitives was continuing and identified Holcomb and Robinson as his collaborators:

> Among the numerous fugitives from slavery who have called on me at different times, on their way to British freedom, was one from Tennessee, who reached Vermont about a year ago. He stated to me that his principal living on his perilous journey to the free States was corn taken from the outstanding stalks. He was blessed with an excellent set of teeth to grind it. His practice reminded me of our Savior's allowing his disciples, when they 'were hungered,' 'to pluck the ears of corn and to eat.' Did our Savior allow theft? Not at all. There is no theft in such cases.
>
> I don't know how well the fugitive would fare in the region of Windsor—where the Abolitionists are so sure of getting mobbed—or wherever the Chronicle or any other Colonization influence bars sway. But if they crowd the poor

victims of their hate to 'dreadful straits,' outhouse who are thus recreant to yearning nature be the responsibilities, and not on the victims of their inhumanity and barbarity.

My present dwelling place is situated on one of the slave's by-paths to freedom. I hope always to be thus situated, while slavery continues, and my life is spared. I entertain no fear of injury from them. I have far more confidence in them than I have in Jesuitical editors and popular religious leaders who would throw obstacles in the way of their escape.

About ten days ago three noble looking young men, on their flight, called on me and took supper. In the evening I was going out about a mile and a half to attend an Anti-Slavery meeting and invited them to go with me. They said they should like to go—they knew all about slavery and would like to know about Anti-Slavery. So, inasmuch as they were fatigued and footsore with walking, I harnessed my number one-horse wagon and carried them. They manifested much gratification at the sympathy they discovered for themselves and their perishing fellow beings which they had left behind in bonds.

I felt no alarm during the night, lest they take my horse or other property and go off with it. Brother Holcomb lodged two of them and gave them breakfast; and I have heard no complaint from him. When they were ready to depart, I gave them some bread and cheese, and instead of manifesting any disposition to wrong me any way, they gave me, and my family severally, a hearty shake of the hand, and involved God's blessing upon us. (And by the way I am confident their prayers will avail us quite as much as some others might that would be far more pretending). If brethren J. A. Allen and R.T. Robinson, to who

I directed them on the same by-way, have been in any way harmed by them, I shall have sorrow and disappointment.[260]

Corroborating Murray is an 1896 letter from Robinson's son, Rowland E., to Wilbur Siebert.

> I remember seeing four fugitives at a time in my father's house, and quite often one or two harboring here. One of the four carried the first pistols I ever saw, and another the first bowie knife. The farthest station south of us that I know of was at Brandon, Vt, and was kept by Orson S. Murray, editor of the *Telegraph*.[261]

Robinson continued in his letter to identify numerous other collaborators, including one across Lake Champlain who was sent fugitives on McNeil's Ferry. This should not surprise anyone. By 1837 Vermont had 89 antislavery societies with approximately 8,000 members.[262] The antislavery societies were the driving mechanism that established the Underground Railroad and the antislavery lecturers and newspapers were its engine of communication.[263] Though Vermont was somewhat desolate and far removed from the Mason-Dixon Line, it does not mean it was an unlikely destination for fugitive slaves or even those who were chasing them. Especially after the Fugitive Slave Law of 1850, when the federal government established special courts and gave additional legal powers to federal marshals in northern states, the possibility of "slavecatchers" coming to Vermont to apprehend fugitives became a real problem.[264]

```
┌─────────────────────────────────────┐
│        Executive Committee.          │
│  R. T ROBINSON,    J. A. ALLEN,      │
│  JEDEDIAH HOLCOMB J. F. GOODHUE,     │
│  O. S. MURRAY,     J. W. HALE,       │
│  O. J. EELLS,                        │
│         H. F. LEAVITT, Ex Officio.   │
│         E. D. BARBER,   "    "       │
│         M. D. GORDON,   "    "       │
│  Cor. Sec. E. D. BARBER, Middlebury  │
│  Treas. B. F. HASKELL, Cornwall.     │
└─────────────────────────────────────┘
```

Vermont Telegraph, March 7, 1838

Suffice to say that Murray as well as many of the abolitionists and members of the anti-slavery societies were aiding fugitive slaves in the state. Note that Murray, Robinson, Allen, Holcomb, and Barber, who were identified by Murray as co-workers in the Underground Railroad, were members of the Vermont State Anti-Slavery Society's Executive Committee.

More evidence of the correlation between antislavery society members and Underground Railroad agents can be found by identifying known participants in the Underground Railroad who were Vermont delegates to the 1839 American Anti-Slavery Society annual meeting. In addition to five in the executive committee identified by Murray, there were Alvah Sabin, identified by Murray in his 1838 account; Austin Beecher, the "AB" in the 1838 Chittenden County report; Laurence Brainerd[265]; Nathan C. Hoag[266]; Chauncey Knapp[267]; Jonathan P. Miller[268]; Cyrus Prindle[269]; and Guy Beckley.[270]

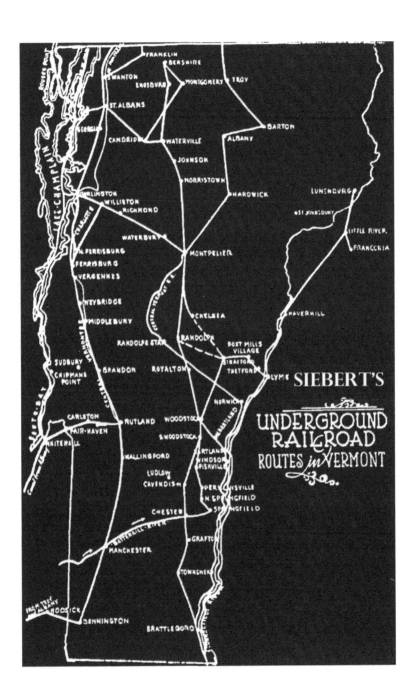

Chapter 16

Death Under His Roof

On the afternoon of August 13, 1839, Murray was at his office, folding newspapers for mailing with ten-year-old son, Marsena. Wife Catherine and oldest son, eleven-year-old Carlos, had gone in their wagon to Pittsford, a village eight miles north, a good hour's trip each way. Six-year-old Harriet, four-year-old Catherine, and the baby Charles were being watched by the babysitter. Orson took a break to check on the kids. The babysitter was frantic; she couldn't find Harriet. Orson called out to the neighbors for help, and a crowd of villagers gathered.

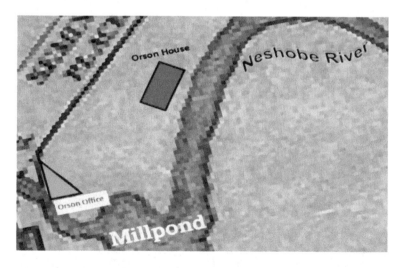

They scoured the grounds, but she was nowhere. Then their worst fears took hold. Orson's land set on a millpond. They became desperate and began searching the pond. For more than an hour, they hoped for a miracle until one of them using a pole with a hook attached caught hold of her dress. He pulled her up like a fisherman making a catch, her lifeless body dangling.

"I write you a few lines, hastily," he wrote to his readers, "to inform you that our Harriet Maria sleeps with the silent dead! [She] had been with us nearly through the Bible, at our family devotions, and always ready . . . to converse about God and her soul . . . . But the Lord has removed her from our embrace. And it becomes us to know and to realize that he had a right so to do . . . . And whither— dear brother and sister—whither should we go under such a calamity . . . if we had not the Christian's God?

"P.S. You will be anxious to know how she got into the pond . . . . From all the circumstances, we think it probable that she was plucking flowers which grew on the bank near where she was found."[271]

Harriet's untimely death caused other concerns like inflation's increase in the *Telegraph's* price, the success of missionaries in India, the sometime critic "C's" farewell to Brandon and its "superior organ of intelligence," and the *Vermont Chronicle* attack on Colonel J.P. Miller, one of the state's foremost abolitionists, who had been converted at one of Murray's lectures, to pale to insignificance. A poem authored by L.H.S offered some solace on the last page.[272]

> O sweet disciple, may He succor thee—
> Till to that radiant clime they spirit soar,
> Where storms shall shred the rose
> And toss the bark no more.

Harriet's death did not cause Murray's faith to waver.

Two weeks later he was back to attacking the hypocritical religious community and its denominations and organizations. He condemned Archibald Mclay, an agent of the American and Foreign Bible Society, who claimed to be neutral about the issue of slavery.

118

It was reported that while acting as a travelling agent for the society in the south, that he agreed with southerners to withhold the scripture from the slaves.

> It is but an act of justice to my brethren in the south, to say, that I have never met with a Christian . . . or even a man of the world, who expressed a wish to withhold the sacred scriptures from the slaves. And I have witnessed the slave reading the Bible in the presence of the master, and with his decided approbation . . . . I have assured all who have made inquiries on the subject that, as a Society, we have no connection with slavery or anti-slavery, farther than to receive the voluntary contributions of all who love the word of God . . . . I take pleasure in saying, that our single object, by the grace of God, is to give the word of life to all nations without reserve, to the utmost extent of our pecuniary ability.[273]

Maclay also denied a report in a southern newspaper that the society supported abolitionism.

Murray countered that Maclay's declaration that he had never met a Christian in the South who wished to withhold scripture from the slaves, "will be about the same as if he had said that the slaves of the South, as a general thing, have free access to the Bible. Now those who are at all acquainted with the laws and practices of the slave-holding States know that it is far otherwise. In most of the States, it is a high misdemeanor punishable with great severity, to teach slaves to read."[274]

In fact, Alabama, Georgia, Louisiana, Mississippi, North and South Carolina, and Virginia all had passed anti-literacy laws and whites found teaching slaves to read or write could face fines, floggings, or imprisonment. For example, in Virginia, the location of the brutal Nat Turner Revolt in 1831, the law specified:

> [Every] assemblage of negroes for the purpose of instruction in reading or writing, or in the nighttime for any purpose, shall be an unlawful assembly. Any justice may issue his warrant to any

office or other person, requiring him to enter any place where such assemblage may be, and seize any negro therein; and he, or any other justice, may order such negro to be punished with stripes.[275]

But even in the North societal pressure placed restrictions on educating black students and there had been riots at schools which did admit black students in New Hampshire and Connecticut.[xx]

There was never any suggestion of Murray's faith wavering. In his prospectus the next month for the *Telegraph*'s coming year, he anticipated business as usual, "I need only say, it will continue to be very much what it has been. To others, it may suffice to say it will be devoted, principally, to vital piety—practical holiness—the purification of human society from all manner of sin—the salvation of lost men." He also announced the hiring of a traveling agent, H.A. Sumner, to manage business matters and subscriptions and made an appeal for continued patronage despite the *Telegraph*'s recent increase in price.[276]

Unfortunately, less than a month into the new year, he was afflicted by a second tragedy. It was not as sudden but with little warning.

"Died, in this village on the 23d instant, of Croup, after a distressing illness of about 60 hours, Catherine Lucretia, daughter of Orson S., and Catharine M. Murray, aged 4 years."[277]

Again, Orson turned to God to offer solace, quoting scripture: "All flesh is grass, and all the goodliness thereof is as the flower of the field: the grass withereth, the flower fadeth; because the spirit of the Lord bloweth upon it . . . but the word of our God shall stand forever," Isaiah xl: 6-8 . . . . Innocent babe!" he cried out, "The memory of thee is sweet. Thou hadst no fear of death. Thou art in

---

[xx] In 1833, a mob destroyed the school run by Prudence Crandall in Canterbury, Connecticut; the incident in New Hampshire was the riot at the Noyes Academy described in Chapter Six.

120

better hands than mine—in the hands of Him who is too good to be unkind, too wise to be mistaken, and too just and holy to do wrong. My great loss is thy greater gain . . ."[278]

Death is so unpredictable and so devastating to those who lose their loved ones.

Graves of Harriet & Catherine Murray in Brandon. Credit: Rev. Sara Rossig

We can only surmise how Murray felt when death came under his roof a third time within nine months in April of 1840,[XXI] "each time with appalling suddenness."[279] Having hired H.A. Sumner to take care of business, he was able to work through some of his angst by taking a trip to New York for the American Baptist Anti-Slavery Convention and the annual meeting of the American Anti-Slavery Society.

[XXI] Murray does not identify the person (likely a relative) who died.

Chapter 17

A Non-Government
Woman's Rights Man

Murray practiced Temperance throughout his life, and discussion of Temperance issues and reports of its meetings were a regular part of his coverage. What became a greater concern was Women's rights, especially their right to voice their opinions publicly. It was an issue over which the antislavery movement split in 1840, and another issue along his path to disbelief.

A letter was sent to the *Telegraph* following that split, denying the right of women to speak in public and participate equally with men citing both the Old and New Testament. It was in response to earlier articles by Rowland T. Robinson and Jedidiah Holcomb, who upheld this right. The following are extracts from "C," who wrote the letter, and Murray's retort.

"I will cite you to a single passage only," C wrote, [from the Old Testament] 'The woman shall not wear that which pertaineth unto a man, neither shall a man put on a woman's garment.' Deut. 22: 5." [Where] in the New Testament . . . is the duty of woman to mount the rostrum for public instruction on any subject, recognized?

C then cited another from the New Testament. 'Let your women keep silence in the churches ; for it is not permitted unto them to speak; but they are commanded to be under obedience, as also saith the law. And if they will learn anything, let them ask their husbands at home; or it is a shame for women to speak in the church. Cor. 14: 34, 35.[280]

Murray responded: "What has he produced, from this source, to forbid the public action of females in works of philanthropy and

122

religion? Why, a single passage, which forbids women, not to advocate the cause of Christianity and humanity . . .

Murray added: "Considering my brother's appeal to the civilized world, I might have reminded him that the civilized world "uses" queens, female theatre-actors, and female teachers-of-science. How this same civilized world that has such usage, should be so horrified at the idea that females should take any public part in teaching morals and religion, I am at a loss to know . . .

As for C's quotation of Paul speaking to the Corinthians, "let your women keep silence in the churches." Murray asked C to identify a single Baptist church that prohibits women to speak and insisted there were none.

"And the fact that no one thus practices is at least practical evidence that no one thus believes."[281]

In a later letter a different reader voices his strong opposition to Murray's views, stating unequivocally, "I do not believe that women have such rights, as the gift of nature, or of grace, in civil or religious affairs . . . . I believe in the perfect equality of the rights of the two sexes; that is, that woman's rights are equally precious with man's, and no more to be disregarded or infringed than man's. But her rights are not the same . . . . It is undeniable that God has made as plain a distinction between the right of male and female."

He also disputed Murray's claim that women are allowed to speak in the Baptist Church.

> Now it is contrary to my experience and observation, as a general thing in the Baptist denomination . . . that females either speak or vote in church meetings; and with few exceptions attend church meetings.

> Let the woman learn in silence with subjection. But I suffer not a woman to teach, nor usurp authority over the man, but to be in silence . . .' 1st Tim. 2: 11, 12, 13 . . . .' Yet brother Murray

123

tells us the Scriptures have not undertaken to settle the question whether females should take part in the governmental affairs of religious or moral bodies.[282]

Murray countered: "Either I am in ignorance, as to the case, or he is . . . . If he knows of a Baptist church which does not allow its female members to speak . . . in the meetings of the church . . . and to vote in receiving and excluding members, on religious and moral questions . . . will he inform where that church is?"

Murray disputed the reader's claim that Scripture commands women to remain silent, citing Paul's words, " 'And I entreat thee also, true yoke fellow, help those women who labored with me in the gospel.' I ask what he supposes the labor in the gospel, performed by these women consisted of. Does he believe it was all performed in silence?"[283]

These debates mirrored what had been occurring in the antislavery movement for the previous two years. Female antislavery societies had been in existence since at least 1833, and women had participated in men's societies but were not considered members. However, female societies had grown significantly and by 1838 there were more than 100 female societies with more than 6,000 members.

In 1838, the New England Anti-Slavery Society, which had been founded by Garrison and was the forerunner of the American Anti-Slavery Society, agreed to allow women to participate as members at its meeting for the first time. The vote was unanimous in favor, though some evangelical members had reservations. Oliver Johnson later wrote of that time:

> We felt sure that, after the first excitement was over, they would be reconciled to so reasonable and inevitable a change, which we did not doubt would vindicate itself by the happiest results. But there is nothing more obstinate than prejudice, and, when fortified by a dash of temper, it does not readily yield to argument. The press was clamorous in its denunciation of the

new fanaticism; and the pro-slavery clergy attacked us on all hands as having openly repudiated the authority of the Scriptures and cast contempt upon the Apostle Paul. They urged all this vehemently, in the hope of creating a division in our ranks, which they thought might prove fatal to our movement.[284]

At the American Anti-Slavery Society's annual meeting that year, it resolved to oppose any "religious or political test for the purpose of rendering the anti-slavery cause subservient to the interests of a sect or party."[285] But this was only the beginning. At

TABLE 5	FEMALE ABOLITIONISM				
	Number of Female Antislavery Societies				
	1832	1833	1834	1835	1836
Maine	0	0	1	0	0
New Hampshire	0	0	2	2	2
Vermont	0	0	0	0	0
Massachusetts	0	3	3	7	9
Rhode Island	0	0	1	0	1
Connecticut	0	0	1	0	1
New York	0	2	1	8	0
Pennsylvania	0	1	0	0	2
Ohio	0	0	0	6	1
Total	0	6	9	23	16

	1837	1838	Undated[a]	Total	Members, 1838
Maine	2	0	0	3	140
New Hampshire	4	0	0	10	895
Vermont	1	0	2	3	—
Massachusetts	13	4	9	48	2418
Rhode Island	1	0	1	4	260
Connecticut	1	0	3	6	133
New York	7	0	1	19	1711
Pennsylvania	0	0	0	3	152
Ohio	1	2	6	16	671
Total	30	6	22	112	6380

[a]Female societies without founding dates.
SOURCE: *Fifth Annual Report of the Executive Committee of the American Anti-Slavery Society* . . . (New York, 1838), 129–52. Because membership data were not reported for many female antislavery societies, the figure in the table substantially underreports actual membership.

its annual meeting the next year, the question of equal participation of women in the society was the main topic of discussion. A significant number of delegates were opposed including Lewis Tappan and James Birney. A vote was taken on the second day of the meeting with 184 in support and 140 opposed. Attempting to counter this, Rev. A. A. Phelps introduced a resolution that women could be delegates of the society but would not be able to "speak, act on committees, fill offices." Gerrit Smith rebutted this with a forceful statement and concluded, "If a woman can do my work best, I wish to be at liberty to select a woman."[286]

Two weeks later, the Massachusetts Abolition Society formed. It split from the American Anti-Slavery society and its associate societies, stating that the woman question was unrelated to the issue of slavery and that because many of its members considered it "a thing forbidden by God" that it would not permit the participation of women at its meetings. They added that they believed it would "impair the public confidence in our integrity and multiply hindrances to the eventual success of our efforts."[287]

As the months approached the next annual meeting of the American Anti-Slavery Society, more antislavery societies shifted their allegiance to the "new organization." It was not merely because of women's rights. Two of the society's leading members, Henry B Stanton and James Birney, wanted more involvement in political action. The society had always been politically active like its petition-to-Congress campaign. But Garrison had moved away from political action and shifted to a non-resistance, non-government position. Finally, there was the deep animosity between Garrison and clergy because of his vicious criticism of their failure to condemn those clergy with pro-slavery views and renounce their connection with churches of their denomination in the South.[288]

Adding fuel to the suspicions that a conspiracy of sorts was in the making was the divestment of the society's newspaper, *Emancipator*, and its sale to the New York City Anti-Slavery Society.

Ostensibly for financial reasons, it had been arranged by Lewis Tappan, one of the society's most vehement antagonists of equal female participation. *The Liberator* was not the "organ" of the society because Garrison had not wanted the society to be influenced by his paper and vice-versa, allowing for freer expression for both. Consequently, the sale left the society without a newspaper representing its views, at least temporarily.[289]

Another revealing development was a convention of abolitionists in Albany, New York a month earlier to organize an abolitionist political party, which the Garrisonians strongly opposed. Its leaders were Gerrit Smith, Alvan Stewart, and William Goodell, editor of the influential antislavery newspaper, *Friend of Man.*

Murray reported its nomination of Birney as its candidate for President as well as its resolutions that included:

[As] abolitionists, it is our duty, and as Americans it is the duty of all—instead of supporting a first, second, or third party—to rise above all [parties], and unite as patriots, philanthropists and Christians, to put down the slavocracy of all parties, and put up the principles of the Declaration of Independence, at the ballot box and everywhere, by every lawful, constitutional, moral and religious influence.[290]

The last week of April Murray went to New York City to participate in the American Baptist Anti-Slavery Society convention in New York on April 28-30. More than 700 Baptists, 400 of them clergy, had called for it. The delegates numbered 110. Murray was appointed to the Committee Sending Delegates to the World Antislavery Convention in London; he also was the convention's secretary, a position generally second only to the president in hierarchy in reform societies at that time.

As would be expected he gave a lengthy report of the convention's purpose and actions, excerpts of which are provided.

"The object of this convention was, to take measures for the purification of the Baptist church from the sin of slavery . . . . It was supposed that Baptist abolitionists have some means for reaching Baptists on this subject that a promiscuous body of abolitionists do not possess—just as a circle of relatives . . . have power, not possessed by their acquaintances."[291]

Murray explained that they weren't a group of dissenters but members who hoped to uplift the church's moral integrity. He acknowledged the possibility of alienating some members, "of leveling down," but that they would not sacrifice their principles simply to be agreeable to its members. Among its foremost concerns was the position being taken by southern Baptist churches on the issue of the education of slaves. They also lamented the prejudice against free "colored" in the North and the use of the "negro pew" in northern churches. Concern was expressed about religious newspapers and their reporting of the truth about slavery. While not identifying those with whom they had complaints, they did single out those in the religious press who were a beacon of truth, including the *Vermont Telegraph*.[XXII]

Not only did important Baptist ministers like Nathaniel Colver address the convention, but also the important Presbyterian abolitionists, Charles Stuart of England, and Lewis Tappan of New York. Rev. Colver who had recently participated in the Albany convention that called for an abolitionist political party, something opposed by Garrisonians like Murray, was nevertheless appointed to be one of the society's three representatives at the World Anti-Slavery Convention in London in June.[292]

[XXII] In addition to the *Telegraph*, they included the *Christian Reflector* in Worcester, MA; *Zion's Watchtower* in NYC and *Baptist Vindicator* in Perry, NY; and the *N.H. Baptist Register* in Concord NH. Those of other denominations mentioned were the *Evangelist, Zion's Watchman*, and *The Luminary* in NYC; and the Observer in Hudson, OH

The convention's keynote address by society president Rev. Elon Galusha was likely authored at least in part by Murray. It concluded with a strong appeal to sever the church's connection with those who accepted slavery:

> Finally, if you should . . . remain deaf to the voice of warning and entreaty, if you still cling to the power-maintained privilege of living on unpaid toil, and of claiming as property the image of God which Jesus bought with precious blood, we solemnly declare, as we fear the Lord, that we cannot and we dare not recognize you as consistent brethren in Christ; we cannot join in partial, selfish prayers, that the groans of the slave may be unheard; we cannot hear preaching which makes God the author and approver of human misery and vassalage; and we cannot, at the Lord's table, cordially take that as a brother's hand, which plies the scourge on woman's naked flesh, which thrusts a gag into the mouth of man, which rivets fetters on the innocent, and which shuts up the Bible from human eyes. We deplore your condition; we pray for your deliverance: and God forbid that we should ever sin against Him by ceasing so to pray.[293]

Meanwhile, two weeks later, the American Anti-Slavery Society would hold its annual meeting. Because of a rumored attempt to dissolve the society by those who wished to supplant it with one supporting more active political action, the Garrisonians arranged to ship hundreds of female delegates to the 1840 annual meeting who would be able to vote against this. Oliver Johnson reported:

> Under the circumstances . . . the friends of the old organization in Massachusetts felt compelled to take some efficient measures to defeat what they thought an unworthy plot to change the whole character of the anti-slavery movement and place it upon a sectarian basis. What they did was charter a steamer to take from Providence to New York as large a

number of delegates [who would vote on the side of women as they could persuade to attend]. They put the fare at a low rate and sent out a rallying-cry through The Liberator to all who desired to keep the good ship Anti-Slavery on her right course.

Over 400 delegates, many of them women, went to New York in the steamer "Rhode Island," prepared to do what they could to preserve the integrity of the anti-slavery movement. A happier crowd I never saw, and surely a more respectable body of people never went on board a ship. They were all animated by what they regarded as a high and noble purpose. They were one heart and one mind, of "one accord in one place." Songs and speeches filled up the evening hours until time for sleep, when such as were fortunate enough to obtain berths retired for the night. Those less fortunate appropriated to themselves such portions of the steamer's floor, in cabin or on deck . . .[294]

Lodgings weren't much better in the city, as more than 1,000 delegates, double the number of the year before assembled for the meeting in the Carmine Presbyterian Church.

The breakup of the society was expected and resolutions from the Methodist Episcopal Church, and the Pittsburgh and Allegheny Anti-Slavery Society expressing regret at the conflict were read in the hope that the differences could be resolved. But the climax of that first day came with the vote to approve the nominations of the business committee. Among those expected for the first time to be named was a raven-haired Quaker woman whose drab dress belied her beauty; her nomination was expected to cause a furor. When Vice President Francis Jackson named the nominees, there were disquieting murmurs:

"Chairman William Lloyd Garrison . . . Amos Phelps . . . Charles Burleigh . . . Ichabod Codding . . . Rowland T. Robinson . . . William L. Chaplin . . . Charles W. Gardiner . . . Charles W. Denison . . . Lewis Tappan" . . . and, finally, hesitating a little longer than he had for the others, "Abby Kelley."[295]

Some delegates leaped in protest. Tappan insisted that women were not allowed to be members of the society and that when the society's constitution referred to persons, it meant men not women. Abby stood up from her pew and cried out into the tumult, "I rise because I am not a slave."[296]

Jackson called for a voice count. But there were too many yeas and nays, and they were so loud it was impossible to determine the result. Slips of paper had to be passed out so the delegates could record their votes.

There was silence in the church hall as Jackson prepared to announce the final tallies.

"Opposed to Miss Kelly, 441," he said and there was cheering.

When it stopped, he looked at the men congratulating themselves and smiled.

"In favor of Miss Kelly, 557."[297]

At once, in formation, several hundred men rose from their pews and stormed out, including their leader, Lewis Tappan. The next day they met and formed the "New Organization," the American and Foreign Anti-Slavery Society, which was founded on the use of political action to end slavery and in contrast to the "Old Organization, prohibited the membership of women. Many of its members were clergy, who had been alienated by Garrison's growing anti-clericalism. Like the new Liberty Party, which many in the AFASS would support, they believed that slavery was a fundamental

131

violation of the Constitution. Arthur Tappan, the president of the AAS, who had not attended the annual meeting, was made President.

Garrison was totally opposed to forming a political party. He believed that it would nullify the power of moral suasion to end slavery. He sought to avoid any connection with political parties, or even the promotion of political candidates with abolitionist views and stressed that those with differing political views could still agree on the single issue of antislavery.

It's not clear if Murray remained in New York for the AAS annual meeting, which was two weeks after the American Baptist convention, but H.A. Sumner was still helping to manage the business operations, so it's possible he did. It's also possible he may have needed some time away to process the grief over the recent deaths in his family. He was listed in *The Liberator* as being one of the AAS board of managers, and while he published *The Liberator's* account of the AAS meeting rather than writing his own, he did provide his own comments:

> My opinion has been one and the same, from the beginning and that is, that the Anti-Slavery platform, laid in 1833, in the Constitution and Declaration of Sentiments adopted by the Convention, which organized the American Anti-Slavery Society, is broad enough for every true abolitionist in the land to stand upon. Every man, woman, and child, from whatever state or section of country, of whatever color or clime, of whatever party in politics, or sect in religion, may consistently, confidently, and confidentially, gather under the broad banner then and there thrown out, and battle against the common foe of freedom and humanity.[298]

He then repudiated a claim made by one of the defectors that the society had never intended to allow the participation of women, recollecting that Lucretia Mott spoke at the first meeting in 1833 and no one was opposed. "I believe there is common ground for all persons, of whichever sex, and of whatever class, sect or denomination— and that ground I believe to be occupied by the American Anti-Slavery Society."[299]

A week later, at the New England Anti-Slavery Convention, the following was among several resolutions in response to the formation of the "New Organization":

> Resolved, that all attempts to narrow down or destroy our noble platform, whether by new-organization or disorganization, are to be regarded as hostile by the true interests of freedom, and should be frowned upon, and unqualifiedly opposed by every true friend of the slave.[300]

Murray would remain steadfast in his support for Garrison and the Old Organization and fully committed to the Non-Resistance movement, whose principles he would unwaveringly follow the rest of his life. He was a non-government, woman's rights man.

Chapter 18

Murray Turns Away from the Church

It's difficult to pinpoint when Murray began to turn away from the Church and become a raving atheist, as some considered him later in life. His transformation seems to have been gradual but there were signs during the early *Telegraph* years. For instance, early on, letters complained that the paper wasn't religious enough, that too much attention was given to antislavery. Murray generally justified this by saying that all reform movements, like antislavery, which involved the "golden rule" and concern for others' rights and welfare, were the proper concerns of a religious newspaper and obliged coverage—other examples were women's rights, temperance, non-resistance, treatment of American Indians, vegetarianism, the water cure, capital punishment, sexual mores, etc.[301]

His spiritual transformation appears to have been motivated by the hypocrisy of the nation's churches regarding slavery. How could a Christian "countenance" slavery, how could a cleric own slaves, how could a church allow its brethren to hold human beings as property? These gnawing questions and his intransigent opposition to the relationships many church leaders had with slaveholders led to his removal to Ohio.

Murray followed the lead of his philosophical mentor, Garrison, who was waging an unabated war against the nation's churches, a battle that led to the previously mentioned split in the antislavery movement,[302] a battle that would leave Murray on the outside looking in at the duplicity of not only the Baptist Church but all religion.

Murray's obstinacy not only drew critics but enemies. For instance, his continuous feud with E.C. Tracy of the *Vermont Chronicle*, which started when he denounced Murray after an antislavery lecture in Windsor, Vermont in 1835.[303]

After Murray began publishing the *Telegraph*, there appeared regular "deprecations" of Tracy, who was opposed to the abolitionists and reserved special loathing for Garrison. Tracy was a confirmed Colonizationist, and his brother. Joseph Tracy, who previously had been the editor of the *Chronicle* for six years, later became one of the American Colonization Society's directors.

Tracy's sarcastic report of the New England Anti-Slavery Convention in June 1836, which he admitted that he didn't attend, exposed him to Murray's wrath.

If Tracy "did not visit it," protested Murray, a participant, then where did he hear that "nobody was very well satisfied with it"?

Murray proceeded to compare Tracy's comment with reports of those who attended.

"Has he heard the *Boston Daily Advocate*, which has the ablest, most independent and impartial editor of any political paper in Boston, who visited the convention daily, and semi-daily, throughout the session?"

The *Advocate* described those attending "as respectable, attentive, and as truly moral and religious an assembly as any public occasion ever called together in [Boston]."

The *Lynn Record* wrote, Murray added, that the convention "was one of the most affecting and deeply interesting meetings we ever attended —calculated to dispel the gloom which is hovering over the liberties of our country, portending its speedy downfall, [revealing] the glowing patriotism, the thrilling soul stirring eloquence of the talented young men who are now coming upon the stage of life."[304]

Murray asked, "Has Mr. Tracy heard any of the above or anything of similar language from a score of other papers? Does he know that [the] meetinghouse, where the Convention was held, was

135

so filled that the broad aisle was frequently crowded with persons standing, in session hours, to the last?"

"It is doubtless true that . . . .all who hate the Anti-Slavery cause, all who envy Anti-Slavery men were not 'well satisfied' with the triumphant success of the Convention. But that is no warrant for the conclusion that 'nobody was very well satisfied with it.' Such a representation is a most glaring misrepresentation."

Murray went on to reference nine other issues of disagreement with Tracy, including his attacks on Charles Stuart and Garrison, and concluded with the following:

> [There were also] some paragraphs of rant and spleen against Mr. Garrison . . . The conduct of these men must be highly amusing to Mr. Garrison, while he is sustained by such resolutions and such men as are daily gathering around him . . . . we pity those who from envy or other black passions are constantly traducing him . . .[305]

The following January, he made an even stronger attack on the *Chronicle* referring to an article it had reprinted from the *Richmond Whig* that suggested if the abolitionists didn't stop their agitating, it could lead to Civil War:

> [The] furious, fiery farrago from a shameless defender of robbery and plunder, is copied into the Vermont Chronicle without note or comment. From the . . . pro-slavery sentiments and violent spirit towards abolition, notorious of that print, we are led irresistibly to the conclusion that the design, of the editors in copying the article was to swell the frantic uproar, the insane, murderous clamor against abolitionists . . . [306]

Two weeks later the *Telegraph* reprinted an article from *Friend of Man*, which discussed the attacks by religious, pro-slavery editors on abolitionists.

The anti-abolition editors, and particularly the religious ones, have kept up an unceasing cry against abolitionists, for two or three years past, on account of the 'unchristian epithets' with which they have assailed the slaveholders; and all because abolitionists have denominated slaveholders as "robbers, man-stealers, plunderers of the poor.

The article identified Tracy as the editor calling attacks on slaveholders "unchristian."[307]

Throughout Murray's time with the *Telegraph*, there were snipes and jabs at the *Chronicle*, continual diatribes against clergy who would not support immediate unconditional emancipation, refused to condemn fellow clergy in the South who owned slaves, and considered Colonization the best solution to the problem of slavery.

Continually, Murray exposed the hypocrisy of those who preached Christian doctrine yet praised acts of violence. Exemplifying this was an article reprinted from the *Colored American*, by noted New York Underground Railroad conductor Charles Ray, and to which Murray added his own remarks. It was a commentary on a report of the holy war being fought in Liberia by black Methodist Episcopal missionary, Rev. George Brown. The report had been published in many newspapers in the northeast, including the *New York Evening Post* and *The Liberator*.

He speaks of cutting [natives] down "like mowers cutting down grass;" [wrote Ray] of "pouring a stream of lead upon them from the window, as fast as two boys could load the muskets," of "throwing buckshot into their bowels, hearts, and brains, like a tornado;" of their being "blood and brains in every direction" . . . of picking up fingers by the wayside of the "blood pouring forth freely . . . All this he speaks of with criminal indifference, as though he had been in battle with a horde of wild hogs. We regard it as glorying in his shame: it exceeds anything we ever heard of from a professed Christian. We pronounce it deliberate murder.

"G. S. Brown, for Rev. or brother we cannot call him, [Ray continued] is a professed Christian minister a missionary sent out and supported by the Methodist E. Church of this country. Better, far better would it have been for G. S. Brown, with all his associates, to have been killed, by them at the onset, before an attack, than to have been guilty of the course he took . . . .

Is this the way to Christianize Africa? To associate musket, powder and ball, with missions and missionaries?[308]

Murray agreed with Ray:
What are cannons, muskets, swords, and bayonets made for? Expressly to slaughter human beings with. What is military training for? To learn human beings the art of human butchery. G. S. Brown. then, has only been carrying out most consistently, the contemplations and designs of his Christian education! . . . . He has been taught and verily believed, no doubt that under some circumstances it would be his duty to slaughter his fellow beings and having found himself in the proper circumstances, while engaged as a Christian missionary, he has now done just what he might have been expected to do . . . . Out, out upon- such Christianity. It is not Christianity . . . . It is the grossest, the greatest possible outrage upon the character of the Author of Christianity.[309]

The following week Murray blasted Brandon Congregational minister, Harvey Curtis, who had debated with him in the pages of the *Telegraph* about the issue of non-resistance. Curtis had become a contributor to Murray's arch enemy, the *Vermont Chronicle*, and defended Brown's right to kill others in self-defense.

I know not but even Harvey Curtis himself, the staunch advocate of defensive war, and the Editor of the *Chronicle* who tacitly endorses his sentiments, may be horrified at the horrible and bloody transaction at Liberia, in view of its having been performed by a missionary. They have not as yet . . . expressed anything of the kind. If they should undertake the expression of such a feeling or sentiment, they will do themselves credit and me a favor.[310]

Murray's disagreement with the established churches is summed up well in the following editorial that appeared not long after.

The time has fully come for Christians to rise and rid their hands and their garments of innocent blood. The conduct of the church in the 19th century on slavery, when it shall have become a matter of history and the foul abomination shall have been wiped from the earth, will be gazed upon with wonder and astonishment. There is everywhere exhibited such monstrous inconsistency, such palpable self-condemnation, such stifling of conviction, such tampering with conscience, such outright infidelity, as ought to shame as many as claim to be rational, and alarm all who profess Christianity or common honesty . . . .

We are told that it is a matter with which the church should not be disturbed! And, generally, the same persons who would not have the church disturbed with it, have objections equally strong against bringing it into politics. There is great alarm lest the church should be divided by the agitation of the subject. Would you divide the Northern from the Southern church? Many at the North, if they be required to disfellowship our "Southern brethren" will far sooner separate from the Northern ultraists.

Allow me to suggest that . . . ... at [your] next church meeting let a resolution be adopted, something like the following: Resolved, that we cannot receive to Christian fellowship and communion those who practice slaveholding, or those who partake of their evil deeds by apologizing for them or keeping fellowship with them. . . . The northern apologist for slaveholding is quite as guilty as the southern slaveholder.[311]

Adding fuel to Murray's furor was a visit to Brandon by none other than Rev George Brown himself, only three months after the account of his report of the warfare in Liberia had been published. Brown had returned to the U.S. for a visit and had been commissioned to do a lecture tour through northern New York and Vermont to raise money for the New York Colonization Society. The publicity he had received in the newspapers earlier that summer drew as many as 300 attendees at a meeting in Chestertown, NY, the week before.[312] While there is no record of the attendees in Brandon, we know that one of those attending was Murray.

In his journal, Brown wrote:

I have just returned from a camp meeting in Brandon, Vermont. We had an excellent meeting, too . . . . But while the preachers were gathering the collection, I was attacked by an Abolitionist, who barefacedly charged me with being a murderer because I fought in the battle at Heddington. He even desired the Presiding Elder to let him go on the stand and inform the people that they were giving to a murderer. But the Presiding Elder rejected him. This man's name was Murry, the editor of the *Vermont Telegraph*. He raged just like the Cannibals in Africa.[313]

While Murray did not report what he said at the meeting, it likely echoed the sentiments of this earlier editorial about Brown:

"When will there be 'peace on earth,' if they who set themselves up, and are looked up to, as religious guides and teachers, continue to advocate the lawfulness and Christianity of manslaying under certain circumstances? Never-never."[314]

Nevertheless, Brown reported a collection of $61 (more than $1700 today)[XXIII] about half of what he collected at Chestertown.[315]

Murray was not without supporters. The seventh anniversary meeting of the Vermont Anti-Slavery Society in January 1841 echoed Murray's disdain of clerical refusal to condemn slavery and their support for Colonization. At the opening of the meeting, the society resolved that "we consider the American Colonization Society, one of the peculiar institutions of the South, the tendency which is to rivet stronger the fetters of the slave and to fasten these prejudices already existing against the colored man."[316]

The next day Murray introduced a resolution that "those ministers who, with all the light they now enjoy in regard to the sinfulness of slaveholding and the suffering of the slave, oppose the cause of immediate emancipation, or remain silent on the subject, are unworthy of countenance as religious guides and teachers." It was passed by a 3-1 plurality.[317]

Murray's battle against the Christian apologists of slavery naturally led to the continuing erosion of his faith. In June 1841, he reprinted an article describing an "Ultraist" that he called a "noble testimony."

"[An Ultraist] is one who goes beyond others, those . . . eagerly desirous to press forward any cause much more rapidly than public opinion may deem necessary, expedient or proper. An ultraist is always in advance of public opinion. He pursues with wonderful energy and perseverance some object, which he believes will vastly benefit a portion of mankind, or happily the

---

whole human race. And he may be prompted by the action of his reasoning powers, by the impulses of a high moral and religious principle, by an elevated sense of right, or strong feeling of benevolence.

An ultraist never looks back—he never looks around, but always straight forward. He aims to establish some favorable principle or accomplish some daring object. And his mental energies are concentrated for the accomplishment of that specific purpose . . . . Opposition only induces him to press forward with increased energy. Indeed, he will hardly be checked by the most formidable barriers which caution, or expediency may interpose. His real character is seldom truly interpreted by the great minds of mankind—and monuments are erected to his memory. A man can hardly be an ultraist unless he possesses moral courage enough to disregard the scoffs and sneers and censures of the world.

Without ultraists, the moral world would stand still—there would be no improvement—no one would step before his neighbor for the purpose of exploring unknown regions or clearing a path which would lead to good. Let ultraists be encouraged, instead of being despised and condemned. Let us examine their labors, listen to their arguments, and if they have struck out a right path, let us follow them."[318]

Indeed, this perfectly described Murray and it justified his strong support from the abolitionists. One of the organizers of the Vermont Baptist Anti-Slavery conventions, he called the convention in Waterbury in October of 1841, "among the most important movements that have been made for the advancement of the great and glorious cause of human freedom now in progress in this country." He proclaimed that "the Baptists of Vermont had been in the advance" of others in the denomination in their support of antislavery.[319] A committee headed by Murray drafted twenty-one resolutions that condemned slavery as sinful and called for the suspension of fellowship with both slaveholders and those in the North who supported them. The resolutions were upheld by a large majority with the final one making the most emphatic statement:

> Resolved, That the time has fully come to suspend Christian fellowship between us and slaveholders and their abettors, until they repent and reform that we cannot receive them into co-operation in religious worship, or in the use of means for the conversion of the world, until they forsake their ungodliness and inhumanity.[320]

However, Murray's aggressive style and desire for separation not merely from Baptists who were slaveholders but from those who permitted slaveholders to remain in the church was viewed by some to be unchristian. This was reflected in his disapproval of the annual state Baptist convention two weeks later, stating "It was not a convention of the people, but of the aristocracy." He reported that the moneyed interests did not support reform, the primary motive of the *Telegraph*,[321] and his intuition was correct. Little did he know that a committee was appointed behind the scenes to supply the state Baptists with a new religious newspaper that "suited to promote the piety and edification of our churches [and] that the want of such a paper was felt and acknowledged from one extremity of the state to the other." Among those on the committee was the man who had financially backed Murray's purchase of the *Telegraph* and one of his first and foremost supporters, John Conant.[322]

Vermont Baptist Journal.

On March 2, 1842, the *Vermont Baptist Journal* published its first issue, replacing the *Telegraph* as the state denomination's newspaper. Now, Murray had a very vocal and visible enemy at his doorstep. As attacks on his character and disapproval of the *Telegraph* became more frequent, things began to unravel for Murray. The *New York Baptist Register* reported: "[For] some time we supposed that the wildness and contentious spirit of the *Vermont Telegraph* . . . was becoming a weariness to the great proportion of the judicious brethren in that State . . . However, we are glad to see [another paper started as the organ of the Baptist denomination]."

Murray was quick to retaliate, charging the *Register* with being a pro-slavery publication.[323] Among outlandish charges against him was an attack by a Vermont Congregational minister in the form of a criminal indictment, later withdrawn, of Murray for printing the *Telegraph* on the Sabbath.[324]

As Murray feared, the *Vermont Baptist Journal* (VBJ) started to put out editorials that gave comfort to southern apologists, comments that were ludicrous in retrospect, insisting that most of those in the South opposed slavery, claiming that "Thousands there are at the South who have nothing to hope, but everything to fear from the continuance of slavery. Again, there are thousands of others, who, *though holders of slaves,*[XXIV] are sick of the whole system. They detest it, and long for deliverance from it as from apolitical, pecuniary and moral evil . . . . [They] are on the side of emancipation.

[XXIV]By 1860, 30.8 percent of the free families in the confederacy owned slaves, according to the Federal Census. That means that every third white person in those states had a direct commitment to slavery. And as we now know they would fight a war to maintain it.

They have already embraced the essential principles of abolition and are arrayed against us only because they don't understand us."[325]

Murray responded, calling the *VBJ* worse than the *Vermont Chronicle* because it had never claimed to support abolitionism as did the *VBJ*. He went on to say, "They profess for good—they practice for evil. They profess for holiness—they practice for sin. They profess for peace—they practice for war. They profess for liberty— they practice for slavery." Then he concluded with a long tirade that filled up half the newspaper.[326]

The feud continued throughout the summer. Most discouraging was when in early September of 1842, or thereabouts, he was disfellowshipped by the Orwell Baptist Church. Its pastor, John Ide, had helped him organize the Vermont Anti-Slavery Baptist conventions over the years.[327] Continual character attacks followed, and in one such demonization, he was described as the "wild, ultra, madcap editor of the *Vermont Telegraph*." This was written by Rev. John Peck and published in *The Liberator's* column, "Refuge of Oppression," highlighting the problems being faced by abolitionists.[328]

An attack by such a prominent and influential Baptist missionary and preacher carried much influence. Peck who had settled near Alton, Illinois, following his missionary period, was the editor of the Baptist journal, *The Pioneer*, and was present during some of the confrontation that led to Lovejoy's murder. In his report in his journal, he condemned Lovejoy for murdering Bishop, but never mentioned that it was the mob that fired the first shots.[329] While Peck did not approve of slavery, he also did not approve of abolitionists. In fact, it was reported that he disagreed with the abolitionist views of Baptist minister Nathaniel Colver, whom he had baptized in 1817.[330] So, it is hardly surprising that he would attack Murray. Pro-slavery was at war with abolitionism, and this was another example.

The forces of evil that had found a target in Murray had a rippling effect.

Chapter 19

Signs of the Times

While Orson S. Murray was battling more foes than he would be able to defeat, there still were some in Vermont who held him in high esteem, like the *Universalist Watchmen*, edited by Christian preacher, Eli Ballou.

> Mr. Orson S. Murray . . . is one of the most independent, bold freemen of the age. He thinks freely, and dares to express his thoughts, however new they may be, or however heretical they may be considered, by the professedly orthodox in religious and social matters . . . . We cannot but admire his free and independent spirit—his frankness and Christian disposition.

Ballou followed with Murray's unexpurgated thoughts on William Miller, whose prediction of the Second Coming would occur in five months.

> "The excitement that is spreading and rising in connection with this subject, in various parts of the country, is very wonderful," wrote Murray, "and portends much evil to its deluded victims. Unless the leaders get out a new prophecy—as I think they will—and put off the time to a period more remote, it may be expected that there will be scores and hundreds of lunatics, made such by the overwhelming excitement.
>
> . . . .
>
> "It is no cause for wonder that these who view that Omnipotent, Omniscient and Omnipresent to be anything else but Mind, everywhere present and eternally the same, should be looking out into the clouds for Him, or expecting Him to

come next year and do things contrary to His established and immutable laws."[331]

Murray would provide only sparse coverage of Miller thereafter, but despite the opposition from many newspapers and clerics, Miller had come a long way. While not a charismatic person, he steadfastly believed that Christ was coming. He was so precise with his knowledge about the Bible and the prophecies that if his premises were correct, Christ surely was coming. As one observer commented many years later, "He did not shout or rant the way so many revivalists do; he made his impression by his earnest manner and his serious way of addressing his listeners. When he talked, people had to sit right up and listen — they couldn't help it," adding that "many men who one would never suppose would be influenced by him or his theory would often be converted at once and get completely under the spell of the delusion."[332]

In November of 1838, Miller wrote a letter to his son about a lecture in Montpelier, Vermont, "There was great excitement on the subject in this place . . . . There was a great breaking down and much weeping. Some souls have been born again. I can hardly get away from these people. They want me to stay another week. . . . "[333]

Miller was continually requested as a speaker at many churches not so much because the pastors agreed with his theory about the Second Coming but because the controversy brought many new members to their churches and inspired revivals that led to many conversions.

By the end of 1839, he had delivered more than 800 lectures and people were flocking to hear him.[334] Earlier that year, Baptist minister T. Cole of Lowell, Massachusetts had heard of Miller's success and invited him to lecture at his church. He was expecting a distinguished cleric when he met Miller at the train depot.[XXV] As he

---

[XXV] The rail line from Boston to Lowell was completed in 1835, one of the nation's earliest.

watched the passengers exiting from the cars, he didn't see the man he expected. But then he saw an old man shaking as if he had palsy[XXVI] with a white beaver hat and camlet cloak and asked if he were Miller.

Miller nodded and Rev. Cole led the way, thinking how could he invite someone like this to speak at his church? However, once Miller began speaking and demonstrated his amazing command of Scripture, and the sincerity and confidence in his belief in Christ's coming, Cole became a Miller advocate.[335]

Up to this time, Miller's success had been in small towns. And most editors either were not convinced of his theory like Murray or simply ridiculed him. This changed when he was invited by Congregational minister Joshua V. Himes to speak at his church in Boston in November of 1839. Himes thought that if Miller's theory was true, then the whole world should know, and he became Miller's most ardent follower. In 1840, he began publishing the monthly, *The Sign of the Times,*[336] which featured Miller's writings and lectures.

Following its first issue, Miller went on a lecture tour for nearly six months, delivering 327 lectures. In Portland, Maine, the pastor of the Christian Church, Elder L.D. Fleming wrote:

> There has probably never been so much religious interest among the inhabitants of this place, generally, as at present. A number of rum-sellers have turned their shops into meeting-

---

[XXVI] Miller's mother had palsy.

rooms, and these places that were once devoted to intemperance and revelry are now devoted to prayer and praise. There is nothing like extravagant excitement, but an almost universal solemnity on the minds of all the people. One of the principal booksellers informed me that he had sold more Bibles in one month, since Mr. Miller came here, than he had in any four months previous. [337]

Miller's years of reaching out to the public with lectures and publications was coming to fruition. Despite being often ridiculed, other preachers became attracted to his ideas and wondered if Christ might be coming. If so, people needed to prepare for the day of judgment when the world would be consumed in fire, their fears allayed by the belief that those who were righteous would soon know eternal happiness.

Many of these converts to Millerism were abolitionists and temperance advocates like Himes. Their preaching acted like a synergistic effect that mushroomed the movement. They included Joseph Bates, a Congregational minister and abolitionist, who shifted his focus to Millerism and in 1842, took a hazardous journey to Maryland to preach the Second Coming; Rev. Charles Fitch, another abolitionist and pastor of the First Free Congregational Church in Boston, who began corresponding with Miller in 1838; Josiah Litch, a Boston minister, who began preaching about Miller's theory after hearing him lecture in Lowell; Congregational minister, Henry Jones, a Temperance agent interested in biblical prophecy; and the charismatic preacher, Elder Jacob Knapp.

Elder Knapp is still preaching to large audiences at the Baptist meeting-house in this town, (Concord, N. H.) Upwards of fifty have been converted, and on Sunday last, five were baptized, by immersion, near the free bridge. From two to three thousand persons were present to witness the ceremony.—*Hill's Patriot.*

Other notables preaching the Coming were George Storrs, Nathaniel Southard, Edward Kirk, Henry Dana Ward, N.N. Whiting, Samuel Snow, James White, Ezekiel Hale, Elon Galusha, and Joseph Marsh, all abolitionists and temperance advocates.

An interesting anecdote comes from the childhood of Marsh's daughter, Jane, who was six in 1843.

"That the trumpet might sound any moment we children were in no danger of forgetting that summer, for, although a day had been set for the End, there was a possibility of another mistake in calculating periods, in misinterpretations, in missing links. That it would not do to run any risks in disobedience was heavy on our infantile minds . . . . but that the day was coming nearer that would burn as an oven, we never forgot.[338]

At the same time some of these exponents of Millerism came to be a problem because some of them began distorting what Miller was preaching and twisting it into their own version of the Second Coming. Among the noteworthy was John Starkweather, an assistant pastor at Joshua Himes' church. When he added in the element of physical manifestations as a sign that one was among those who would be saved from the fires of the great conflagration, all kinds of jerks and fits started to manifest among his listeners. Miller and others worried that such aberrations would hurt the movement and outsiders would see them as fanatics. Himes confronted Starkweather, who broke away and started his own group.[339]

In 1842, a series of Second Advent Camp Meetings that drew thousands daily increased Miller's huge following. The first one occurred in New Hampshire in August. Poet John Greenleaf Whittier, who attended, described it:

> The white circle of tents; the dim wood arches; the upturned, earnest faces; the loud voices of the speakers, burdened with the awful symbolic language of the Bible; the smoke from the fires, rising like incense — carried me back to these days of primitive worship which tradition faintly whispers of, when on hilltops, and in the shade of old woods, Religion had her first altars, with every man for her priest, and the whole universe for her temple.   The spot was well chosen. A tall growth of pine and hemlock threw its melancholy shadow over the multitude, who were arranged upon rough seats of boards and logs. Several hundred — perhaps a thousand people — were present, and more were rapidly coming. Drawn about in a circle, forming a background of snowy whiteness to the dark masses of men and foliage, were the white tents, and back of them the provision-stalls and cook-shops. When I reached the ground, a hymn, the words of which I could not distinguish, was pealing through the dim aisles of the forest. I could readily perceive that it had its effect upon the multitude before me, kindling to higher intensity their already excited enthusiasm. The preachers were placed in a rude pulpit of rough boards, carpeted only by the dead forest leaves and flowers, and tasseled, not with silk and velvet, but with the green boughs of the somber hemlocks around it. One of them followed the music in an earnest exhortation on the duty of preparing for the great event.[340]

Daily coverage was given of a four-day camp meeting in Newark, New Jersey, in November, with Miller himself as the featured speaker.

At its close, Father Miller, as he was now being addressed, said to his followers that he would not see their "dear" faces again until the resurrection morning--which he expected to be soon though he did not know the exact day.

He told them to love Christ--to study their Bible, and wait until the next year, when they would all meet in heaven. There was much sobbing, especially among the ladies, as Miller gave them his parting blessings.

"May God dwell with you until the coming of Christ, and then may we all dwell in his kingdom forever," he called out. [341]

Miller then stood at the center of the church. Many of the women there shook his hand and some kissed him. Finally, he departed in a wagon, amid much singing and praying. Such veneration showed how devoted his following had become. [342]

As the fateful day approached, there was great unrest among the Millerites, who numbered by conservative estimates more than 50,000. [XXVII] [343] There were many reports of those who had given up all material possessions as they prepared for the blessed event. A summation of Miller's doctrine, which he had written on the first day of the New Year was published in the *Signs of the Times* and other newspapers:

> I believe Jesus will come in the clouds of heaven. The body of every departed saint will be raised . . . That the righteous who are living on the earth will be changed from mortal to immortal bodies, and those raised from the dead, will be caught up to meet the Lord in the air, and so be forever with Him. He will come to deliver his children from all bondage, to conquer their last enemy, and to deliver them from the power of the devil. He will destroy the bodies of the wicked by fire, as these of the old world were destroyed by water that shut up their soul in the pit of woe, until their damnation.

[XXVII] Extrapolated from our present population, that would be more than one million

When the earth is cleansed by fire, Christ and his saints will then take possession of the earth. And the time is appointed when these things shall be accomplished. God has revealed it to those who desire to understand and are ready. I am fully convinced sometime between March 21, 1843 and March 21, 1844, Christ will be coming.[344]

William Miller's Chart of Prophecies
williammiller1844.com

William Miller

Tension was evident in Washington, D.C., where placards announcing Miller's appearance were mistakenly posted. It led to the gathering of an angry mob of thousands, upset because Miller was not actually in D.C. A week later, in Philadelphia his lecture was cancelled because of concerns about unruliness.[345]

As the Millerites prepared, Miller continued his lecturing. During the last week of January, he was in Burlington, Vermont, where it was reported that he described what would occur during the Second Coming: "A small bright spot will first appear in the east, which will gradually expand as it approaches the earth. By and by, a small cloud will appear before the luminous ball, and between it and the earth. On this cloud will be seen the Son of Man, standing erect, his figure plainly visible to the spectators on the earth."[346]

Coincidentally, the announcement of just such an astronomical event was reported about a week after Miller's lectures in Bennington in the *Baltimore Sun*.[347]

The first reports in Vermont of the comet occurred in the March 3 issue of the Vermont Mercury, which rejected the idea that it was a "precursor" of any "dire calamities."[348] Comets had come before, most recently, Halley's, in 1835. This one's tail was not as wide but longer.

Astronomer Peter Smyth's painting of the Comet of 1843

Miller who was lecturing in Milton, New York, near Saratoga Springs, became ill about the middle of March. He was suffering from what was described as a rash that manifested as numerous carbuncles on his body. He was taken to the home of a local follower where he was given care while he awaited the fateful day until he was taken home by his son.[349]

There are no reports of his condition during this time while reports of the approaching comet multiplied in the newspapers though with few associations to the Millerites. The March 28, *Rutland Weekly* reported the following:

As the present day appears to be one of more than usual excitement, it can be no way surprising that these believers in a general conflagration of our earth in 1843, should indulge in terrific forebodings, and their belief strengthened by the present appearance of a comet, which is now visible in a south-westerly direction, but indicates nothing more than a harmless, though a very magnificent visitor to our system.[350]

After arriving home, Miller wrote Himes, "I am now at home; I am very weak in body but blessed be God! My mind, faith, and hope are yet strong in the Lord — no wavering in my belief that I shall see Christ this year. . . ."[351]

Ascension Rock outside his home where it is said he awaited the Coming

So, the first date of reckoning had passed but there was the year ahead to face and Miller's efforts and those of his fellow clerics had just begun. The Millerite movement would grow stronger in the next two years as Miller continued lecturing, and he was being called Prophet Miller. His faith in his prediction never wavered and his followers grew more fanatical, and some continued to give up their homes and possessions as they hoped and prayed for the coming of that fateful day.

When March 21, 1844 passed without Christ's appearance, Miller was devastated. He remained in seclusion at home and did not get out of bed for four days. Finally, he wrote to Himes:

> I am seated at my old desk in my east room, having obtained help of God until the present time. I am still looking for our dear Savior, the Son of God from heaven. . . . The time as I have calculated is now filled up and I expect to see the Savior descend from Heaven. I have now nothing to look for but this glorious hope. I am full in the faith that all prophetic chronology, excepting the thousand years of Rev. 20 is now about full. Whether God designs for me to warn the people of this earth any more or not, I am at a loss to know. . . . I feel almost confident that my labors are about done; and I am with a deep interest of soul looking for my blessed and glorious Redeemer. . . . This I can truly say is my chief desire. . . . It is my meditation all the day long. It is my song in the night. It is my faith and hope. "I still believe the time is not far off![352]

Miller's faith that the time was not far off never wavered until the day he died in 1849, and his followers would start a new denomination that continues to the present day, The Seventh Day Adventist.

As for Orson S. Murray, his rationalist mind could no longer hold back. Some weeks after March 21, 1843 had passed, he came out with a scathing rebuke of Millerism. While he later reported news about the "Adventists," this editorial was a good reflection of his final view on the subject.

> The moral and mental desolation sweeping over the land in connection with this subject is deplorable. It will furnish a page for the history of the times, to be read with humiliation and sorrow. It will be a thunder-speaking comment on the popular theology that has obtained, such an ascendency over the mind

of this generation. Soon it will be seen to be, what in reality and fact it is, the maturity, in one direction of a system of materialism which is a terrible pestilence walking in darkness and a destruction wasting at noon day, more to be dreaded and deprecated than cholera and plague.

Nothing is plainer to my own mind than that Millerism comes from modem theology . . . . It is now nursing in the arms of the priesthood and lap of the church. They have already branded it with lunacy and idiocy to be sure. But that is nothing. They may ostracize it. Still, it will be their own child. Say what they will and do what they will—it will yet be seen that the child is every way worthy of its parentage. At some future time, life and health being spared, I shall undertake to show that such an event as is called second advent," " the end of all things," " the final consummation of all things," is not to be looked for, is never to be expected, is only a figment of addled brains."[353]

While the fervor of Millerism would continue for almost two more years, Murray left the subject, for the most part. He had far more pressing problems.

Chapter 20

The Inconvenient Truth

The loss of support from the Baptists did not deter Murray. He had already been actively soliciting subscribers but now he would begin increasing these efforts by taking to the road and lecturing about the unchristian and immoral stand they had taken. His primary focus was not antislavery. It was now religion, the Bible, the hypocrisy of the clerics and the lack of Christianity practiced by the sectarian denominations, especially his own which had forsaken him. However, his presence was not always welcomed.

And criticism seemed to come at Murray from all sides. For instance, letters to the editor about being faithful subscribers and cancelling because Murray was moving too far ahead of them with his ideas and principles, like the following:

Mr. Murray: Sir: I take this opportunity to request you to discontinue my paper. If I mistake not, we are about even in our accounts. "I have ever taken the *Telegraph*. Have got some subscribers for the same. Have formerly been pleased with the straightforward, independent course of the Editor; but of late think there is too much departure from original principles. Find it will not do for the common people to look to their leaders neither in religion or politics, for examples; but they must weigh, think, and act for themselves. A word to the wise is sufficient This from, yours, H. M. Baldwin. Hinesburgh, Aug. 6, 1842.[354]

Often, he was attacked for his unconventional interpretation of Scripture, as for example, quibbling about such esoteric issues as the requirement for circumcision as commanded in the Old Testament.

Such matters pushed Murray to suggest that the Bible was not divinely inspired but the words of mortals. To make matters worse, he never accepted any criticism and usually responded in a lengthy rant about how wrong his critics were. He was becoming increasingly bitter about his fortunes and the unjust criticism. Instead of relenting with his pressure, however, he pushed back harder, which turned him into a pariah, especially among church leadership.

One of his trips on the road in his attempt to sell the moral leadership of the *Telegraph* was made with fellow reformer, Benjamin W. Dyer, who lived 40 miles up the road in Braintree.

Murray was on his way to Williamstown, his first stop, that also included Groton, Passumpsic, and Danville. A roundtrip approaching 200 miles through the scenic wilderness that was Vermont and still is today. At a juncture in the road, he met Dyer and his wife, out on errands. Dyer had already published articles in the *Telegraph* on vegetarianism and was a non-resistance man. Murray asked Dyer to join him, and Dyer's wife urged him to go.[355]

Not surprisingly, they were met with resistance in Williamstown and Groton, though his reception in Williamstown turned out well. Not so in Groton. A Williamstown congregant had gone there ahead of them and deprecated Murray. After discussion among the church leadership, he was finally granted 30 minutes to speak. He summarized his words in his report: "Selfishness which lies at the foundation of all slavery, everywhere and in all forms, can only be overcome by benevolence; and the violence of the system, by peacefulness . . . evil must be overcome with good."[356]

In Passumpsic, they stayed with Jonathan Lawrence, a Grahamite,[bb] but were not allowed to speak at the Baptist Meeting House. But a good turnout was received at the Congregational

---

[bb] Follower of the diet principles of Sylvester Graham, which was in vogue among the progressive intellectuals of the time. It consisted of bland foods with whole grains, fruits, vegetables, and no spices, meat, alcohol or tobacco.

meeting house. "Selfishness, proselytism, and idolatry," these were what characterized the churches of the time, he declared. They do not save its followers from sin. They do not practice Christ's teachings.

In Danville, Rev. Cheney opened the house and enthusiastic meetings were held. Evil can only be overcome by goodness, he again exhorted.[357]

After returning home, he attended the Addison County Baptist Association Meeting. He knew he would not be welcome. The leaders of the meeting were among those who called for the *Vermont Baptist Journal* (VBJ) to replace the *Telegraph*. In fact, one of the orders of business was to discuss starting another newspaper to represent the Baptists. The VBJ was struggling, probably in part because of the unceasing attacks on it by Murray.

In his report in the *Telegraph*, Murray sarcastically mentioned that he fell asleep during the opening sermon: "I received much refreshment from the sleep and was thereby prepared to attend to the conference with interest."[358]

Thereafter, he rose and went into a rant:

"Genuine Christianity puts down all rule and all authority. It allows no one to rule over another, or others—and no one to be ruled over by another, or by others. It requires each to rule himself and leaves him responsible for himself to God."[359]

Rev. Ide, once one of his closest associates, told Murray that he was out of order, but he refused to stop speaking, saying his right of free speech was being abridged. Then one of the elders, James Ten Broeke, walked over and physically forced him to sit down.

The meeting resumed with a speaker from the American and Foreign Bible Society, known for its anti-abolition views and reluctance to give bibles to slaves.

Of course, it was almost a reflexive action on Murray's part to rise and contest the speaker. Again, he had to be restrained. Amidst the chaos, a vote was passed in favor of censuring Murray and silencing him.[360]

A reflection of how far Murray's fortunes had fallen in Vermont was the organizational meeting of the Vermont Baptist Anti-Slavery Society later that month. Murray who was the leading figure in Vermont's antislavery movement ten years earlier and the organizer of the state's first Baptist antislavery conventions now was on the outside looking in at the organization of its antislavery society. And there was no mention of it in the *Telegraph*.

A full report, however, was published in the first edition of the *Vermont Religious Observer*, the successor to the failed *Vermont Baptist Journal*, which also published the report of the meeting that transferred the obligations of the *Journal* to the *Observer*. Its position was much more accommodating to church members in the slaveholding states than the earlier conventions led by Murray. While it took a strong stand against slavery, it did not cut ties with its colleagues who owned slaves or tolerated slavery but sought "to aid in forming a correct abolition sentiment in our churches . . . at the South, and to exert our influence for the elevation of the free colored population of our country."[361]

VERMONT OBSERVER.

Murray attacked the "Vermont Observer," saying it was the same paper, only with the named changed.[362] Nevertheless he soldiered on. With all the chaos in his life, he crossed paths with the other man causing chaos, much greater chaos than the localized one created by Murray, William Miller. The Second Coming was approaching, and Miller was speaking at the Methodist Church in Brandon. Murray offered no criticism of Miller, who spoke about the inspiration of the Bible, but others there were offended simply

163

by Murray's presence. One of the elders became visibly upset when it was noticed that Murray was in the church and stormed out, saying he was not about to "hearing the Devil preach!" Of course, this wasn't going to deter Murray who launched into another attack on the churches.[363]

On Thanksgiving, 1842, Murray and his wife, Catherine, were invited for dinner at the home of Jacob Spear, the father of Benjamin Dyer's wife. He doesn't say who was caring for the kids, though there were plenty of relatives nearby. His oldest, Carlos, was now 15, and his youngest, Roselinda, named after his mother, a toddler of nearly two.[364]

His commentary about his visit, which was enroute to his next speaking engagements in West Brookfield and Williston, reveal his radical views of diet:[XXIX]

> It was such a sight as my eyes never beheld before. The occasion afforded a feast for the mind--the soul . . . . The table was plainly and well furnished, from the kingdom of fruits and vegetables, uncontaminated with blood, unstenched with dead carcasses . . . an occasion for rejoicing to the beasts and the fowl.[365]

It was a festive occasion. The presence of all of Spear's nine children and some of the grandchildren suggest that Brother Dyer and his family were there too, for his wife was one of the nine. It was "a day on which people make a god of their bellies," Murray wrote sarcastically.[366]

His lectures, however, did not come off well. In Williston, he caused chaos by insisting that no rules should limit the speakers, stating:

[XXIX] In 1834 Murray gave up eating pork and most animal products. However, after four years he once again began eating some beef and dairy ("Diet—My Own Practice," *The Regenerator*, April 1852).

The common practice of governing meetings, by moderators and rules of order, is wasteful of time and destructive of good order . . . inconsistent with free discussion, and . . . a hindrance to truth. It is part of a system of violent restraint upon human liberty, which no one has a right to impose . . . It would therefore be useless . . . for this meeting, or any human beings, individually or collectively . . . to set up any authority over me. I hold to self-government . . . mutual forbearance, patience, and kindness.[367]

One can understand the exasperation many were feeling with Murray, who now was refusing to abide by anyone's rules. Nevertheless, his refusal to give up the *Telegraph* pushed him to do more meetings.

In January, he traveled with his wife to Bristol. It was the first stop on a series of lectures that also included Starksboro and Williston. He put an announcement in the *Telegraph* and sent a notice of his lecture in Bristol with Luman Scott, a church member who was going there on an errand.[368]

However, when Murray arrived at the appointed time, only a few had come to hear him. Apparently, the notice had not been posted, though Scott assured Murray that he had delivered it to Pastor Hurlbut. When Murray confronted the pastor, he said he had received the notice but was against Murray preaching at his church.

Murray was taken aback because Hurlbut had been his friend, had stayed over at his home when traveling, had been given space in the *Telegraph*. Apparently, orders had come down to him that the Baptist Church did not want to allow Murray to speak in Vermont.

In Starksboro, on the other hand, there was a receptive audience; in Williston, where they stayed with his cousins, Sela and Dorcas, the churches were not open to him, but a friend helped him obtain a private hall which filled up to hear him.[369]

The opposition Murray was facing was insurmountable, and yet the next week, he scheduled another speaking tour to Charlotte, N. Ferrisburgh, Panton, and Cornwall.

Before heading to Charlotte, he stopped in to attend the ninth annual meeting of the Vermont Anti-Slavery Society, which had diminished in influence because of the rise of the Liberty Party in the state. Certainly, Murray was a contributor to the society's instability, but the fundamental differences on political action and women's participation were far greater influences.

Harvey Leavitt, the current president, introduced the subject of electing a president for the new year. Murray and others quickly offered up Rowland T. Robinson, but Leavitt objected. While there was no question of Robinson's antislavery credentials, Leavitt cited other opinions of Robinson with which many society members disagreed. It caused an uproar, and John Orvis, an ally of Robinson and Murray, was removed from the meeting after being out of order. In the end, Robinson was chosen as the new President. But at the end of the meeting Murray withdrew his membership.[370]

The rancor facing Murray continued to grow. At the Baptist church in Charlotte, he was forcibly removed from the pulpit. "The popular and prevalent religion, or theology, of this country, at the present time, I view to be sadly wanting in Christianity, to be essentially material, idolatrous, infidelic, blasphemous and atheistical," he began.[371]

A man approached Murray and ordered him to stop speaking. When Murray ignored him, the man along with others "seized him by the collar and arms and dragged him out."[372]

Some days later, he spoke on a Saturday evening and the Sabbath in Whiting. On Saturday, his topic was biblical reform. His main proposition from which the rest of his ideas followed was that the bible was not divinely inspired. It was the first principle that supported his other disagreements with Scripture. The next morning, he emphasized his defiance by a public display of chopping

166

wood on the Lord's Day of rest outside his place of lodging, and as you might recall, Orson was quite expert with an ax.[373]

The end had come for Murray in Vermont. He could not continue like this. A letter from his colleague, Charles Burleigh, to Rowland T. Robinson reveals the depths of his situation. In the beginning of the letter, Burleigh is discussing Jedidiah Holcomb resuming the publication of the state antislavery society newspaper, *Voice of Freedom*. In doing so, he segues to a notification Holcomb received about the business failures of Murray.

> A letter came from Brandon today, directed to [Holcomb], which I opened as usual, thinking it related to Voice business, but it proved to be an announcement that O. S. Murray has failed, his property been attached, and an officer started off in pursuit of him to take the horse he has with him – and it seems he is somehow connected with Orson, so that he may lose by his failure . . . . I was very sorry to hear such news concerning Orson. But the priests will no doubt rejoice with exceeding great joy, and perhaps regard it a special interposition of Providence, on behalf of their sacred order – another proof that no weapon found against Zion shall prosper. I am sorry, not only on Orson's private account, & that of his family, but also for the very reason which I suppose will give the priesthood joy, – viz, that his faithful, bold and free paper will have to stop.[374]

But it was now not merely public disapproval of his ideas that he was up against but legal obstruction. While the paper was stopped only temporarily for two weeks, it was a harbinger of things to come. A lengthy narrative in the *Telegraph* told the story.

Murray explained that seven years earlier he was helped in purchasing the *Telegraph* by the "prince of the aristocracy."[xxx] Now,

---

[xxx] John Conant. Murray adds that Conant was not part of the scheme to use foreclosing Murray's debt to close the *Telegraph*.

both financial and clerical influences had stymied the free speech of the *Telegraph*. Nevertheless, Murray resisted and "a clandestine movement was made to buy accounts of its creditors, for the purpose of turning a key upon it and staying its progress or stopping it in its course."[375]

This action occurred while Murray was in Danville, 90 miles from Brandon, where he was staying with friends. During the night, two men had taken his horse. He learned that one of them was the deputy sheriff from Brandon and that they were staying at the local tavern.

Murray went to the tavern and confronted the deputy. He admitted to the claims but said he was not opposed to keeping the *Telegraph* office open.

With the help of friends, he was taken home to Brandon. It was claimed that the legal proceedings were brought because of outstanding debts that Murray had. But Murray insisted that it was solely due to the content in the *Telegraph* and its reform mission.[376]

Murray then enumerated the outstanding debts in question and indicated that none of his creditors had sought immediate payment. He insisted that the four individuals suing were put up to it by someone else, a person or persons who wanted to force the closing of the *Telegraph*. And they waited until he was out of town to put their plan into action. Those creditors trusted Murray because he was a local person with a good reputation who had built his trust over the years.

In his lengthy explanation of his circumstance, Murray squarely put the blame on the church and the clerics who did not agree with his views. They wanted to shut down the *Telegraph*. But then Murray showed that stopping its publication would also punish his creditors who were making the suit but who suddenly lost trust in Murray despite the good credit he had built over his lifetime. They too had been hoodwinked because unless it continued publication, he would be unable to pay them, and they would lose their investment.[377]

Murray then revealed some of his financial circumstances:

When I commenced publishing the *Telegraph,* I was three hundred dollars in debt, which I had sunk in the Anti-Slavery cause, in its infancy . . . I did not receive as much money during three years as is now paid to an agent in one. In connection with publishing the *Telegraph,* I soon paid up the three hundred dollars and advanced in a few years five times that amount beyond my liabilities. At length I was beset to print a book the memoir of two Baptist ministers. On the representation of two living Baptist ministers, on whose words I depended, I proceeded with the work, but found myself deceived and disappointed.

It stands now a dead loss of at least $600.

Baptist priests and people who have stopped the *Telegraph* and are doing it all possible violence, owe me quite extensively. I have lost by numerous bankrupts (of subscribers).[378]

And this was true as Murray had published numerous notices of delinquent subscribers, some who never paid him.

I have never sued, and never shall . . . . It has for a long time been my desire to dispose of the property in my hands and pay my creditors. But the hardness of the times has greatly depreciated the value of property and destroyed the market. The fault is less with me than with those who have defrauded me, that all my engagements have not been fulfilled. I have never for a moment abandoned the idea of paying all I owe.[379]

Murray concluded that the *Telegraph* had been rescued for the time being:

Twenty-six men, of the bone and sinew and muscle of the town of Brandon, have come to the rescue, as good neighbors and as human beings, and have signed a receipt for the property. Thanks to them I should be happy to publish their names but have not consulted them generally on this point. Many others would have gladly joined them in the work if it had been necessary or convenient to give them an opportunity. Some of the receipters are among my principal creditors in town; again, I say thanks to them. And on behalf of the friends of free discussion, I assure them they shall not suffer.

Shall one press stand in the world untrammeled by sect, unbiased of organization or party unawed by combinations in church or in state? The *Telegraph* shall thus stand or thus fall.[380]

Against all odds, Murray continued to fight but started to look for a way out. "Many times, during a few weeks past," he wrote, "I have indulged the feeling of a strong desire to attend the meeting to be held here tomorrow for the promotion of Universal Inquiry and Reform; but have seen no way that my desire could be gratified, on account of my extreme poverty."[381]

Once again, Murray was helped by an abolitionist friend who offered to pay his expenses.[XXXI] They went together and started out in Murray's horse and carriage to Union Village to visit with his old friend, Rev. William Arthur, the Baptist preacher whose son was Chester Arthur, who would be elected vice-president and become president in 1881 after Garfield was assassinated. They crossed the Green Mountains and descended into charming Union Village with its beautiful Free Church and Arthur's high-steepled Bottskill Church, just up the block from it.

[XXXI] This friend, who is not identified, apparently was going to the antislavery convention because Murray uses the pronoun we in narrating the story.

"He manifested so much cordiality and charitable feeling," Murray wrote, "that I was led to ask him if he thought an audience could be obtained for me to address that evening."[382]

He said yes at once, and his lecture on "reform" was scheduled at the church.

Bottskill Church

"I endeavored to be practical, and to point out several errors in existing institutional arrangements and proceedings which claim to have for their object the redemption of mankind from sin and suffering and in their stead suggested the adoption of practical love and good will," wrote Murray.

But Rev. Arthur objected. Not only in private but publicly. He said he would never have allowed Murray to speak if he knew he held such views—apparently. he hadn't been reading the *Telegraph*.[383]

Murray moved on. The abolitionist friend and Murray took his team to Troy where they left it at a stable and took the steamer to New York. They didn't arrive until the closing day of the antislavery convention. But Murray's primary reason for his trip was the convention of the Society of Universal Inquiry and Reform. Though he didn't say this directly, it is likely he saw the group as a possible means of escape from Vermont—a group of individuals whose philosophy and ideas were like his own.

Murray had published a full account of its first convention held in Oakland, Ohio, in February.[384] In the report, though he didn't attend, Murray is listed as a Vice-President. However, there were many others listed as members in absentia, all of them prominent reformers, including some from England and France like George Thompson and Harriet Martineau.

171

Murray actively participated in the reform convention's New York event to which he gave high praise:

I have had part in many heavenly meetings, but this exceeded them all. Violent organization and government were set aside. No despotic moderator to command. No absolute rules of decorum to shackle. No aristocratic business committee to gag or control. No concession to the authority of numbers by voting-No strife for places or preferments. No jealousies. No contentions. No recognition of color, caste, creed, sect or sex. Of course, there was the best of order, the greatest harmony, the largest goodwill. Forbearance and kindness characterized the proceedings throughout. The utmost liberty was conceded to all, of whatever views.[385]

Murray wrote at length about his view of the cause of human disharmony. He vilified the system of private property and suggested that eating meat affected one's moral choices. But what was more significant were the leaders of the society, five of whom were part of a group that traveled 700 miles by wagon to the convention, including the society's president, Abram Brooke of Oakland, Ohio. The others were Abram Allen and John Wattles, also of Oakland, Valentine Nicholson of Harveysburg, and Edwin Fussell, of Pendleton, Indiana, who hailed from Chester County, Pennsylvania, and was the nephew of noted Underground Railroad conductor, Dr. Bartholomew Fussell – all also participants in the Underground Railroad. The others were Amos Welsh, John and Maria McCowan, also of Harveysburg; Rebecca Nichols of Lloydsville, Belmont County, Ohio; and Sara Dugdale and Elizabeth Borton of Green Plain.[386]

Among accounts of this journey from Ohio to convention, which were published in the *National Anti-Slavery Standard* and *The Liberator*, is the following:

The wagon ought to be described . . . to enable our readers to see what righteous zeal can do, when it simply resolves to go forward. It [has] a flat top and covering, on which to carry baggage. A hammock was slung at night, on which the men slept---the women resorting to houses in the neighborhood. Eight persons can be accommodated with lodging on board this 'Great Western' land ship. The carriage is known by the name of LIBERATOR, because of its extensive service in aiding fugitives to liberate themselves from southern bondage. It picked up two on the voyage and gave them a considerable life freedom ward. It was decorated with evergreens, some of which were distributed among the friends in this city, who preserve them as interesting memorials of the journey.

The travelers carried their provisions with them; and as these consisted of Graham bread and apples, they considered it as quite luxurious. Thus they journeyed on, through pleasant and foul weather, to Concord, where they . . . were to stop a couple of hours, [and] it was concluded to have an anti-slavery meeting [which] was addressed by John O. Wattles . . . The whole distance ... was over seven hundred miles. Who would not gladly have shared the toils and pleasures of that journey?[387]

Miniature of The Liberator, Friends Museum, Waynesville OH

Whether or not they met at the convention, Murray did not say, but they would play an important role in his future. For now, Murray was setting his sights on moving to New York, where he hoped to get a more appreciative audience. Six weeks later, he announced that he would be moving there where he would be starting his new paper. He called it, *The Regenerator.*

THE REGENERATOR.

It will be its design to be devoted, as it has been the design of the Telegraph since it came under my control, to the promotion of the highest interests of the human race. It will labor for the *regeneration* of mankind.

After another trip to New York City, in September, Murray explained that while he would be starting publication of *The Regenerator* there because of its accessibility for distribution, he wrote that he would looking elsewhere to settle.[388]

As Murray prepared to leave Vermont, his close associate in reform, Jedidiah Holcomb, and his brother David Murray were resuming publication of the state antislavery society's newspaper, *The Voice of Freedom*. It began in the offices of the *Telegraph* and Murray graciously offered the use of his printing press until eventually selling it to them. In time, the *Voice of Freedom* would move to Montpelier. Meanwhile, Benjamin Brierly, Murray's nemesis at the *Baptist Journal* and *Religious Observer*, stepped down as its editor before the final issue of the *Telegraph*.[389]

In December of 1843, Murray left Vermont in sleighs with his wife and six children for Albany, and from there took a steamer to New York City. They moved into temporary quarters in Brooklyn.[390] His accounts had been settled and he was looking for new horizons.[391]

Depiction of Legendary Ohio Woodsman

Johnny Appleseed

Credit: Library of Congress

Chapter 21

The Beginning of the Regeneration

The Regenerator will be the organ of no sect or party. It will be devoted to free inquiry after all truth. It will be confined neither to a negation, nor to an affirmation, neither to destruction, nor to observation, neither to aggression, nor to repulsion neither to building up, nor to tearing down . . .[392]

Regeneration is a continuous process. We see it in the cycles of the seasons, in the renewal of a married couple's vows, the rebirth of a flower, the revival of an old idea, the rejuvenation of an old friendship, the resurrection of the Phoenix rising from the ashes, and so it was with Orson S. Murray, who was reinventing himself as he moved from his native Vermont.

He needed to escape the hostility and contention created by his unconventional ideas and harshly critical nature. Many of his friends and supporters in Vermont had deserted him. Now he was looking for a regeneration and a more congenial home for his radical newspaper. As he had stated in his Vermont publication, the *Telegraph*, he was undecided where and chose Brooklyn, across the harbor from New York City, as a temporary location.[393]

At that time, the community of Brooklyn was growing rapidly from the influx of Irish and German immigrants. The burgeoning metropolis of Manhattan offered work and easy access with a regular ferry service that had been in operation for more than two decades.

Brooklyn ferry circa 1840 (Steele engraving, public domain)

The Murrays moved to a rural location on the eastern outskirts. "There were no paved streets in Brooklyn at that time," wrote son Charles, who was then six years old. "There was an apple orchard nearby, and ponds with plentifulness of cattails."[394]

Murray located his new paper, the *Regenerator*, at 29 Ann Street in Manhattan. Within a few short weeks he published its first issue on January 1, 1844, with the motto, "Ignorance the Evil – Knowledge the Remedy." In his prospectus, Murray stated that the paper was "devoted to universal inquiry, general improvement, and perpetual progress . . . a channel for free thought and faithful expression devoted to no one idea" … or servant of any sect, party, faith, creed, or constitution . . . "Free inquiry is the ground . . . . All can, therefore, through this medium express their own views and sentiments for themselves."[395]

Murray had managed to maintain his subscription list and with a large audience in New York, he increased it to 1900 subscribers.[396] While not totally impoverished, he was watching his finances. The

178

New York Tribune said the "no-government, anti-everything" Murray was someone for whom wealth was not the primary motive, "an oddity in our City, and his long beard attracts more attention . . . than his ultra-Radical doctrines will [attract] subscribers."[397]

Beards and facial hair were not yet in fashion as they would become in the years leading up to and during the Civil War, and it is not clear when he adopted the long hair and beard. However, son Charles who was born in 1837 wrote, "My father early conceived the idea that the shaving of the face and close cutting of the hair was unfavorable to health and inconsistent with natural conditions. His adoption of the unusual practice in those days in these particulars made him an object of special observation, in his movements, wherever he appeared."[398] Murray himself addressed what had become his characteristic trademark, his long hair and beard, in a lengthy commentary in one of the last issues of the *Vermont Telegraph*, writing, [S]ome have undertaken to say that the wearing of the hair and the beard must be inconvenient and uncomfortable. These generally know little or nothing about it, having had little or no experience. Few with whom I converse have worn their hair and beards to any considerable length or taken any proper care of them as to cleanliness. An

179

experience of five months enables me to testify that it is less trouble to take proper care of any beard than to shave it off. Then, if I may be believed, it is my positive testimony that the enjoyment of it is a great luxury . . . . The truth is no reason can be given for this constant use of shears and razors about the human head. It is monstrously unnatural and must be vastly hurtful. All that can be said for it is, it is the fashion to do it (Shaving)."[399]

Editor Horace Greeley also complimented *The Regenerator* adding that it evoked "a spirit of kindness and love breathed through all its sharp condemnation of the existing order of things which proves that the Editor and his correspondents have profited by their Christian education, though . . . they say, [have] outgrown the institutes of Christianity. We think no man will be the worse for reading this paper, though many of its editor's ideas are very much out of the way."[400]

Though the *Tribune* was generally positive in its comments, Murray bristled at its criticism. "Church, government and property, as they go on, are one system," he countered, "a trio of monsters, born of ignorance and bred in perverseness. They have engendered and produced violence, hate, tyranny, and oppression. They have labored reciprocally and mutually."[401]

A review of *The Regenerator* by William H. Burleigh described Murray as someone who is "very wild in many of his notions—and a very unsafe leader." Murray disagreed: "Of course, he holds to the leading and being-led system. I do not. Am no leader. Will neither lead nor be led. Think it is time for human beings to begin to stand on their own feet and walk for themselves uprightly. They have already been led too long."[402]

Meanwhile, personal tragedy, which had haunted his family with the deaths of their two young girls, continued to stalk the Murrays. Catherine's father passed away at age 73 in Orwell, little more than a month after their move. It was a transitional period for the family.

In the April 29 issue of the *Regenerator*, Murray veered farther from the mainstream, arguing that laws are arbitrary and tyrannical, and that "creeds and constitutions" prevent progress.[403]   Two months later, he expressed his disdain for worship on the Sabbath.

[It] is a day for gluttony and lounging. For extravagance of dress, decoration, and display. For smothering thought and suppressing speech. For the promotion of creedism and caste. For filling the world with fear and torment, with hatred and maliciousness, with anything but knowledge and good will. For exalting useless forms and senseless ceremonies, over moral excellence, and practical goodness.[404]

But more significantly, the *Regenerator's* pages included continuous reports and correspondence from reformers in southern Ohio, among them Abram Brooke of Oakland; Valentine Nicholson, of Harveysburg; and John Wattles, then living temporarily in Ohio, leaders of the Society for Universal Inquiry and Reform. All three were interested in the commune movement that had developed among reformers. Brooke and Nicholson had purchased land in central Ohio for a community they called Prairie Home. Wattles sent Murray a glowing, poetic description of it.

Lo there, there the Lord shall deliver
And souls drink of that beautiful river
That flows peace for ever and ever
Where love and joy shall ever increase

Wattles added, "[The] four rivers, the Euphrates and its tributaries, that flowed through paradise that was planted 'eastward in Eden' could scarcely have afforded more beauty to the beholder and more utility to the dwellers there, than those that run through this beautiful valley."[405]

The idea of an Eden-like utopia that Murray imagined in Prairie Home was what he was searching for. The idea of improving humanity and the welfare of all was his goal, as it was for most of those involved in the Community movement. Among the lifestyle practices subscribed to by its followers was a commitment to the Grahamite principles of healthy eating. No animal products—no meat or dairy—no stimulating beverages like coffee or tea, no tobacco or alcohol, which he had long renounced. Hot liquids were to be avoided as was salt; uncooked foods were recommended with cold water the ideal drink, after consuming solid food and properly masticating it with saliva. Cold baths were the prescription for good health. Sex was to be kept to moderation and release of male seed was considered to weaken the body. Fasting and chastity were considered useful in maintaining health and preventing disease.

One cooked food Murray would not forsake was bread: "unbolted (unsifted) wheaten flour and sifted corn meal."[406] A series of articles about breadmaking with Henry Pratt, a bread maker in New York City, who left his samples at *The Regenerator's* office appeared in the paper.[407] The following treatise, sections of which are extracted below, shows the diversity of Murray's interests.

> His bread must be beyond all calculation wholesome, above anything I have seen in market. If the population of this City could eat such bread as he makes beyond doubt the general health would be vastly improved. But all this is not saying that I believe he still cannot improve, particularly in the use of the principal material, the flour . . . . He states it to be the "first time" he has made bread from the entire, wheaten flour . . . . This being the first time he has made bread from the entire flour of the wheat, how could he be well and discreetly prepared to decide against its use, especially in connection with such concessions as he makes.

He says it yields the exact proportion of bread to flour. When he says the "dough was very stiff indeed; and cut like a board," he is liable to be misunderstood by those unacquainted with the facts in such matters. Taken with his other statements, this fact is one of the highest possible recommendations . . . It shows that it has a superior degree of life, of power to resist the unnatural action upon it for decomposition, previously to taking it into the mouth for the use of the system. His statement as to its "fresh, vinous, sweet, smell" is further testimony to the same point, showing a greater amount of vitality and less advancement in decomposition . . . . Every step in this grinding, fermenting, and baking process, is so much violence.to vegetable vitality, and of course so much diminution of power to contribute to animal vitality. The stiffness and strength of the dough, as compared with other, shows that the life has not been as much dissipated by the separating process. Its sweet smell shows that it has not been as much rotted by fermentation.

From all his concessions and voluntary statements, oral and written, it is evident to me that his opinion was formed, or rather his feelings, habits, and prejudices are fixed, condemnatory of the entire flour, before he began the experiment with the seven pounds which I furnished him for the purpose.

Brother Pratt, it is of one piece with your adherence to salt. That is, your decision I think to have been made out after the same manner. In both cases your opinions seem to have been very much one thing with your habits and practices, with too little examination and too little reference to facts. Just as it has been too much with human beings generally, regarding most of their eating and drinking.[408]

It was characteristic of how Murray thought to point out how Pratt's preconceived notions about the coarseness of unsifted flour colored his conclusions about the quality of his bread, in the same way that preconceived ideas color the conception of the truth.

Murray published his last *Regenerator* in New York on June 22, and shortly afterwards, his family left for Prairie Home while he concluded his affairs in New York With Catherine were their six children: Carlos, who was sixteen; Marsena, fifteen; Charles, seven; Rachel, five; Roselinda, three: and one-year-old Ichabod. Charles Murray later wrote that they traveled by steamer to Albany, then by packet boat to Buffalo on the Erie Canal. He said there was a party atmosphere on the packet. From Buffalo, they took a steamer to Sandusky, then proceeded by rail to Tiffin, where they boarded wagons without springs. He commented that it was an extremely rough and rocky ride to West Liberty in Logan County.[409]

But Wattles' description of Prairie Home was a romanticized portrait. A.J. MacDonald, another visitor, also called it a beautiful location but pointed out its fatal flaws.

Half of it was thickly wooded and the other half prairie with rich soil, he wrote. About 130 residents occupied two, two-story frame buildings. Many were Hicksite Quakers, and most of them did not eat meat, and were conversant in such topics as the water cure treatment and phrenology, the fad which claimed the shape of the skull determined personality. Sheep were raised for their wool, and there also was a sawmill and a grist mill along the stream that ran through the property. A large shed that seated about 40 persons was used for meals.[410]

However, conditions were far from ideal. Both mills were in disrepair. And it was so overcrowded that people who wanted to join were being turned away. MacDonald described it:

At that place there seemed to be much confusion; too many people and too many idlers among them. The young women

184

were most industrious, attending to the supper table and the provisions in a very steady, business-like manner; but the young men were mostly lounging about doing nothing. At bedtime there were too many persons for each to be accommodated with a bed, so the females all went upstairs and slept as they could, and the males slept below, all spread out in rows upon the floor. This was unpleasant, and as the sequel proved, could not long be endured.[411]

Charles Murray's memoir made no mention of Prairie Home. We only know his family stayed there because of Valentine Nicholson's autobiography. We also know their stay was brief because of the unsatisfactory living conditions and they ended up at the home of Abram Brooke in Oakland to await Orson's arrival.[412]

Meanwhile, before leaving for Ohio, Murray made one last visit to Middlebury, Vermont. He would not return to New York until some years later. One can only speculate about the reason for his trip, though it might've been for financial reasons or perhaps to retrieve possessions left behind. While there, he gave a lecture articulating his "radical" ideas. The same account was published in both Middlebury newspapers.

[The] great Orson S. redeemed, regenerated, and disenthralled from the iron bands of sectarian discipline stood forth first as infidel and then an Atheist. Recognizing but his own inclination, his person as he appeared on that night in a coarse frock, hair reaching to his middle and a beard which the great Mogul himself might have envied, well represented the principles which be advocated, and the utter abandon, to which he had arrived. He commenced to a crowd of curious men and boys, by assuring them, that he did not regard them with contempt and knew how to make allowances for their prejudices. He congratulated himself on having broken the shackles with which his mother had bound his infant mind. He

185

denounced the Christian Religion as the "Juggernaut of ignorance and nonsense," and recapitulated his objections (any one of which an ordinary Sunday School scholar might have refuted) against the doctrines of our religion . . . . He went on in such a tirade of blasphemy and abuse that we were compelled to leave the house.[413]

Chapter 22

The Perilous Journey to Ohio

Departing from Vermont, Murray began his journey to Ohio. He had dreams and ambitions. He was going to transplant the Regenerator which he hoped would become the first "Free paper," where all ideas could freely be expressed and truth not orthodoxy would be its mission, a paper that would be the voice of a sprouting Community movement seeking a living arrangement that would lead to human perfection.

He hauled his precious press and possessions in a wagon to upstate New York where he hopped on the Erie Canal for the 350-mile journey to where he would board the steamer Robert Fulton to Sandusky, Ohio.

While Murray was embarking on a new chapter in his life, Rev. William Miller, was still clinging to the hope that Christ would come and save the righteous and punish the sinners. In a letter to Joshua Himes, the editor of *The Signs of the Times*, he wrote:

> I have now much more evidence that I do believe in God's word; and although surrounded with enemies and scoffers, my mind is perfectly calm and my hope in the Coming of Christ is as strong as ever . . . . If I have erred, it has been on the side of charity, of love for my fellow man, and my conviction of duty to God.[414]

A new religion based on his theories which called itself the Seventh Day Adventists had emerged, and it continues to the present day. Miller himself would pass away in 1849 convinced that Christ would still come, only that his calculations were in error. Yet his irrational passion would have lasting impact with an established religion the result. Murray would only make passing reference to Miller in later years.

Three months earlier, Murray's family already had journeyed in the very boat he was boarding. A strong northeast wind had been driving up Lake Erie for several days, but on the evening of his departure on the 18th of October, a sudden shift of the wind took place. It blew from the opposite direction with a tremendous force never known even to this day along the eastern section of Lake Erie.[415]

Murray later wrote about it: "No language can describe the awfulness of [what] I am about to speak."

The steamer had left at seven in the evening, the wind blowing moderately. It was steady and continuous, and it gradually grew. It was making him seasick. He went below deck but it worsened. He went back up and the fresh air dispelled his nausea; but he had become drowsy and fell asleep.

Sometime, more than an hour later, he was shaken awake. The ship was tossing in the waves as a ghoulish gale gusted over and howled. Water splashed onto the deck and blew him across. The careening ship was riding up monstrous waves and down rollercoaster chasms. They swooshed and continued to lash at him. He reached for a dangling rope attached to the deck and held tight. It felt like the boat would capsize at any moment. Passengers below deck were screaming and praying as he clung to the rope. Water continued to thrash about and began pouring into the cabin and below deck. Parts of the deck began falling away. Then he heard a cracking of wood as the main sail washed away. The ship was at the mercies of the elements as Orson's body swung like a rag doll, pummeled by the ferocious waves.

Death continued to howl and somehow out of the cauldron snatched a thirteen-year-old girl child from the outstretched hand of her mother who was inside one of the cabins above deck. It sent her into the churning waters, her cries ignored by its indifference.

Orson was flung off to the edge of the boat as it swayed, and the lake whooshed and whirred and squealed as it thrashed upon him. Somehow he hung on, grasping for life and gasping for breath.

The terror persisted and a board floated within reach. He grabbed it, in case another upheaval might toss him off. For five endless hours, the storm continually halted, then resurged, yet the ship somehow remained afloat. Finally, it exhaled and slumbered into calmness.

The *Robert Fulton* coasted onto a nearby beach, luckily avoiding rocks that would've caused even more damage and death. All luggage was lost, including Orson's printing press, though parts of it would later be recovered. It was one of several ships that lost passengers and cargo. The wreckage was devastating not only to boats in the region but to businesses and residents near the shore, demolishing more than 200 homes and some warehouses. In addition, two other children on the boat had drowned, and a rumor circulated that Murray also had drowned.[416] Not surprisingly, as the storm caused the deaths of 89 on land and sea.[417]

For a week, Murray searched up and down the coast for his press and other possessions but to no avail. As he reported: "The main casting of the press was lost, and at least one hundred dollars besides in cash[XXXII] . . . including some of the delicate parts of the printing materials . . . [and] a keg of ink." Other salvaged parts were sent to New York for repairs. His losses were great but he was fortunate to have supporters of the paper in western New York, Pliny Sexton of Palmyra and Griffith Cooper of Williamson whom he visited and who provided "liberal aid."[418] He then visited his parents and other relatives who had moved to Springville, N.Y.,[419] about 30 miles south of where the Fulton ran aground. After another week, he set out for Ohio, carrying what little he had salvaged from the wreck including some small parts used for his printing press.

His first destination was Little Valley, about 30 miles south, on the Alleghany River, where he considered taking a raft to the Ohio River near Pittsburgh. There, he could take a steamer to Cincinnati.

> [I] found that a boat was at the place to carry butter and cheese to Pittsburgh and Cincinnati. As this promised me better accommodation than a raft, I stayed and aided in finishing it and getting the freight on board, which occupied about three days. We then set off but had not proceeded half a mile down the current before the boat, attempting to pass over a dam, lodged and remained fast. I stayed and helped some hour in

---

[XXXII] Approximately $4,000 today.

endeavoring to extricated it but in vain, then left and found my way overland to Warren, PA

That's a journey of about 50 miles but Murray makes no mention of how he got there. While steamboat passage was available to Cincinnati, there were no steamboats in, so he decided to join on a skiff with a couple of hunters on their way to Iowa.

> Their traps, guns, and other baggage, with themselves myself and baggage, gave the little bark, at least a full freight for such a voyage. So near was it sunk to the level with the surface of the water, [and] in passing rapids the ripples would frequently dash in.

He also mentioned the hazard of rocks that sometime could be rising near the surface of the water. He wasn't worried as he was a capable swimmer and thought he could easily get ashore if the skiff crashed, adding, "But there was nothing of Lake Erie in it." After enduring the shipwreck, this was just a trifling. He also mentioned taking turns at the oars and remarked on the good feeling the exercise gave him and the freedom he felt not having to depend on public transportation. It was a 200-mile rowboat ride.

> It took us between four and five days, the rate being between 40 and 50 miles a day. We found cheap and comfortable lodgings for the nights, among the settlers on the shores of the river. It was a rude mode of traveling but not a less agreeable one to me on that account. The cost was trifling. But what was more we were free . . . not under the tyranny of the ignorant, licentious, and mercenary who have too much to do with controlling the traveling conveyances in this country.

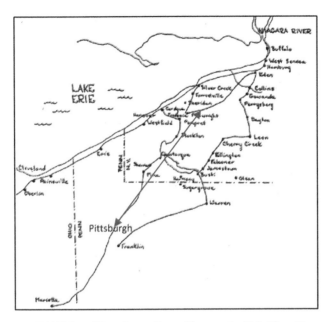

Western NY UGRR, red line shows Orson itinerary to Ohio River Steamer

In Pittsburgh, he took a steamer on the Ohio River. Stopping in New Brighton, 30 miles downriver where he spent the night, he became acquainted with locals who were familiar with *The Regenerator*, and they organized a meeting at which he spoke. New Brighton was an abolition town and friendly to his views.

The next morning he boarded his steamer for Cincinnati. He paid the economy fair, deck side, sleeping two nights "on the soft side of a board" with no covering but his unbuttoned overcoat. It was a 500-mile journey and he was restless to get to Ohio.

From Cincinnati he took the railroad another 25 miles getting off near the home of Henry T. Butterworth, of Maineville, who took him in his carriage to Harveysburg and the home of his brother-in-law, "the excellent Valentine Nicholson."

The following day they went to the home of "beloved Abram Brooke" in Oakland where his family awaited. It was now a month after the shipwreck and two months since leaving Vermont.[420]

Chapter 23

Coming to Ohio

Despite the failure and dissolution of Prairie Home, where he had planned to base the *Regenerator,* and his hardships enroute to Ohio, Murray was pursuing his dreams and regenerating his life. He was only 38, in the prime of life, not about to abandon his dream to publish a truly free paper open to all opinions and ideas.

Things were looking up. He had found two friends whose dreams matched his, Valentine Nicholson and Dr. Brooke, "a tall, thin man, with gray hair, and beard quite unshaven. His face reminded me of the ancient Philosophers," noted one visitor to his home at that time. "His only clothing was a shirt and pantaloons; nothing else on his body, head, or feet . . . . His comfortable parlor . . . was neatly furnished and had a good supply of books and papers. Our breakfast consisted of cold baked apples, cold corn bread, and I think potatoes."[421]

Both followed similar diets and placed great value on books. Both were avid abolitionists: Nicholson and Brooke much more active than Murray in the Underground Railroad.

While Murray viewed money as a means to an end, Dr. Brooke had gone farther and given up the use of money. He gave his physician services for free, and in turn for his own necessities merely requested from them those whom he thought would be able to supply them. Formerly the postmaster of his community, he had resigned so that he would not have to use money.

A.J. MacDonald, a printer and native of Scotland, who after his own failed attempts to form a community traveled around to other communities of the time, put his observations into a 700-page plus memoir that testified to the validity of Brooke's ability to support himself without the use of money:

> I remember when in Cincinnati, one Sunday afternoon at a Fourier meeting I heard Mr. Benjamin Urner read a letter from Dr. A. Brooke to some hardware merchants in Cincinnati (the Brothers Donaldson in Main street, I believe), telling them that his necessities required a variety of agricultural tools, such as a plow, harrow, axes, etc., and requesting that they might be sent on to him. He stated that he had given up the use of money, that he gave his professional services free of cost to those whose necessities demanded them, and for anything his necessities required he applied to those whom he thought able to give. Mr. Urner . . . informed us that the hardware merchants very kindly sent on the articles to Dr. Brooke free of cost, which announcement gave great satisfaction to the meeting.[422]

The Murrays moved in temporarily with the Nicholsons in Harveysburg while Orson began searching for a more permanent location to settle and resume publication of the *Regenerator*.

Nicholson was sympatico with Murray. Along with the Liberator's wagonmaker, Abram Allen, Nicholson was the most prolific Underground Railroad operator in the area. He revealed in an anecdote the first time he aided a fugitive slave.

> The first fugitive slave that I ever met, I think, was in the spring of 1831. I lived then in Clinton Co., and had been to a township election, and on my return towards home I met a colored man traveling on foot carrying a small bundle in his hand. When I came up near him, I spoke to him and asked him if he was a slave escaping from the South. He said "Yes, sir, that is just what I am." I then asked him if he would tell that fact to every stranger who might ask such a question of him. He replied, "Oh no Sir, I was sure that you was Quaker soon as I seed you, and I know that all Quakers, are good friends to all colored people."

He was not in a very safe neighborhood for one in his situation. I took him off the main public road and put him on a road leading more towards the North Star and gave him directions where to find other Quaker friends who would give him safe counsel.

In the next passage, he refers to himself in the third person:

The Friends in Cincinnati sent them up Foster's Crossings in the Butterworth neighborhood, sometimes, and to Springboro or Harveysburg, at other times, according to the emergency of the case . . . . In the first mentioned neighborhood one of the trusted friends of the slave was William Butterworth. In the same vicinity was Henry T. Butterworth [Nicholson's brother-in-law]. At Springboro lived Edward Potts and John Potts, and Warner M. Bateman . . . [Valentine Nicholson] was known to be a reliable and trusted friend of all those escaping from Southern bondage and consequently most of those escaping from Cincinnati . . . were delivered to his care.[423]

In all, Nicholson and his wife Jane may have aided as many as 2,000 fugitive slaves, for in a later memoir she wrote that one year she counted 86 and some years there were more, and this was over a period of 30 years.[424]

Nicholson also was one of the primary financial backers of Prairie Home and deeply involved in progressive movements. He had lost a $1,000 investment in the community after its dissolution and return to its owner.[425]

During his time at the Nicholsons, Murray traveled to the port of Sandusky. He had learned that the type for his press had been salvaged from the shipwreck and been brought by the steamboat company there. As testified by friend Nicholson, Murray spent time chopping wood to supply the needs of his family. "Such is O.S.

Murray's mode of becoming enabled to re-establish the press," wrote Nicholson, noting that lesser individuals would've given up.[426]

When Murray returned, he cobbled together a temporary press and printed a two-page *Regenerator Extra* on January 1, 1845.

In it, he discussed the circumstances that led to his current situation, his plans for the future of *The Regenerator*, his need for donations to fund his operation, and his hopes and dreams for the Community movement.

> I did not at the time [referring to his published letter about the shipwreck]… feel like saying much about the loss of property in connection with so much peril to life, and loss of life itself to so many—and because it was difficult to arrive at anything definite concerning it.[427]

Fortunately, the aid that he had received from Pliny Sexton and Griffith Cooper, whom he visited after surviving the shipwreck, had enabled him to continue to Ohio and pursue the publication of *The Regenerator*. But he was still financially stressed and upset about the dissolution of Prairie Home, which he had hoped to use as the base for its publication. "One principal object in removing West with the Regenerator," he said, "was to find and . . . rest upon [a Community] . . . . An opportunity for realizing this desire was promised and expected at [Prairie Home]. In fact, the friends had gone so far as to prepare a printing office; and they would have had all things in readiness on their part in season. But about the same time of the shipwreck on Lake Erie, Prairie Home was dissolved."[428]

Murray's mission in life had become the *Regenerator*, and its regeneration. He wanted it to be the voice of the Community movement. And he explained why "Community" was so important.

My convictions as to the correctness of community . . . are not shaken. [First] I must be shown that human interests are not one and inseparable. That mankind [is] not a brotherhood. That war is better than union and cooperation. That confusion and discord are preferable to order and harmony. That it is desirable to have antipathy displace sympathy. That contention, destruction, and misery, are worthy to be cultivated rather than reconciliation, salvation, and happiness.[429]

But he had his doubts about realizing this dream. He wondered if enough "knowledge and goodness" were in existence to make it happen. Nevertheless, he asked for readers to contribute support.

Let *The Regenerator* . . . be established upon the soil, and free thought shall have one permanent medium of communication that can be depended on . . . It will be independent of the lethal hindrance of all unnatural and arbitrary organizations. It will be free, like the soil it stands upon.[430]

In the *Regenerator Extra* Murray's matured opinions were offered in a detailed and unexpurgated form, as they had been expressed in the first issue of *The Regenerator* published in New York a year earlier. Only a couple of supportive articles by friend Nicholson punctuated the pontifications of Murray.[431]

It is believed that the time has fully come for the world to have one Free paper . . . . Such a paper has never yet existed . . . All the papers now . . . are partial . . . . Not one of them . . . devoted to free discussion . . . One is an organ for this sect . . . another for another [They exist] to . . . promote exclusiveness. To

197

confine to limited views . . . . To create disharmony. To distort. To exaggerate. To magnify faults on the one hand and excellences on the other.

In a word the press, like other instrumentalities in the interests of existing institutions is made to be a tool—a dependent, cowering, cringing slave.[432]

No institution was spared by Murray's derision. Even his first causes, Temperance and Abolition felt his sting.

It is not an uncommon thing for a Temperance lecturer . . . to be seen with a pipe, a cigar, or a cud of tobacco in his mouth—and then filling his stomach with dead flesh, grease, gravy, unripe vegetables, salt, pepper, spice, ginger, nutmeg, cloves, cinnamon, vinegar, and washing down the whole with scalding tea and coffee. Our Temperance taverns and stages are selling and serving up all these and other pernicious things, while they are denouncing their neighbors and murderers for adding to them the single item of alcohol . . . . They inflame the blood and create every hurtful and abominable lust.

The Abolition ranks are chiefly filled up, as to numbers, with those who are exercising tyranny and oppression in various forms and ways . . . . They virtually deny to others the right to live by extorting from them a price for the privilege of filling their stomachs and keeping their hearts and lungs in motion. Such are they who are boisterous for freedom. Their cries of robbery and piracy against the slaveholder chime very much with the cry of murder from the selling of salt, pepper, tea, and tobacco, against the seller of rum.

What's the use of declaiming against war and violence, and at the same time supporting a Jesus-faced religion, the gate of whose temples are always open for blood shedding?[433]

198

He also offered disdain for government.

Let an invention come in that should clash with the interests of the government—no matter how perfectly demonstrated to be true—no matter how useful to humanity—it would find an enemy in the government at once. It is not the business of governments to promote, and the interests of mankind, but to promote their own interests.

The truth is, there is nothing in our church and state establishments which recognize man as being formed for improvement. They are dead weights upon him. They retard his progress. They suppress his nobler, his onward and upward aspirations.

It is a mistake and a delusion to suppose that these institutions, as such, aid general improvement. They have always been nightmares upon knowledge and humanity. Advancement has been made despite them by the native energies of manhood in individuals, struggling up from under their overwhelmingly oppressive influences.[434]

His most scathing remarks were hurled at religion.

[Religious institutions] are the genuine children of ignorance . . . . It is in their very nature to be opposed to the increase of knowledge beyond their control . . . . The religions of the world have shown themselves to be one thing. They are a trio of tradition, superstition, and bigotry . . . .

[All] religionists set their religion above all others. [They] hold all other systems to be idolatrous.

All religionists are intolerant . . . . They hate one another . . . . Hence the propriety and necessity of separating between religion and practical goodness. Each religion being an enemy to all other religions, and of course producing enmity between the devotees as religionists, how can there be any identity between religion and goodness?

In carrying out the hatred which it creates, it has always kept the human family in violence, often extending to enormous blood shedding. Thus, religion and goodwill to men are two different and distinct things.[435]

The Regenerator, he wrote, will base its work on constant and faithful self-examination.

[We must] look within ourselves and improve what is placed there by the everlasting laws. Not trusting mysteries. Not humbling and degrading himself with impositions. Not yielding blind and besotting obedience to commands. Not bowing down to images and things of imagination. But lifting our head and loving the good that we behold. Walking in the light of knowledge. Living faithfully to our convictions of truth and duty. Taking a step in advance as often, as fast and as far as we see the place and the way, and thus gaining strength and station for taking another, and another still.[436]

This paper is to be a channel for free thought and faithful expression. To be devoted to one idea. The servant of no sect. The organ of no party. The defender of no faith. The establishment of no creed. The expounded or no constitution. The interpreter of no oracle. The instrument of no dictator. The mouthpiece of no dogmatist. The advocate of no exclusive interest. It will be devoted to the interests of all. Will seek the good of creation. The harmony of the universe. The happiness and usefulness of every living susceptible being and thing.

Free inquiry is the ground. The wish and desire to learn as well as be heard. To receive as well as impart.[437]

Murray was exuberant and energized. He was on a quest to regenerize the human race. Three months later, the Murrays and a small band of supporters who believed in his community mission moved to a parcel of land owned by William Butterworth, next door to Nicholson's brother-in-law, Henry T. Butterworth in Maineville, Ohio.

Chapter 24

The Product of the Soil

As long as money makes the distinctions of society; as long as money is representative of labor: as long as buying cheap and selling dear exists, so long they who produce all things by their labor, [men] must toil without hope. By this unequal distribution of wealth, palaces have been allotted to the few and hovels to the many . . . yet multitudes are suffering for the necessity and comforts of life, we, the working men who have built houses have no roof of our own to shelter us. We that weave the cloth and make the clothes have not enough to keep us warm. We that have reaped the harvests have no bread to eat. Why is it so?[438]

Such words could've been written by Murray. He published them in the Regenerator without criticism. He elaborated on this perspective when he discussed the product of the soil, the free use of property that he felt should be shared as the foundation for his dream of *Community*.

"The products of the soil. To whom do they belong?" he asked. "To individual men? Or to universal man? . . . . . Everything belongs to Humanity. To lay violent hands on a single thing, fix value on it, convert it into individual property, and take it into individual possession, is robbery of the common treasury. To set up an individual interest against the common interest is treason and piracy against mankind . . . . I say again, individuals are not their own. They belong to the family. They are a part of the body."[439]

In search of a potential Eden of possibility, he found an inviting location near the home of Valentine Nicholson to establish his community. Pear, apple, cherry trees, vines with berries, watermelons on a 127-acre strip of hilly land thick with timber; glowing with summer sun and a creek rivulating down to the Little Miami River, one of many tributaries that flowed into the mighty Ohio. A perfect place to rejuvenate his life from the soil. Called Fruit Hills, it was where Murray and his merry band of rebels were settling, and while he didn't choose the name, it fit perfectly with his vision of rebirth.[440]

Fruit Hills

"It is now plain that the human family is destined to be of one mind and one soul," he wrote, appealing for others to join him. "[Because it] loves and seeks communion and oneness . . . . Who then will aid such an undertaking?"[441]

Those who moved with him supported the community vision and publication of *The Regenerator*, which he hoped would become the voice of the community movement. He believed that "the scattered fragments" of the defunct and dying communities should gather in smaller, more stable units.

"Let there be community of communities,"[442] he urged.

On March 20, 1845, the Murrays moved to Fruit Hills with ten other adults and two other children with expectations of more to join them.[443] Their land sat across the river from the homestead and mill of retired Ohio governor, Jeremiah Morrow. The Little Miami Railroad ran along the edge of the property at the riverside, at that time extending another 10 miles upriver to Morrow. In four years, it would connect with the Mad River Railroad in Springfield, completing railway passage all the way to the port of Sandusky[XXXIII] on Lake Erie.[444]

William Butterworth had drawn up a note for $30 an acre to be paid on credit by the community (about $120,000 in today's money).[445]

There were some "old cabins to live in," Murray continued, "in a crowded state and plenty of work to do."[446]

Fruit Hills was a remnant of the failing community movement, a kind of last gasp. Still, Murray was hopeful: "Who will share with us in such a work? Who will lend a helping hand when a given amount of aid will be worth much more than at a later period?"[447]

[XXXIII] Writing to UGRR historian, Wilbur Siebert, Robert Corwin of Lebanon, Ohio, stated that after 1850, this railroad often transported fugitive slaves from Cincinnati to Sandusky (September 11, 1892).

As A.J. MacDonald noted: "The members [of Prairie Home] then scattered in various directions. Several were considerable losers by the attempt, while many had nothing to lose. At the present time I learn that there are men and women of that Community who are still ready with hands and means to try the good work again."[448]

Soon after arriving in Fruit Hills, Murray resumed *The Regenerator.*

Son Charles wrote of this time: "I was in my eighth year when my father located on his farm, and the beginning of my printing office experiences occurred shortly thereafter. At that time there was but 36 miles of railroad track on the Little Miami Railroad (Morrow was about ten miles north and Fruit Hills about 26 miles from Cincinnati), which passed through my father's farm . . ."[449]

Charles also wrote of another regular chore that he was responsible for when he turned eight years old, lugging the copies of *The Regenerator* to the post office for mailing to subscribers: "I was sent two miles away from the farm with frequency to the post office at Twenty Miles Stand, crossing the river, passing by the flour and lumber mills of Jeremiah Morrow, an early Governor of Ohio, and member of Congress."[450]

The fertile soil of Fruit Hills was not the only consideration for Murray choosing it. Maybe even more important was that it was near a post office, not only for mailing his newspapers but for receiving his subscriptions to the many newspapers whose articles he reprinted, not the least of which was Horace Greeley's *New York Tribune.*

Here in this bucolic countryside, the ax-wielding Murray joined in with clearing the land and plucking the fruit off the trees. And getting back to his calling to spread the truth. Among those who we can be almost certain who joined him were David Thomas and Robert T. Thorburn, who made significant investments in the enterprise, Thomas contributing $40 ($1300 today) and Thorburn $100 ($3250 today) and whose residence was listed as Fruit Hills in the "Receipts" columns of *The Regenerator* in the months of April and July 1845.[451] Others included G.W. Rollings, John Hurford, Joel P. Davis, Pennock Pusey, Joseph Gregory, and C.D. Lewis, the latter three who contributed articles.

Robert Cheyne, who lived at Fruit Hills after the dissolution of the Community, wrote 22 articles, commentaries, or letters during the period from October 1846 to May 1850, moving there early in September 1849. An immigrant from Scotland, his 1846 letter used a Boston, Massachusetts address, and it appears that he lived in Fruit Hills during the Community period, judging by his acquaintance with Carlos Murray shown in his letter of August 1849.[452]

Murray listed two children in addition to his own among the original merry band, so it is likely there was another woman besides Catherine among them.

Those who came stayed for various periods, mostly young men, then moved on. Rollings told a friend that members of Fruit Hills left because of "not being satisfied with the proceedings, and not finding the climate suitable to health —there being no females of any consequence at Fruit Hills, and of course, no society."[453]

Murray focused on survival and adapting his new life to the virgin countryside. In the first issue published at Fruit Hills, John Wattles offered his encouragement: "I trust that the community (Prairie Home) has not failed, but only awaits a place for redevelopment . . . . We learn by the things we suffer . . . . But to the work before us. The sun is shining on a new age."[454]

And plenty of work there was: clearing the heavily timbered land for planting, plowing, constructing living quarters, helping Murray to get out *The Regenerator's* message. In a response to a family who inquired about the possibility of joining, Murray wrote:

> We are in present need of more help . . . We could have any desired number, at any time, if we had commenced and gone on differently. If we had published . . . that here was a place for all manner of human beings to congregate . . . or if we had fixed

on a creed and published it — there would have been no lack of number at Fruit Hills. But we have done neither. A few of us began under the conviction that the power to do good does not necessarily depend on numbers . . . Our apprehension was that we were in danger of having too many, rather than too few . . . . The history of attempts at cooperative proceedings, thus far . . . cautions us.

He informed them of the community's concern for animal rights and its vegetarian views:

We have commenced here without hogs to be butchered and cows to be robbed of their calves. All the animals to be enslaved to us, and to whom we are enslaved are three horses, which aid us in performing labor . . . While we bought hay and grain for them, before the grass grew, it cost as much to feed these horses as to feed 15 human beings.

Our food is delivered from the vegetable kingdom. Our clothing cannot be, altogether, at present . . . . Our accommodations are now scanty. And we are expecting more to join us . . . But room can soon be provided for others.

However, he reassured those who might have divergent opinions about the openness of the community.

As we have no creed, no constitution, no laws, no government . . . so we have no form of prohibition, no terms of trial . . . . We see no reason why you might not aid the enterprise, and our mutual happiness and usefulness be promoted by family union.

At present there is need for more production than consumption. Our land is not redeemed, but we feel confident it can be . . . . If you come, the sooner the better.[455]

Among those who took a short residence at Fruit Hills, John White described his 25-day stay: "Having now for several weeks past partaken of the hospitalities and mingled in the labors and good cheer of the little band of reformers, on Fruit Hills, I can now take my departure." White described a positive and life-affirming experience. "I am truly rejoiced to have met with one family of mankind possessing sufficient practical faith in human capability." He praised the vegetable diet without salt and cold-water bathing. "I declare that under the regime alluded to, that I have enjoyed better health than I ever have before."[456]

One of the members, Joseph Gregory, who also was the business agent for a short period for the enterprise and listed a Fruit Hills address briefly, provided a detailed description of the property.

Fruit Hills, as a farm, consists of 127 acres of surface, 25 of which is bottom land of deep soil and great fertility. There are about 36 acres of table land, generally level, lying about 800 or 100 feet above the bottom. On this stand the present buildings and orchard. This upland has excellent soil for gardening and general tillage. The remainder of the land is not so well adapted for general cultivation, being hillsides of every conceivable aspect and surface. It is covered with the finest of timber, including an abundance of poplar—the best building timber the region affords—oak, ash, black and white walnut, hickory, sugar maple, beech, button wood, elm, and many other kinds. This timber land is of equal richness with the other and appears adapted for the growth of fruit of every kind suited to the climate, especially apples, peaches, grapes, raspberries, and strawberries, and to which a portion of it will be appropriated this autumn and next spring. For grapes there appears the greatest adaptation, there already being hundreds of indigenous vines growing on the trees.[457]

C.D. Lewis, who was part of the community for the longest period, described the fairness and integrity of its operation. "I was among the first of those who collected at Fruit Hills and was the last to leave . . . . Many came penniless, who, on their departure, received money sufficient to defray all the necessary expenses of a journey to such places as they wished to reach, in some cases considerable amounts." Lewis added that for Murray some only brought increased financial hardship. "[They] were consumers not producers, because of their inability to perform, advantageously, such labor as needed to be done. The Community was an affair of expense and exhaustion to" the Murrays, he said, concluding his support saying, "I have the most unbounded confidence in your integrity and generosity.[458]

In these first years in Ohio, Murray was confident that he could make his community work, that he would publish the first free paper, open to all free thinkers and be an outlet for all opinions to advance the cause of truth and improve the well-being of humanity.

As he wrote, his principal objective was "to free the press by freeing the soil and connecting the two, that they may co-operate for the universal good."[459]

Chapter 25

The Underground Railroad and Fruit Hills

Murray's abhorrence with religion and its tyrannical influence eventually became the most important theme in his life. It was the hypocritical stance of the churches and its clergy in failing to condemn slavery that led to his break with religion and his eventual infidelity. Having left Vermont, he was now freer to give vent to his views. In his first issue at Fruit Hills,, clerical matters were addressed in a letter from a Vermont subscriber who discussed a report in the Vermont newspaper, *Voice of Freedom,* questioning the Christianity of a minister who prosecuted three young men who disturbed his religious service, as well as an editorial in which Murray vehemently denied that he resorted to prayer during his encounter with life and death during the shipwreck, a claim that was being circulated by the *Vermont Observer*, the paper that had replaced the *Telegraph* as the voice of Vermont's Baptists.[460]

While Murray was active in the Underground Railroad in Vermont, and he continued his passionate interest in antislavery and fugitive slaves up through the Civil War, there is no mention of his active participation in Ohio.

Nevertheless, Fruit Hills did sit in the middle of its activities. His two closest neighbors, William Butterworth, who sold him Fruit Hills, and brother Henry Thomas, both were active and helped hundreds. Also, as already mentioned, the Nicholsons who may have helped 2,000 fugitive slaves over a 30-year period.

It's also fitting that one of the original members of the Fruit Hills Community, Joel P. Davis, was one of the most active local Underground Railroad agents. Davis listed his address as Fruit Hills in the first Regenerator published there. Born in 1822, Davis of

Oakland, Ohio, wrote in 1892 of his activities to UGRR historian Wilbur Siebert. He began participating in 1836 with his older brother Isaac, transporting fugitives from stop to stop. One of his frequent destinations was the home of Valentine Nicholson when he lived at Clark's Run in Greene County before he moved to Harveysburg.

According to Davis, there were two routes north from Cincinnati during the years of 1836-to-1846.[XXXIV] The west route along the Lebanon Turnpike led to the home of John Van Zandt, who was caught with fugitive slaves in 1842. Found guilty, Van Zandt was beset with bankruptcy and illness that led to a premature death.

Another led to Springboro where John and Jacob Bateman, Franklin Farr, and John Janney hosted fugitives. Because of three confrontations with slaveholders passing through that area in the late 1830s (all of which Dr. Brooke had played a major role, spending a night in jail for one),[XXXV] as well as the prosecution of Van Zandt, whose home was along that route, fugitives thereafter were passed farther east to Oakland and eastern sections of Warren County.

Most prominent was the Oakland mechanic Abram Allen and son David. Allen was known for constructing a double-decked carriage pulled by four horses. It had a mechanism that struck like a clock after every mile. It became known as the "Liberator" for its continuous service transporting fugitive slaves.

Others identified were the other Brooke brothers, Edward, William, Samuel, and James; Artemas Nickerson, and other "boys," Mark Haines, and H.D. Thompson, who was Davis's cousin. The main route from Oakland went through Port William, Paintersville and Jamestown (Greene County). At Paintersville, they brought

---

[XXXIV] Davis moved to Indiana in 1847, eventually settling in Iowa.
[XXXV] Brooke moved to Marlboro, Ohio in 1853 and was involved in a major slave rescue there in 1854. In 1858, after rumors that he was going to be arrested for violating the Fugitive Slave Law, he fled for a time to Canada.

fugitives to William Whitney and Lindley Coate; at Port William, there was William Osborn and in Jamestown was Simeon Johnson, who took the fugitives to Green Plain and the Dugdales.[461]

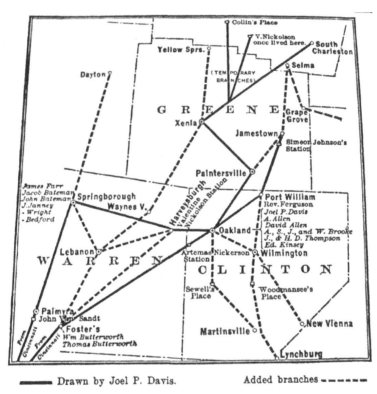

Drawn by Joel P. Davis.   Added branches ━ ━ ━ ━ ━

Underground Railroad map Davis sent to Wilbur Siebert

Activity through Maineville and the Butterworths is well documented from a number of sources: Siebert, family letters, local histories, and accounts.

Henry Thomas Butterworth's wife Nancy was a Wales and her sister Jane married Valentine Nicholson. It was a double wedding. William married Elizabeth Linton. All these families, the Wales,

Lintons, and Butterworths, are reputed to have aided fugitive slaves. Henry Thomas recalled those days shortly before his death in an 1892 letter to Wilbur Siebert:

> We [once] had two women, one man and some children on hand and had them concealed for some time and it was becoming unsafe to keep them longer . . . I had two good horses and a good wagon with high sides and a good set of bows and cloth. I put the bows on and then stretched the cloth on and tied it thoroughly down. . . . . After thus being all fixed I stored in a lot of hay for the poor creatures to lie on. Then after leaving all the children [the fugitives' children] for fear of their crying and betraying us, I put in two carts for my daughter Mary and I to sit on. By this time, we had heard that a pro-slavery boy by the name of Andrew Davis had somehow got a knowledge of the whole thing and had, perhaps for a sum of money, made it known to two persons who would do anything they could to catch the flying slaves. The names of these two persons [were] David Coddington and James Foster. We had heard of our betrayal; I prepared for it; the river was high. My destination was to take them to an uncle of my wife's by the name of Turner Welch residing at Harveysburg . . . . The bridge here at Foster's must be crossed and was a toll bridge. Joseph Whitney took the toll at the west and James Foster kept a store at the east end (just before they came to the bridge). We had our Quaker school teacher, Robert Way, to go with us to see if we should run the gauntlet . . . just as we expected out came the two men [Coddington and Foster].

Foster called out to him . . . Got any chickens, got any eggs, got any butter.

Butterworth shouted back as he passed by, "I am not going to market I am after fruit trees," and handed Whitney the toll without stopping.

He heard Coddington say to Foster, "I'll be damned if there ain't niggers in that wagon."

Bridge at Foster's Crossings, site of currrent bridge by Monkey Bar in Maineville

Butterworth had thought they would follow him and kept looking back but they made it safely to his wife's Uncle on the north side of Caesar's Creek. He did not consider it safe to keep them that night, so he sent them over to Harveysburg up on one of the many hills in that area, and Butterworth returned home to see about the fugitives' children. He gave the task to his neighbor, a man by the name of Carroll who lived only a mile away with whom he had a regular arrangement regarding the transport of fugitives.[462]

Robert Carroll recalled one of the nights he transported fugitives:

One early morning I was told to go up in the haymow. On doing so I was somewhat startled to see half a dozen black persons hidden away. That day they lay hid, and their food was carried to them with secrecy. About 9 o'clock that evening we hitched up, [and] cautiously loaded the vehicle with its human freight, and carefully fastened down the curtains. Thomas Butterworth was there and assisted. It was raining; the sky was still clouded and the roads wet and muddy. We went at first by a lane, across the farm of Butterworth, another of the brothers ... We soon struck the main road and turned our course towards the North Star .... We drove along at a round pace, always on the lookout for pursuers, and it must be confessed, somewhat nervous. Now and then we stopped, and by the struggling moonbeam's misty light, carefully scanned the road in both directions. We crossed Todd's Fork near the site of Morrow; drove past Rochester and Clarksville and on through the night to Harveysburg, where we arrived just after daylight. As we traveled along the stories of the blacks were told.[463]

A quick review of subscribers during the first three years of the Regenerator in Ohio reveals a dozen who were known participants in the UGRR. This is not to say that Murray was an active collaborator in Ohio as he was in Vermont. But it is quite obvious that the activity was common in his neighborhood.

One of his subscribers, John Janney of Springboro, was interviewed by Siebert about his participation. According to Janney, Abram Allen in nearby Oakland aided 3,300 fugitive slaves. This cannot be confirmed but it lines up with claims of Levi Coffin who estimated that number in his memoir, so the numbers may be conflated. Coffin began sending fugitive slaves up through Clinton County in 1847 when he moved from Indiana to Cincinnati. We can be certain, however, that it was a large number, and if Valentine Nicholson's number is accurate, then it may be in that range.[464]

Another subscriber, Perry Dakin of Oakland was identified in a letter to Siebert by his son, Dr George Dakin, who incidentally was the son-in-law of Abram Allen. He wrote that his father started his participation with Abram Brooke.

I made my first trip [in 1838] with my father when I was 12 years of age. From that time until I left the state in 1853, I was actively engaged in the work. We generally traveled in covered wagons with a guide ahead on horseback. I became so well acquainted with the road to Port Williams [Clinton County] and Jamestown [Greene County] that I could travel it the darkest nights and signal, by a low whistle, to the drivers behind, although it was rough, and there were frequent hills and valleys and bridges and angles. During the later years, several young men of the neighborhood joined us, and we [would bring the fugitives] on horseback . . . After the Fugitive Slave Law was passed, the sentiment changed so rapidly that we often went by daylight . . . The Anti-Slavery people in that section of the State were mostly Quakers, and we never carried any [guns] although there were many times when slave-hunters were in the neighborhood.[465]

Another important anecdote regarding UGRR lore in relation to Fruit Hills was that reported to Siebert by attorney R.G. Corwin of the prominent Corwin family of Lebanon, whose uncle Thomas Corwin was Governor of Ohio and a U.S. Senator.

Corwin wrote that he recalled fugitives at his father's house as early as 1820 when he was a boy and that from 1840-to-1850, fugitives were there "almost every week and sometimes every day of the week." After that, more use of the railroads was made.[466] This is an especially important nugget of information for that railroad that went all the way to Sandusky, a major UGRR terminal whose boats took fugitives to Canada. And it stopped at Fruit Hills four times daily, according to the 1845 report of Joseph Gregory.[467]

There is no report of fugitive slaves being hidden by Murray at Fruit Hills, but it was certainly happening all around him and if called upon, he undoubtedly gave assistance.

Chapter 26

Free Paper for Free Thinkers

A totally free paper for free thinking, this was Murray's goal. To free the press by freeing the soil. To make the paper the product of the soil. Finances, however, were a constant struggle, and he needed the community to support the publication of *The Regenerator*. Continually, he was appealing for subscribers who were delinquent in their accounts to pay because he could barely afford the paper on which it was printed.

"We have a heavy payment to make on the first of August. How many subscribers will forward their subscriptions before that time? The Sooner it is done the better."

Two issues in a row in June, he made this exact appeal on the front page of *The Regenerator*.

"Our necessities are greater at present, and will continue to be during the present volume, than at any future time."[468]

It wasn't a good time for Murray, who received word in June that his father had died after being poisoned from skinning an ox.[469] How ironic it must've been for Murray who must've been exasperated learning this, considering his views of human cruelty in its use of animals for labor and food. Such opinions, like those on religion, were definitely out of the mainstream. Consider this social practice of the day in southern Ohio as reported in *Beer's History of Clinton County*.

> "Of all the sports of hunting in early times, the bear hunt was the most exciting. This usually occurred accidentally. I never knew a bear hunt to be regularly organized. Someone in the neighborhood would accidentally discover a bear, and, if at a

217

time when the animal was fat and worth possessing, he gave the sound of a horn, known in the neighborhood as the signal of the discovery of a bear, and the call for help to capture the prize. Instantly, almost, men on horseback, with rifles and dogs, were on hand. The sound of the horn indicated the course of the bear, and thither the neighbors hastened.

The dogs would keep on the track of the bear, but, unless they could cause him to take to a tree, they could do nothing with him but to keep his trail and enable the hunters to follow. If they ventured to attack him, they were soon repulsed— sometimes killed on the spot. At last, after many hours' chase . . . the exhausted bear would take to a tree, around which the dogs quickly gathered, and, by their united noise, gave assurance to the hunters that Bruin was at last treed. The signal- horn sounded and the hunters were soon on the spot. If it was still light, the bear was soon brought down by an unerring rifle . . . . The event ended with skinning the bear and cutting up the carcass into as many pieces as would give each hunter his portion, and usually sending a part to each family in the neighborhood.[470]

This report was contributed by attorney A.H. Dunleavy of Lebanon with whom Murray was acquainted. Whether or not, there were bear hunts in the Maineville area during the time Murray lived there was never mentioned in *The Regenerator*. But the inhumane treatment was the topic of an eight-part series called "Men and Other Animals" written by S. Whipple of Utica, N.Y. which was published in *The Regenerator* shortly after the death of Murray's father. Whipple reasoned that the existence of all living things was dependent on the destruction of other living things, in what we now call the food chain that comprises the ecosystem; that because humans have superior intellect, we are better able to understand the suffering and pain of other living things. He theorized that the greater sensitivity we have to the pain of other living things, even insects, the less likely we will commit violence against each other. He further deduced that human violence would not cease until we stopped committing violence against animals and using them for food. It was a position that Murray was in full agreement with. Whipple concluded:

> [W]hen men have so far advanced its conscientiousness and benevolence, as to sincerely regard the dispensing with the use and abuse of domestic animals as desirable, for moral as well as physiological and economic considerations, many, and perhaps all the ideas entertained by [Community life] But I apprehend the vision of the present race will never be greeted with a sight so glorious as would be such a consummation. The present generation of men, and we know not how many generations after, will trudge along nearly in the path trodden by their fathers, perhaps straightening a bend here and avoiding a hill there, by slow degrees making the road of life smoother and straighter; what the final results will be, it is only in our power of the present time to conjecture.[471]

Despite his revulsion of the act of skinning an animal, he expressed his respect for his father stating, "In my Father's acts towards others, the generous, the magnanimous and the humane were leading traits."[472]

The news of his father's death contributed to the pressure felt by the comings and goings of community members. His family was shouldering the burden. All three of his sons helped to get *The Regenerator* printed: Charles, who was nine, Marsena who was 17, and the oldest and closest child to Orson, his son, eighteen-year-old Carlos. They also were working on the farm with the other community members.

"It is requiring too much of us," wrote Carlos who had begun writing for the paper, "who do the work of editing and printing, that we get our food, fuel, rent and clothing from the land by our labors on it, with our hands, clear the claims of the previous owner, and publish the paper too. There are too few of us. There is no proper apprehension as to the smallness of numbers who are performing the labors at Fruit Hills.[473]

Finally, in the February 8, 1847, issue, Murray confessed to the dire straits of *The Regenerator.*

The amount of land is 127 acres . . . . But for our present number, we should have chosen to take less than half the amount we now occupy. And we should now choose to dispose of more than half of it.

The undertaking was in good faith. The object was [to connect] the press and the soil, and unite them for improvement and progress—to extend family relations on the ground of affinities. For its attainment, we believe the highest ground has been taken at Fruit Hills.

The commencement here was with the expectation that several were to join, with the anticipation of productive laborers, to pay for land and erect comfortable buildings. Some of these means were brought together, and in the expectation of the enlargement of some, borrowing was resorted to.

But it was soon found that the affinities were not strong enough. Separation commenced.

[Those who left took what they had brought]. During the first volume of the Regenerator, we had between a dozen and a score of beginners, dabbling in types, coming and going. This has been tedious and exhausting for the editor and to the youths who have had to go forward in the printing. Much of the work on the farm has been of the same sort. Most of those who have come and gone, were almost entirely wanting in practical knowledge of the business necessary to be performed here. Thus, a very few of us have been taxed and burdened continually. Often, we have found our strength increased with a decrease of numbers. All has been suspense every moment. At no time have we known on what or whom we could depend for carrying on the farming during a single season of the year, or the printing during a half or quarter volume.[474]

Murray persisted in bringing the latest developments in the human search for the truth and betterment. Another topic he began to feature was the water cure treatment, which derived its basic tenets from Grahamism and its advocacy for the use of cold water, including excerpts from the newly launched *Water Cure Journal* published in New York. Fruit Hills' devotion to Grahamism was mentioned by John White in the report of his 25-day visit during the summer of 1846.[475] The following summarized it in a review of *The Handbook of Hydropathy* by Dr. Joel Shew, the editor of the *Water Cure Journal*:

> The water-cure system, more than any other, implies all due attention to the more important consideration. the prevention of disease. A few simple rules being observed—judicious daily ablution—cold water the only drink-plain unstimulating food in proper quantity-the giving up of all stimulants—an avoidance of overheated and unventilated rooms a suitable amount of daily appropriate open-air exercise-regularity and moderation in all the habits of life, the certain and natural consequence would speedily prove, throughout society, to be a comparative immunity from bodily suffering and disease.[476]

An excerpt from the Journal included a report of Dr. Shew's treatment of Albany abolitionist Lydia Mott. She was suffering from the "hardening of one of her lungs," which her doctors considered "hopeless." They were doubtful of the efficacy of the Water Cure but gave it their blessings. Dr. Shew described the treatment:

> The wet sheet was used each day. It was wrung from water of a mild temperature and applied according to the usual mode. It produced a soothing and relieving effect, followed by an ablution [washing] in water of a moderate temperature. Four well wrung wet towels were arranged about the chest to meet at the side, making two thicknesses of wet linen upon every part of the chest. Over these towels still another moist bandage was placed and over the whole an abundance of flannels, to retain the warmth . . . The effect of the sheet, the ablutions, and the bandages in removing the pain, preventing general fever, cough, and night sweats was indeed wonderful. She improved astonishingly.[477]

THE

WATER-CURE JOURNAL.

JOEL SHEW, M. D. EDITOR.

"Wash and be Healed."

Published semi-monthly at 56 Bond street, New-York, and for sale by Periodical Agents generally.

One Copy, $1; Three Copies, to one address, $2; Ten Copies, do., $5—invariably in advance.

Newspaper postage only.—Within thirty miles, free.

| NEW SERIES. | NEW-YORK, DECEMBER 1, 1845. | VOL. I.—No. 1. |

BULWER ON WATER-CURE.

WITH NOTES BY THE EDITOR.

The New Monthly Magazine, for September, (1845,) an English publication, has for a leading article, "Confessions seasoned for the mouth, and like all good articles to a periodical, "warranted not to keep," have passed away into the lumber room, where those old maids, History and Criticism, hoard their scraps and relics, and where, amidst dust and silence, things old-fashioned ripen into things antique. The roar

None of Murray's extremist views attracted more animosity than his anti-religion message. This message was and still is misunderstood and it discouraged membership in the Fruit Hills community. The general misunderstanding was that it was life-denying when it was life-affirming. As Carlos once said to him, perfectly explaining it, "They tell us to prepare to die; I think it better to prepare to live."[478]

Even abolitionist friends like William Lloyd Garrison could not accept it and found Murray's "infidelity" disagreeable. A comment from the January 1847 *Regenerator* shows the distance that had grown between the two. While Garrison preached against the hypocrisy of the churches, he still held true to scripture and based his abolition on the Christian ethic we all know as "Golden Rule." Murray, who had rejected the Bible, claimed it was full of lies and deceitful, that the Golden Rule was preached long before Christ, by Socrates and Confucius. In his commentary, Murray derides Garrison for complaining about a tax on a tea set gifted by a ladies benevolent society during a visit to England.

> I have not seen brother Garrison's letter, as the Liberator has long since been withholding from the sight of us "infidels" . . . As for this " tea service," it must have been quite a costly one, that the government duties on it should have been $60. My first thought was that it would have furnished a large amount of bread to the perishing poor, whose condition so excited brother Garrison's sympathies at the time he may have been bringing away under his arm these materials which are indirectly, distantly, more or less, the products of the, labor of these very poor, extorted from them by a governmental arrangement which robs these and puts it into the hands of those, to be made such a disposal of.[479]

The discourses by Murray of his views on religion and the non-existence of God were continuous throughout his life once he left the church. Among the most eloquent and straightforward was written in a letter by wife, Maria. The following is extracted from it:

> I have ceased to worship God, who is so imperfectly known . . . . . Truth, purity, and goodness are dear In me. To see a practical

demonstration of them, in my own life and among mankind, is what I desire; by whatever name they may be called, whether Christianity or Infidelity. To me, these realities now furnish more permanent motives to action than the imaginary things religion formerly did.

I now consider the writers of the Bible fallible men, as I perceive all others to be at the present day. Many of the precepts and examples attributed to Jesus, are worthy of imitation. But I can never . . . again become enslaved to the erroneous ideas held forth by him, of salvation and condemnation . . . . I know too well there is misery in this life, but I can no longer worship a Supreme Being, having arbitrary control of our existence and . . . [who] causes us to suffer here or hereafter . . . . The Bible, or its adherents have never . . . been able to perfect society. [Nor] the God it teaches us to revere. Look but for one moment at the corruption even of the enlightened portion of the world, as it is called. How full of vice and crime. What is there to give us a shadow of a hope that mankind will ever be regenerated by the present systems of religion, which have so long been promulgated with so little success?

Were half the effort made to render life pleasing to ourselves and others, which is expended to sustain a religion that never has redeemed and never can redeem mankind from ignorance and degradation, we might hope for redemption. As it is, most we or I can do, is submit to the condition of things as they are.[480]

The godlessness of Fruit Hills probably doomed its success as a community from the start. But for a brief time, it was a place where people could discuss their beliefs freely and which a small number looked to with hope.[481]

"Through the Regenerator I have received knowledge which has been, and will no doubt continue to be, a lasting benefit to me and my family," wrote Henry Soffe of New York.[482]

"I have seen and perused two or three other numbers of your publication. Such a periodical is destined to do much good in the world," wrote Jacob Lybrand of Monroe, Wisconsin Territory. "It is a desideratum that has been long needed. A paper in which all can express their own views and sentiments for themselves, should certainly be duly appreciated by all, and will be by those who are inquirers after Truth."[483]

"I hope you will be able to continue the Regenerator, for it is much heeded in the world," wrote Robert Cheyne of Boston. "All the others that I know of are devoted to the building up of some ism, bound to some sect or party, and little if anything, however interesting to mankind, can be admitted into their columns, unless it has some particular bearing upon the interests of their sect, or square with the peculiar dogma or doctrine they support. One free paper can surely be supported."[484]

Murray's readers were scattered throughout the North. His short time in New York increased his exposure and circulation. He wrote that he was printing 1900 papers per issue then, which continued as high as 1100 in Ohio. However, he confessed that he was only paid on average for about half the numbers he mailed.[485] As time progressed and as the community movement declined, so his readership. This is reflected by the list of subscribers that he regularly published. It's not known how many papers he was printing in later years and appeals to those who were delinquent in paying for their subscription and for new subscribers to help pay publishing costs continued throughout.

For Murray, it was a bittersweet period of struggle to survive in his new home. But here he was more free and less troubled by those

225

who opposed his infidelity. While his neighbors, the Butterworths and Jeremiah Morrow practiced their religion, still they were good friends, especially the Butterworths who had become like family. A poem submitted to *The Regenerator* during this period captured the perspective of what it was like living at Fruit Hills then:

THE FARMERS HOME.

Still let me live among the hills,
The rocks, the trees, the flowers,
Where I have passed my earliest years,
My childhood's happiest hours.

How oft beneath an aged oak,
Nearby my father's dwelling,
Have I reposed with kindred youth,
Some playful story telling.

The birds above would plume their wings,
And raise their happy voices,
O, sure it is a pleasant place
Where everything rejoices.

Surrounded by the friends I love,
And free from every fetter,
I am an independent man,
And wish for nothing better.

My little children round me sport,
So blooming, bright and healthy,
I often think that nature's gifts
Have made me very wealthy.

My wife is all that she should be,
Kind, gentle, prepossessing.
I'm sure if ever man were blest,
Mine is the greatest blessing.[486]

Chapter 27

Carlos Emerges

Carlos was Orson's heir apparent, and it was evident that he was following in his father's footsteps. As Community members came and went, more responsibility was placed on the Murray boys. Carlos, Marsena, and young Charles who helped typeset the press. They had become the heart of *The Regenerator* with Carlos contributing articles, starting in 1846.

The following written by him provides a picture of the Murrays' life at Fruit Hills:

A pair of wrens have lately built a nest and are depositing their eggs, in our office, in a cupboard near the door, where we file the Regenerator. How much better the feelings we enjoy in the intimacy of these little songsters, than the feelings of those who would shoot, stone, or rob them. I would not exchange them for the wealth of Croesus. Mankind at present seems to be in ways that forbid all such intercourse with the lower animals. They have 'domesticated,' or put in slavery these animals as far as possible. The others they are at war with. This is a sad thing for contemplation. But if they could learn to leave their, destructive ways of living and thus get out of enslaving each other—enslaving themselves to domestic animals and domestic animals to themselves—they would soon be on terms of intimacy with the so-called lower parts of creation, and thereby soften their rude disposition, and as far as possible bring about such a state of things as is spoken of in that book they reverence so much . . . .[487]

Such a comment not only shows the sensitivity of Carlos, but the closeness of his connection with Orson, which was of major consequence in Orson's life. This connection was also apparent in his longing for community, which he expressed in his report to those considering a move to Fruit Hills.

"I consider affinity," he wrote, "congeniality of feelings and ways of doing, in neighborhoods, or any closer relations thar may be entered into by mankind, as indispensable to success and consequent happiness."

He then went into a lengthy description of the advantages those thinking of a move might consider: the rich soil, the price of land, the quality of the water, the dense timber and available stone for construction, He followed with an Orsonesque lecture on healthy eating and drinking.[488] In another commentary, he expressed his love for connecting with the soil.

> I have been in the potato field, digging, and though the potatoes were somewhat rotted, after pretty close confinement in the printing office for some time, the fresh autumnal breeze, the beauty of the fading foliage of the surrounding forests, the indescribable-feelings in connection with all this, has invigorated and strengthened me, and made me to think more deeply on the evils resulting from the separation of a great portion of, civilized, mankind from the knowledge and means of such enjoyment. It appears to me that no one can have the greatest amount of true, beneficial enjoyment, without, immediate connection with the soil.
>
> The time may come, and I hope it will, when so much dividing of labor into professional, mechanical, mercantile, and farming departments, will be seen to be bad in its results. A good and equal division of labor would give the person who tills the soil time to exercise his mechanical skill and time for self-improvement. and the acquirement of general knowledge. It

would also give the mechanic time to labor on the soil, which he needs to enjoy good health and the greatest happiness. What need then of the professions? What need of merchants to enrich themselves by profits taken in exchanging between the farmer and mechanic?[489]

Carlos also showed the empathy that endeared Orson to those who knew him but disagreed with his dislike of city life:

[E]very time I come in contact with cities I feel less inclined to be in business that shall ever bring to my sensation so much that injures my better feelings . . . . Men are social beings and like to be united. . . in order for their greater strength and enjoyment—as the formation of cities show. But they are living one on another, devouring each other continually instead of living for the benefit of each other, the stronger consume the weaker, thus bringing want, misery, and woe instead of happiness, plenty, and peace. They have not the means of producing—therefore are consumers. There will have to be radical changes in the customs, practices and systems that are established in the civilized world before cities will give way to better collections of men . . .

Further on, his description of entering the city poetically evoked his revulsion for the cruelty of eating animals:

"We felt a strong smell as we entered the city, issuing from the slaughterhouses, that [would seem to sicken] any human being so that he would loathe the sight of flesh meat . . . . A short distance back my fellow traveler had pointed me in sight of what [would seem] to cause a human being to shudder if he should ever attempt to tear the tender lamb in pieces after it was cooked. On the side of a green knoll were a score of sheep nipping the grass in very innocence—unconscious of the proximity of three persons busily engaged bartering for them, to take them to market.

On every hand were the loads and barrels of flesh for devouring . . . . It would seem that this wholesale butchering of dumb animals were a more cold-blooded business than even that of war . . . . Certain I am, that if every flesh eater had to kill his food before he partook of it, there would be much less killing and devouring of the poor animals.[490]

This ethic of purification at Fruit Hills was well expressed in a letter from Aquilla Hurford to his son 14-year-old John Hurford, then a part of the Community, describing a business trip to Pennsylvania:

[I]t is heart sickening to the fanatical reformer, to witness the tea, coffee, meat and tobacco consumed by the pious Christians . . . . Some say that they will quit the coffee and meat but cannot quit the use of tobacco. Some say that it would kill them if they deprived themselves of their coffee for the space of one week. Some say they could not live if it was not for their tobacco . . . . There are but few books in the majority of the farmers' houses . . . Some of their libraries consist of an old Bible, a hymn book, four or five old almanacs, a political paper, some religious tracts, and some comics pictures, among which is a drawing of an orthodox devil, and this they have put in the most prominent place for their children to behold frequently that they may scare them with it to keep them from going to hell. The people are very pious here. They are full of religion. It is religion first, then money and land afterwards. Many who think if they have the word of god, it is not necessary to have any other book. They save their money to build meeting houses and pay priests.[491]

On commenting about another visitor's negative comments about Fruit Hills and the pale complexion of its residents, suggesting their poor health, Carlos responded:

[A] confinement of 12 or 14 hours of the day inside of a printing office, with this toil and perplexity harassing continually, would tend to make the confined pale . . . . It depends much on the judge as to what a healthy look is. Some look through greasy spectacles. They will not be able to see very clearly. The persons spoken of on Fruit Hills have not the flush, or redness of skin from stimulating drinks, nor the greasy skin with many a pimple of flesh eaters. But they have a clearness, a purity of skin, which may not be so much a beautiful ideal as an enduring fact—a living reality. There is not so much in reality neither of this pale look as some would make out. Many who visit us are ready to see a striking difference in the appearance of our little band from those they have been accustomed to think had a healthy look. This they are as ready to call paleness or something implying feebleness. But they are compelled to admit the facts that their faces are full enough, their countenances seem bright, yet they soon forget this part of the story in the fogs of their twin savory viands . . . . There are many who have tried the vegetable system without counting the cost, or without sufficient knowledge of all that is required to make so important an improvement upon old systems, who are falling back into old ways. There are also many who do not seem to satisfy themselves about vegetable diet and vegetable eaters but are better satisfied in crying about bran bread, pale faces, [and] starvation. Why is this? I am well satisfied, as long as I can see health around me, among my fellows, and much cheerfulness . . . together with a love of freedom, knowledge, and improvement . . .[492]

Carlos continued to mature and his powers of expression were surpassing Orson himself. It must've deepened their connection and augured well for the future of *The Regenerator*. It was as if he were becoming what Orson had been reaching for in himself.

There is "freedom of the press enough on Fruit Hills," Carlos wrote, "if nowhere else, for expression of thoughts——for or against—on subjects that are called "holy;" subjects that a superstitious reverence, awe, or veneration . . . have made, among the ignorant, too holy lo talk or write about freely. The sceptic, the unbeliever on these subjects has been made to keep his thoughts to himself, or else be held in odium—Thus has freedom of thought been kept out of expression, bowed down, by his holiness.

. . . .

What is this religious feeling, this worship that is so universal? This is brought as proof that it is "natural," is necessary to our wellbeing . . . Well, if it be so, why is not idolatry as much to be regarded as holy as godology?

. . . .

These avowals may seem horrible, sacrilegious, blasphemous even, in the eyes of my religious brethren who worship their unknown, invisible, arbitrary, almighty god. But why my feelings, sayings, or doings towards all worship of anything, are any worse—near as bad—as the feelings, sayings, doings of the Christian, who brings the idol of the pagan from other lands and holds it up in derision? He despoils the holy things of other religionists, and wars on their religion.

. . . .

[D]oes not this "innate" worship of idols, of gods, or of "great spirits," as the aborigines have it, all amount to one thing in reality? It appears so to me. It is directed towards an imaginary arbitrary power. This idea of arbitrary power . . . has always been headed and directed by a priesthood, whose living depended on their keeping the people in ignorance; and the more they could extend their religion, the greater was their arbitrary power.

. . . .

The great cry of atheism will be raised. Who can define what an atheist is? The answer will probably be—one who does not believe in any god, or believes there is no god. All that I have to say regarding this is, that if belief comes from evidence or knowledge, I have no belief in an "unknown" arbitrary power that acts contrary or without regard to cause and effect. What unknown power there may be I do not pretend to know, or trouble myself about, or live in fear of. I hold myself ready to receive all evidence and all the knowledge I can of all power and of all else. Of worship and religion, I see not the necessity for myself. I would be charitable towards all religions and all worshipers. I would not persecute them.

The most eloquent expression of Orson's philosophy was Carlos's comment about an article in *The Regenerator* excerpted from *The Green Mountain Gem*:

There is a religion in everything around us—calm and holy religion in the unbreathing things of nature, which man would do well to imitate. It is a meek and blessed influence, stealing, as it were upon the heart. It has no terrors—no gloom approaches. It rouses not the passions and is untrammeled by the creeds and unshadowed by the superstitions of men. It is from the hands of the Author, and growing from the immediate presence which pervades and quickens it. It is written in the arched skies. It is amongst the hills and valleys of the earth, where the shrub-less mountain pierces the atmosphere of the eternal winter, or where the mighty forest fluctuates before the strong winds, with its dark waves of green foliage. It spreads out like a legible language upon the broad face of the unsleeping ocean. It is that which lifts the spirit within, up until it is tall

enough to overlook the shadows of our place or probation . . .
493

Carlos's comment took it one step farther. For him, as for Orson, the existence of spirit is illusory. "My thoughts and "revelations" of the present day, lead me more and more beyond "a world of spiritual beauty," he wrote, "to material beauty and goodness in everything around us."494

An ironic comment considering what was to later transpire at Fruit Hills.

Chapter 28

Infamous Witness

In Josiah Morrow's biography of Thomas Corwin, one of Ohio's foremost 19th century politicians,[XXXVI] there is a story that he was an attorney in a case for which Murray was called to testify on behalf of his client. According to it, the prosecutor made an objection claiming that Murray should not be allowed to testify because he was an atheist and therefore would not be able to swear on the Bible to tell the truth. Corwin argued in favor of his testimony, but the court ruled in favor of the prosecution. According to the story, Corwin's parting message for Murray was, "My old friend, go home, shave, shear, turn hypocrite like the rest of us, then come back and your word will be as good as ours."[495]

The story may be apocryphal, but it was one of the legendary stories that have come down about Corwin, who was known for his witticisms. Murray reported the story of his denial to give court testimony in detail in two issues of *The Regenerator*.[496] It was a long-winded, rambling account common for Murray who was a man of many words.

The date of his court appearance was August 24, 1847. He was volunteering his testimony at the request of a neighbor who had become involved in a dispute with another neighbor. Murray had knowledge of the true facts and had agreed to testify to help settle the matter.

[XXXVI] Corwin was a Congressman, Governor of Ohio, a Senator, and the Secretary of the Treasury in the Millard Fillmore administration. He was serving in the U.S. Senate when the Murray court appearance occurred, but it is not known why he was in Lebanon for this court case.

"I was forced away from home, family, paper and farm, to the Court of Common Pleas, at the county seat, ten miles distant," he wrote.

The object was the obtainment of my testimony in a case of litigation between two brother men . . . . I chose to ride our good horse George, as we call him, who seemed to enjoy the excursion with me as well as he could, separated from home and his mate to which he is strongly attached . . . . It was one of the finest days in that delightful part of the year when summer is closing and approaching autumn is beginning to be faintly seen yet deeply felt. Clear. Calm. Quiet. A most agreeable and wholesome temperature and condition of atmosphere. But with such a day to delight me—with such scenery as the Little Miami valley presents to view, in nobleness of forests, richness, splendor and excellence of foliage—deepness of verdure—fertility of fields—abundance of maturing corn—variety and vastness of vegetation in general—and with all such a philosophy as I now enjoy to sustain me—how could I be unhappy?

However, Murray was being ironic. The incident about which he was writing was not at all agreeable.

The courthouse was a building fit for better use. The room occupied was well lit and ventilated. It was a place worthy to be used for the promotion of freedom and philanthropy, and not to be devoted as it was to despotism and misanthropy . . . . Soon after getting into the court room, I was called upon the stand as a witness. A lawyer arose and objected to my testimony being taken or allowed—the declaration being that the law would exclude it on account of my views of religion.

The lawyer then called a witness to the stand, a clergyman. He swore that during the time he lived in Murray's neighborhood he had often seen him, heard him discuss religion, and had read the Regenerator. He regarded Murray to be an atheist, though he added that he thought Murray was honest and genuine in his convictions.

Corroborating the minister was a passage read in court by the prosecution from the January 12, 1846, issue of *The Regenerator*. It stated in part:

> [Murray had] avoided the use of the word, as far as convenient, as also the use of many others—such as God, heaven, hell, sin, holiness, spirit, soul, angel, devil. 'There are many reasons with me for avoiding their use. They have been used to convey erroneous ideas . . . . To use them as they are commonly used, is to aid in perpetuating error. As for mind, soul, spirit, all is un, known to me. The same regarding deity. I choose not to deny nor to affirm regarding the existence of any of them . . . . None can deny that at best and at most, the whole is a matter of opinion. The most confident and denunciatory religionists in my acquaintance acknowledge and declare the unsearchableness and incomprehensibleness of deity.[497]

The proceedings lasted from 9 am until 4 pm, and Murray confessed that during the tedious arguments he had fallen asleep three times. He concluded with a rant noting that Jefferson and Franklin had argued successfully to keep the word "God" out of the Constitution and considered it hypocritical to be using it in a court of law.

But the gods would plague Murray with greater misfortune when he was driving his team of horses with a wagon load of gravel two weeks later and one of them stumbled and fell, causing Murray to be thrown from the wagon. One of the wagon's wheels partially ran over his upper arm, breaking it, and causing the bone to protrude through the skin. The quick work of a local physician repaired the arm, but it set back his work.

'This calamity comes on us at a time of our greatest destitution of help," he wrote, "for the office and the farm. The arm that is broken was the chief dependence for the press work and the heaviest of the outdoor work."[498]

He later found vindication for the denial of his rights in court, however, in the following report:

[It] is announced that the state of Maine has taken a step in favor of freedom on the subject. This is so indicative of a sound growth of intelligence in that region. A law recently enacted by the legislature of that state reads as follows: An Act relating to the competency and credibility of witnesses . . . .. *Be it enacted by the Senate and House of Representatives in Legislature assembled, as follows:—No person shall be deemed an incompetent witness on account of his or her religious professions or opinions, but shall be subject to the test of credibility: and any person who shall not believe in the existence of a Supreme Being shall be permitted to testify under solemn affirmation, and shall be subject to the pains and penalties of perjury. [Approved Aug. 3, 1847.]* [499]

"May like rays of light soon gleam through the dark volumes of statutes over the length and breadth of all states and nations where human beings are afflicted and oppressed with law and religion," he crowed.[500]

A few years later a new constitution adopted in Ohio declared no person should be prohibited from being a witness on account of his religious belief.[501]

Chapter 29

Dying of the Light

The oldest of the children, on arriving at the age of manhood, finds himself, worn out, prostrated, broken down, the subject of unremovable chronic diseases, produced, brought on by confinement in the printing office. Looking at him, how can the younger brothers and sisters but view themselves to be dangerously situated? Seven days in the week, three hundred and sixty-five days in the year, we are all of us slaves to this work of periodical publishing . . .[502]

The decline of Carlos' health was especially troubling because he had a similar bout with illness three years earlier and went to New York for water cure treatment from Dr. Shew.[503] The evident abilities of Carlos and his devotion to the mission of *The Regenerator* increased Orson's future expectations for it.[504] His health continued to deteriorate, however; he even reverted to eating some food produced from animals[XXXVII] but it did not help. Finally, the family agreed that he needed to see Dr. Shew again, Marsena expressing concern that consumption[XXXVIII] was the cause. Carlos' last commentary appeared in the April 1849 issue of *The Regenerator* concerning an article in the *Practical Christian* relating to a criticism of a Temperance lecturer, a convoluted last sermon, if you will.[505]

On March 26, Carlos set out for New York. Along the way, he wrote a letter that was full of optimism, but after he saw Dr. Shew,

---

[XXXVII] Probably milk and butter not meat.
[XXXVIII] The term then used for tuberculosis.

the good doctor wrote Murray and sadly said the end was near. Both letters arrived in Fruit Hills on the same day. Maria immediately left for New York to be at his side. But she was too late.[506]

> We stop the press . . . and remove other matter, to give place for the following painful intelligence from the New York Tribune:

> In this City, April 19, Carlos O. Murray, aged 21 years, son of Orson S. Murray, formerly a Baptist Clergyman and editor in Vermont, now of 'The Regenerator, Fruit Hills, Ohio. Mr. Murray was an estimable young man, and engaged with his father in the publication of The Regenerator, until consumption drove him to seek relief in the Water Cure treatment, but unsuccessfully.[507]

DIED.

In this village, April 25th, Mr. COREY MYERS, aged 39 years.

In this City, April 19, CARLOS O. MURRAY, aged 21 years, son of Orson S. Murray, formerly a Baptist Clergyman and Editor in Vermont, now of 'The Regenerator,' Fruit Hills, Ohio. Mr. Murray was an estimable young man, and engaged with his father in the publication of 'The Regenerator,' until Consumption drove him to seek relief in a milder climate and the Water Cure treatment, but unsuccessfully.--N. Y. Tribune.

"[Carlos]" Orson lamented, "has contributed no small share in making the Regenerator what it has been. The part he has acted has been more and greater than has been apparent.[508]

He died at the home of James Pierce; while living in Brooklyn, Orson had developed a friendship with Pierce and fellow Quaker, John C Ferguson,[509] who visited with Carlos at the Pierce residence.

Murray later wrote that a few days before his death, Carlos was visited by a priest, urging him to swear on the bible and accept God before his passing. But Carlos was defiant and said he had no use for the Bible.[510] Perhaps, this is something Murray contrived. He wasn't there and he never had said the Pierces told him this. However, Pierce did say he was calm and dignified while facing death and that his only regret was that he could not spend his last hours with his family.[511] Pierce and Ferguson assumed the burden of burying Carlos and consoling Maria when she arrived afterwards.[512]

Orson was devastated. Little did he realize that Carlos' death would be the turning point in his life. "It was shockingly sudden," he wrote. "And momentarily convulsing . . . . He is gone, not to return."[513]

Orson felt guilty; he had overworked Carlos. He wrote that his broken arm had placed an extra burden on him and despite this they continued with the publication of The Regenerator and the farm work, actually producing more than in any year since coming to Ohio. Despite his bouts with illness, Carlos never lost hope despite growing weaker.[514] One report in the Regenerator stated that he was so slight that he weighed only about 100 pounds during this time.[515]

The printing process of that time was not only physically demanding in the placement of the various types, headings, and titles but also intellectually demanding. Mackellar's 1885 manual of typography, *American Printer*, recommends hiring energetic teenage boys to do the job of compositing, the job that had been done by Carlos with some help from young Charles.[xxxix] It provides instructions, for example, on how to stand while selecting the various letters from a type case that resembled a keyboard and

---

[xxxix] Charles wrote (*Life Notes* 21) that he began working at the press helping with typesetting in 1848 when he was eleven. As Orson mentioned in the Regenerator Extra of May 20, 1849, he was doing the typesetting.

placing them on marble slab called the imposing stone from which it would be loaded into the printer.

> The standing position of a compositor should be perfectly upright . . . the shoulders thrown back, the feet firm on the floor, heels nearly closed, and toes turned out to form an angle of about forty-five degrees. The head and body should be kept perfectly steady, except when moving from the Roman to the Italic case, the operations of distributing and composing being performed by the various motions of the arm, from the shoulder-joint alone; and if, to reach a box placed in the further part of the cases, to put in or take out a letter, he should incline the body by a slight motion, he should immediately resume his erect position. The height of a compositor and his frame should be adjusted so that his right elbow may just clear the front of the lower case by the a and r boxes . . . his breast will then be opposite the space, h, and e boxes. Sitting at work should be rarely permitted . . . and then the stool should be a small piece of board fastened to a single leg. Habit will render a standing position familiar and easy; perseverance in conquering a little fatigue will be amply repaid by the prevention of knock knees, round shoulders, and obstructed circulation of the blood and respiration of the lungs.[516]

Orson published many commentaries describing his grief and love for Carlos as well as letters of condolence and praise for him from supporters. They included one from former Fruit Hills Community member, Pennock Pusey, who wrote, "Scarcely an hour passes but my thoughts wander back to you as to a beloved home . . . . Oh, I knew not how dear you all were to me, till I heard of my great loss! My thoughts are with you daily, perpetually and my heart is with you always."[517] Another from Robert Cheyne, whose comments suggested he earlier had lived at Fruit Hills: "Few can have a correct idea of the extent of his usefulness, and of his greatness of character, except such as had some personal acquaintance with him, and with matters at Fruit Hills . . . . It is my opinion, a more extended biography of him ought to be written and published."[518] Another visitor to Fruit Hills from Cincinnati who regularly contributed to *The Regenerator*, David Reddington, a physician and practicing phrenologist, wrote, "I never knew a greater philosopher, he had traced the relations of cause and effect sufficiently to discover his own deficiencies, and that it was best for him to talk or write only when he had, something to say."[519]

"It was hard for me to let go of Carlos," Orson wrote.

At this point, the little Brother of the deceased who is selling the type, while I am writing, tells me the space in the Extra is about filled. The momentary feeling is that of discomfort, at being arrested and limited by such a circumstance. But there is no proper way of avoiding it that I see now. I would have spoken briefly of other qualities. Of his far seeing, in tracing causes and effects. Of his living in advance of the existing generation. Of his views of the diseased and disordered condition of the mass of human beings in their present ignorance and mistreatment of themselves. Of his sympathy with all living things. Of his freedom from bigotry, from the impositions of superstition, and from fears of the unknown. But I must speak of his dying, and stop for the present.[520]

Orson declined to write a biography of Carlos. He said that Carlos was a man of action and not words, but if there were others who wished to publish a pamphlet to memorialize his life, he would not object.[521]

Thereafter, the Regenerator shifted permanently from a semi-monthly to a monthly, skipping its August issue that year.

Chapter 30

The Grim Reaper

Carlos's death coincided with the sale of 48 acres of Fruit Hills to a family of seven from Moriah in Essex County, New York. The family, which included was related to Regenerator contributor, David Reddington, who had developed a personal friendship with the Murrays after visits to Fruit Hills. According to Reddington, the Simonds were congenial with Murray's views on infidelity, and in May, his brother-in-law, Thomas Simonds, came to Fruit Hill and prepared for the coming of his family. On June 12, 1849, Murray sold 48 of the 127 acres he had mortgaged from William Butterworth to the Simonds family for $1,468. It was agreed that the Simonds would reside with the Murrays while they built a house on their new land. Though it provided financial relief, it turned into a personal nightmare.[522]

The problem began because the Simonds could not afford to pay the full agreed upon price and could only pay $1,000 down. Murray, who was selling the land at the same price for which he mortgaged it, agreed to allow them to pay the rest by the end of the year. However, it was only an oral agreement and the Simonds avoided getting a signed document to close the agreement. Further complicating things was that David Reddington's wife, who was only 33 and a sibling of the Simonds family, died of cholera two months after the Simonds arrived. She was buried on the Murray farm. In consideration of their grief, Murray held back on discussion about the payment agreement. When an agreement finally was reached, the Simonds agreed to pay $100 annually to settle the debt with $68 down. It was an acrimonious agreement because the Simonds had agreed they would pay the full $468 by the end of the year. By this time, the Simonds had moved into their own home.

As the domestic dispute flared, Murray continued to obsess about Carlos. Obituaries continually appeared in *The Regenerator*, like the following one.

"Brother Murray:—I have just returned from the funeral of Robert Nelson, of our village, who died yesterday, the 10th of November 1849, in the 52nd year of his age."[523]

A confirmed infidel and a subscriber of *The Regenerator*, Nelson had converted to Christianity just before he died, wrote Thomas E. Longshore of Attleboro, Pennsylvania. "I feel it my duty to notice the death of our Brother." Nelson was a shoemaker, a hard-working "self-made" man who succeeded without the benefit of a formal education and rejected religion and ideas of a hereafter. "He saw the evils and abuses in both church and state and manifested some interest in trying to reform them."[524]

But Nelson had second thoughts when his time on earth was coming to an end. He never was totally convinced he would end when his life expired. When friends offered to pray, he encouraged them to do so. Before his death he called for a minister to whom he accepted Christ as his savior. It was alleged that Nelson warned those who visited him during the late stages of his illness that while his was the "death bed of an infidel," he advised against it. "Infidelity will do to live by," he said, "but not to die by." After his death, his body was taken into a Methodist church and a ceremony held to complete his conversion.[525]

The friend was perplexed, feeling grief on the one hand, but disappointed that his friend succumbed to what he had never believed. Murray was contemptuous: "Others will place what estimate they must on the dying of men. I think living is of more importance."[526] He referred to others like Carlos and another young infidel, the niece of E. Seaver, a subscriber and sometime contributor, who had written that she died with "unusual calmness and composure . . . and made directions for the last act to be performed for her."[527] Murray compared their courage to the fainthearted Nelson. "There was everything before them in life to attach them to it. They had just arrived at an age to make them cling to it. Their characters were irreproachable. They had embraced a philosophy which attached importance to life and living."[528]

Murray turned philosophical:

Religion teaches that dying is the thing. Philosophy teaches that living is the thing.

The former says that however bad a man's life, of whatever length it may have been, it is all sufficient to obtain from him in his dying moments what is termed conversion to the Christian faith. He may have been an oppressor of his fellow beings and a destroyer of happiness all around him, during his whole life— still it shall be well with him if in his dying moments he throws himself upon the Christian religion and expresses his desire to escape its hell and find its heaven.

Philosophy teaches us to depend for happiness on proper conduct towards oneself and towards others—on knowledge of what is to be known and doing what is to be done accordingly. It teaches that what is done——.what the conduct is—during life, is of more consequence than what can be extorted in the shape of a few words by preaching terror at the approach of death.[529]

In that same issue, Murray wrote, "[A] god of the Bible and Bibleists I reject, as I do all other gods in their systems of mythology . . . But on the subject of deity. I only say I do not know—am waiting for evidence."[530] Could he have started to equivocate on his ideas about the hereafter in the hope that he could communicate with Carlos?

Chapter 31

Robert Cheyne Moves to Fruit Hills

Robert Cheyne was living in Cincinnati at the time of Carlos' death. His original move from Boston to Ohio probably coincided with his joining the Community of Fruit Hills for a time.[XL] Now, with Orson seeming to be headed for a breakdown with his continued lamenting of Carlos, Cheyne moved back to Fruit Hills to help *The Regenerator* stay afloat.[531] Sometime within a window of August 28 and October 2, he moved there, based on dates showing his Cincinnati and Fruit Hills addresses in the September and October issues.

Born in Scotland in 1819, Cheyne came to the U.S. with his parents in 1828.[532] His Scottish accent surely added culture to the Community, and he was in complete agreement with the iconoclastic Murray. During his stay, he wrote the following poem that appeared in the January 1850 issue of *The Regenerator*:

Heaven in this Life

This world is bright and beautiful,
None else for us so fair,
And were we true and dutiful,
We 'd seek no Heaven elsewhere.

When superstition's chains are riven,

[XL] See Cheyne's article on the death of Carlos, "A Philosophical Life—Or the Life of a Philosopher," *The Regenerator*, August 1849. Such intimate knowledge of him suggests Cheyne had earlier spent time at Fruit Hills, especially because Carlos reluctantly left to visit Cincinnati.

And freedom we enjoy,
Then will no Vain, false hopes of Heaven,
Nor fears of Hell annoy,

When to ourselves and others true,
And true to nature's laws,
Joy and content will then ensue,
As effect follows cause.
Then jarring discord's sound shall cease,
And passion's deadly strife,
Then will the world he filled with peace,
And Heaven be in this life.

This was in tune with Murray who wanted to live free of cities, governments, and religions ordering his life. In some of Cheyne's commentaries which numbered more than 20, he was perhaps even bolder than Murray in his atheism. The thirty-year-old was the perfect man to come and help. Murray was having problems coping with Carlos's death. In fact, he still would be writing about it in the last gasp issues of *Murray's Review* in 1856.

Cheyne's commentaries rivaled Murray's for their vitriol. His bitterest rejoinder was directed at a review of an eighty-page pamphlet by E.W. Capron of Auburn, N.Y., a supporter of *The Regenerator*, entitled "Singular Revelations. Explanation and History of the Mysterious Communion with Spirits, Comprehending the Rise and Progress of the Mysterious Noises in Western New York, Generally Received as Spiritual Communications":

I have, for some time past, seen paragraphs in the papers in relation to these "mysterious noises." I had also read friend Capron's communication to the N.Y. Tribune . . . in relation to the same matter. I have now read his book, but am not yet convinced, that "departed ghosts are e'er permitted to review this world," At least, if they are, it will be to do something more worthy of "superior intelligences," than knocking in people's chambers in the night time, pinning women together, taking the rings off their fingers, undoing the braiding of their hair, moving about tables, chairs, and other articles of furniture, and such like foolish and fantastic tricks; or anything else mentioned in brother Capron's History. He tells us communication has been held with the Spirits of George Fox, Lorenzo Dow [and others] . . . . Why did he not tell us something communicated by those men?

[It] will take something more . . . to convince me that this affair is not a cheat, an imposition . . . . Why won't you then, friend Capron, use your influence with those shadowy creatures, to induce them to pay us a visit, here, to Fruit Hills? If they do not come, I fear we will continue in our unbelief; we will continue to think, that the notion of a future state, and of spiritual existences, is but a delusion, the creation of a diseased imagination, a figment of a phantom, 'an empty airy nothing,' 'a dream but of a shadow.'[533]

Supporting Murray's complaint with Garrison and his siding with Christianity,[534] Cheyne attacked *The Liberator* for its ads with what he thought were quack medical remedies as well as Murray's former benefactor John Conant of Brandon for being a hypocrite by working his employees on the Sabbath. He also wrote an article claiming that the Jewish religion was superior to Christianity because of its healthier dietary rules.[535]

Among the incidents in which he collaborated with Murray was when they participated in a local debating society, the topic being whether the Bible promotes human improvement and progress. Both Murray and Cheyne were allowed 20 minutes to present their case. Among the participants were two priests, who expressed indignation with their infidelity. The meeting was adjourned, and a second meeting held the following week. Murray did not attend but

Cheyne, who did, was not permitted to speak. That meeting turned into a one-sided attack on infidelity by the priests. Among their arguments was that the Bible is infallible and promotes human improvement.[536]

In response, Murray published a lengthy rebuttal in *The Regenerator*. Not only did Murray clearly show through the story of Genesis that the Bible was false—how could creation be accomplished in six days, or the first woman be created out of the first man's rib—but that it promoted ignorance that led to warfare and the degradation of human society:

> My conviction is that the Bible hinders human improvement—
> Bible religion is the history of the most cruel and desolating
> wars that have depopulated our globe . . . . Its story of creation
> is a stupefying fabrication; [it] teaches fundamental falsifying of
> facts . . . disqualifying for advancement in knowledge . . . . [It]
> teaches dependence on a god, with supernatural power instead
> of trust in human skill and energy [and] is a collection from
> imaginary spiritual writers, of former times, brought together
> and published by priests for their own benefit.[537]

Murray's debate with local clergy may have stirred up the lingering bad blood with the Simonds, who had converted back to Christianity. The Murrays had a favorite spot on their land close to the Simonds property, which they had made known to them. Despite Murray's admonitions against it, the Simonds began tying up their oxen to trees in a favorite spot on the Murray farm.

One day, Anna Simonds, the lady of the house, visited Catherine and asked for some strawberries which grew abundantly on the Murray farm. It led to an ugly exchange after Catherine requested the down payment for the final $468, which they hadn't received. The following day Murray discovered the trees where the Simonds had been tying up their oxen had been chopped down. This led to a confrontation witnessed by Cheyne; John Collins, another Murray farmhand; and young Charles.

Murray had enough and asked if they would sell out if he could find a buyer. They agreed and Murray contacted George Johnson in New Hampshire who earlier had expressed interest in the property. A price was agreed upon and Johnson traveled to Fruit Hills ready to buy, but when he arrived the Simonds changed their mind. It was an impossible situation and Murray steered clear of them for the time until an even more vicious action occurred two years later.[538]

During Cheyne's residence at Fruit Hills, he took a trip to New York City. It led to the writing of a striking article about the killing of horses for human use.

> While strolling in the suburbs of the city," it began, "my attention was drawn toward an oddly shaped cart, on which was a dead horse. I had heard that there was a class of people, who made a business of drawing off dead animals, and I felt a curiosity to know what was done with the carcasses. I saw a number of old wooden buildings and sheds, also a large brick chimney termed a "stack." I approached the entrance, over which was a Sign —"Depot of Dead Animals."

A man who was the owner came out and invited him in to see what was being done. Inside was "a large pile comprising skulls, leg bones, ribs, which were very white and clean, and were piled with great regularity, the skulls and other large bones forming the outside and the smaller bones filling the center.

An old, dying horse drew his attention. The horse was bleeding from a gash in the neck, its hoof, "one mass of disease and putrefaction. I turned from this sight only to see a more horrid one. Here were two Irish boys cutting up another mass of putrefied horseflesh, and throwing the pieces into a large cauldron, under which was a fierce fire.

He learned that dead horses, dogs, and other animals were delivered every day, and the owner said his men were busy all day cutting them up. The owner said there were seven such "factories" in the city, that the hoofs were sold to glue makers, fat to soap makers, and the bones and skin for other purposes. The horse flesh being boiled was fed to hogs which were kept near the factories.

Cheyne continued with his diatribe blasting the flesh-eating habits of Americans, writing that it was no better than the Chinese custom of eating cats, dogs, and rats.

> The whole affair of flesh eating is a disgusting, diseasing, depraving business . . . . such stuff as the carcasses of hogs that have been fed on the flesh of diseased horses and mad dogs, or stall-fed cattle, is not fit food for man. It should be left for the vultures and the buzzards.[539]

Cheyne's byline disappeared from *The Regenerator* after the May 1850 issue in which his last commentary, "Extracts from a Letter," is a lengthy defense of infidelity. He signed off, Fruit Hills, April 17. While Cheyne's tenure wasn't long—seven or eight months—it helped Murray get through a difficult period; he left sometime after May 1850.

Nothing more is heard from or about him in *The Regenerator*. He apparently migrated to Michigan, enlisted in the army during the final year of the Civil War, and thereafter moved to San Francisco where records show him to be a prosperous shopkeeper. In 1908 he died in Michigan where he is buried. [XLI]

[XLI] Information about Cheyne's life outside Fruit Hills was derived from the U.S. Federal Censuses of 1870, 1880, and 1900; the 1880 Voter Registration, San Francisco County of 1880; his State of Michigan Death Certificate; and the U.S. Civil War Soldiers Records and Profiles, 1861-1865, all of which can be found on Ancestry.com.

Chapter 32

Here, Now, and Hereafter

In the March 1850 issue, Murray discussed life after death, commenting on E.W. Capron's publication about "Spirits" that Cheyne had excoriated a month earlier.

"It was my intention to say something on this matter in the last number of the Regenerator. But the space was otherwise occupied before it was convenient for me to get about it." He explained that it wasn't because he did not think it important, but that he was hesitant:

> Until I see evidence of better things in another world than any revelations have ever yet brought to my attention, I shall probably give preference to the things of this world, where my existence is, and my sympathies and interests are . . . If the beloved ones with whom I have bad acquaintance and sweet communion in life, and who have died, are now in existence in a spirit world, and if they are in possession of knowledge that it is important for me to have, and if they have power to communicate that knowledge . . . I must be allowed here to mention the name of my Carlos.

Again, Murray equivocated. If Carlos were out there and could speak to him, of course he wanted to reach out. But if he was out there and had that power, Murray thought that he was sure that Carlos would indeed speak to him. At least, that was his hope. For Murray still had hope, that though he did not believe in the fake God of the Bible, of a divine being in the form of Jesus Christ, he still was unwilling to unequivocally deny a higher intelligence. He was still waiting for the evidence. "Before it can engage my attention, I must see something more worthy to occupy me, as compared with the useful work now in hand. It seems preferable to me to be improving in such knowledge as will enable me better to act my part in producing corn and apples . . ."[540]

With Cheyne gone, Murray turned to the business of Fruit Hills. He was struggling to maintain the farm and at the same time publish *The Regenerator*. But he still had loyal subscribers, who wanted a paper for free thinkers, wanted to push the boundaries of public opinion, and helped pay for its publishing. It was the production from the farm, however, that sustained it and the livelihood of the Murrays. He also contracted out land for farming.[541]

One of his obsessions was diet. In a later issue of *The Regenerator*, he discussed his dietary practices which he followed but not with 100 percent certainty that it was best for his health. Like others who abstain from meat, for him it was as much an ethical as health consideration.

There is a seeming inconsistency in the course I have adopted from time-to-time, he said.

All the way, from step to step, however, my practice has been in accordance with my prevailing convictions . . . . We are diseased—How are we to be healed? We are corrupted. How are we to be cleansed—We are sick. How are we to get well? We have infirmities that are inherent . . . What is the remedy? Who will bring it to us, or point it out to us? If the Bible and the god of Christendom could do it, and would do it, or do anything towards it, my confidence in them would be increased! . . . . In withdrawing alcohol from the system, no nourishment is withdrawn. In withdrawing flesh food, some nourishment is withdrawn. [But] would be better than what flesh food can afford.

He also opposed the use of coffee, tea, tobacco, salt, sugar, and especially alcohol, having to committed to Temperance as a young man. Food from animal sources, he believed, was even more "depraved" than alcohol. Yet acknowledged the difficulty in breaking off from these stimulations.

> My own alimentiveness is so large, the tendency with me was to eat too much while denying myself food. I had grown up in so free use of it. While I loathed and abhorred the idea of returning to the use of milk and flesh meat, the morbid unnatural appetite continued to be unsatisfied with a reasonable quantity of vegetable food.

He admitted he enjoyed meat. Interestingly, one of the charges in the Peterson pamphlet (Chapter 34) was that he was a hypocrite because he ate beef in secret.

> [I] have discarded and abjured the flesh of hogs since 1834. During about four years commencing at that time, I ate no butter, and but little of flesh food of any kind. Carlos and Marsena practiced with me—not from compulsion, but from choice. They were not more held to the course by me than I by them. The rest of the family varied but little from the practice with us. Afterwards we all got to use some butter and beef. Sometime in 1843 we put away all flesh food, butter, and milk, and adhered to this practice about six years, with the slight exception, on my own part, using a little cheese, now and then tasting dried beef, for a few months. My wife occasionally tasted butter and flesh food away from home. When we resumed the use of milk, our children loathed it—as they also did flesh food. We have by degrees again got into the use of flesh and milk—Our youngest child, eight years of age, has never eaten flesh meat, butler, nor cheese. I have not returned to butter, and do not expect to.

Bread was important to him, but it had to be "unbolted" (unsifted) as earlier described in Chapter 21. Murray claimed that a diet free from animal foods and stimulating substances would provide "comparative freedom from pain— cleansing from disease, and intervention against its liabilities. He believed that because of it, his broken arm was able to heal quickly. And he said he was suffering more pain recently after returning to eating meat.

Soon after commencing the use of a small amount of cheese and of dried beef occasionally— irritating my system again with salt, in addition to stimulating it with animal food—I had a felon [infection] on the thumb of my right hand, which pained me more in five or ten minutes—and these pains were protracted for hours and days—than all I was pained by the broken arm. Have since had another felon on the little finger of the same hand. The thumb and the finger are injured and deformed beyond recovery—their usefulness is impaired for life. 1 have not a doubt that those felons were the results of my return to the animal food and salt—as have been numerous other painful conditions I have since fallen into.

He added that his children had been sicker more often since the family returned to eating animal foods. Anticipating the reader, Murray wrote that one must wonder why the family had gone back to their former diet. He said there were various reasons and inconveniences.

The laboriousness and perplexities to which we were subjected, in sustaining and carrying ourselves through a transition from superstition to a better philosophy, at the same time with our dietetic transition, were unfavorable conditions in our experience. Altogether, it was too exhausting a process for us to hold out under. I found myself emaciated and irritable. At these points I am less fortified in my organization and temperament than some others. Our children had inherited constitutions from flesh eaters, and had themselves, all but the youngest, used animal food. With the less stimulating food we found them growing too slowly.

Despite the challenges his family had faced in abstaining animal and other stimulating food, he concluded, "I believe flesh food to be a depraving, corrupting perversion. While I continue thus to believe, my preaching and practice will be in all possible accordance."[542]

Murray had become more introverted during this time, more fixed on his own problems. When President Taylor suddenly passed away after a short illness on July 9, 1850, there was no word of it in the August *Regenerator*. But there were four pages about "The Mysterious Noises." In July, there was a long-winded account written by Capron who claimed he had spoken to Carlos, who told him that he would not approach his father because of his disbelief. Murray ridiculed this.

"Really—really! I must say that there is too little else than pretension when he says that Carlos is unapproachable to me . . ."[543]

The front page of the August issue was devoted to "Mysterious Knockings" and other manifestations that were increasing around the country, in Auburn and Syracuse, N.Y., Ohio, NJ, CT, and Mass, in as many as 200 different places. There were reports in the *New York Tribune* from witnesses who saw chairs lifted on opposite sides of a table and changing positions, flower vases rising and depositing themselves in another room – sometimes as many as 20 witnesses.[544]

258

It wasn't until the September issue that he discussed Taylor condemning the "enormous waste" that resulted from the funeral parades for the President: $500 for a coffin, $1,000 to decorate the East Room where his body rested in state,[XLII] 20,000 yards of glazed muslin to decorate DC, hundreds of dollars for the use of carriages, a procession seven miles long "while thousands were suffering in want."[545]

There also another death that hit closer to home, that of his oldest sister, Emeline, who had died on March 24.

In the next months, Murray continued his usual coverage of topics attacking religion, the bible, and worshipping on the Sabbath; there were stories on women's rights, the water cure, the California Gold Rush, capital punishment, American Indians, the slave trade, Dickens, fertilizer, and planting potatoes and fruit trees. And every issue had detailed accounts of spiritual knockings and mysterious manifestations, and the shock and fascination about departed loved ones who were moving tables and sending signs from the hereafter.

But when he wasn't writing the Regenerator, his life at this time was much like what he described in a letter to a friend in Vermont on a cold February day in 1851.

Yesterday and today, I have been getting up wood, with a sled, on snow. About six inches of snow fell during Saturday night and Sunday, it is now nearly gone. The ground is frozen under it, as much as we often have it in this climate. It rarely remains frozen many days in succession—although it is frequently frozen during the winter months, so as to bear up loaded wagons. But it is not often that we cannot do good business at turf plowing sometime in any winter month. We could have done fine business at it week before last.

[XLII] One dollar in 1850 is equal to about $39 today (2023).

Have had a very mild winter thus far. Much pleasant weather. The mercury in the common thermometer tube was not down to zero until the morning of the last day of January, when it was 4 degrees below. We have commonly had it 5 or 6 degrees colder than this, sometime in each winter preceding the present, since we have lived here. Last year, or rather last winter, we had it once down to 15 degrees below zero—47 below freezing point. I think it was on the morning of the 29th of December.

One of the greatest objections with me to this climate is the sudden, often, and great changes in the weather. I have observed a variation of 30 degrees in 24 hours—from a given hour in a day to the same hour the next day. In our coldest winter weather, it rarely grows colder more than three days together, after a change, before it turns warmer; and it is not infrequent that in a week from the most intense cold which we generally get, we have it warm again almost like summer. A large part of our January just gone has been like the fore part of a pleasant New England April—some warmer and drier. Part of the month has been a good time for making maple sugar.

Another of my objections to this climate, which I may have spoken of to you before, is the lateness of frosts sometimes in spring, after much warm and growing weather. But I am becoming attached to the climate on the whole. And Maria, I think, is more so than I am. The shortness of our winters; the [less] intense coldness. The long, pleasant autumns. The early opening and blossoming springs—and early fruit-ripening summers. Apples and most other fruits . . . ripen a month earlier here than there. Such grapes as we have here cannot be produced there. Then peaches—when we get them. But they are often put so far forward in our warm autumns, or warm spells in winter, as to be afterwards killed with coldness.

260

Everything, however, grows so much more rapidly and certainly here. Fruit trees can be produced in a lesser number of years. Grain can be raised with half the labor.

What I have now said is not to be taken as any disparagement of my native soil and climate, or complaint against them. If I were there now as I was once, with the knowledge I now have of everything here, it is probable I would stay there and not come here. But I have now no thought of returning to remain.

This was a surprising admission. He had regrets about moving to Ohio. It certainly had been a period of struggle and tragedy. And his troubles weren't over. Nevertheless, he still had concerns about the Fugitive Slave Law which he mentioned and the bad blood between the North and the South. He hoped that better days were ahead.[546]

Chapter 33

The Mysterious Manifestation: Carlos Speaks

In the next issue, Murray pushed back on the claims of the spiritualist, Capron.

The mischief and harm in connection with what is mysterious often is, that so much is assumed and affirmed of the unknown, as if it were known . . . it is their imposition upon others that is most objectionable . . . when they come to assume for their opinions and their conjectures that they are facts—that they are revelations from infallible sources—that they are communications to material beings from spiritual beings.[547]

Butterworth Residence

Murray was skeptical about spiritual beings but curious. He wondered like so many Americans were wondering. As it was reported in the *New York Tribune* and reprinted on the front page of *The Regenerator*:

> Few of our readers except those who are themselves engaged in the great business of ghost-seeing, spirit-rapping, table jumping, speaking in tongues, mysterious writing, and other phenomena of the kind, are aware of the extent to which these practices and revelations are continued in this free and independent country.
>
> There is hardly a rural parish, or a city, which does not count its "mediums" and circles of explorers into this department of the misty unknown. Everywhere, the curious and the credulous are receiving high moral and spiritual commonplaces from their defunct uncles, aunts, grandames, and posterity.
>
> Dear, believing souls exult at the new winks, and blinks, and squeezes of the hand, and slaps on the back, vouchsafed to them from the transmortuary world; and the aspiring and hopeful long for the greater revelations that are promised, but never received, from the same dubious source. Those wiseacres who proclaim that the delusion is exploded, and triumphantly knock their knee joints or crackle their toes by way of demonstration, receive little attention and make no converts. But the ghosts do. They go on conquering and to conquer.
>
> The number of their disciples multiplies from Maine to California. If it be all a delusion, there was never one more widely disseminated, and it is time for those who deprecate its influence and deny its spiritual claims, to really explode it if they can. It will not do to wait till it dies out of itself, for, as we hear, scores of people are actually made crazy by it, and the received faith with respect to the life of man after death is being so widely and dangerously undermined.

The "spiritual manifestations" are very remarkable, and seriously require explanation of another sort than the [self-evident] verdict of solemn ignorance that they are all humbug.[548]

Murray was reticent to call them humbug. He had hoped that somehow, someway despite his rational powers of dissent, that Carlos might be out there waiting to speak to him. And it happened one night at the home of the Butterworths.[XLIII] Friends and family had gathered there to commune with a Medium, likely brought there by Valentine Nicholson, the brother-in-law of Nancy Wales Butterworth, who was obsessed with spiritualism. Murray counted fifteen in all. He and Catherine arrived after the supper party.

"Three tables were arranged, or placed together, through the central part of the room," Murray wrote. "We were requested to have our hands on the tables—the object, as we were told, to form and electro-magnetic circle."[549]

During the supper, rappings had been heard. The Medium suggested the gathering should announce names of those deceased persons whom they would like to speak with. They received an affirmative sign at the mention of Carlos Murray.

Before they began, the Murrays were told that Carlos was ready to speak to them and that they should pose a question. In Murray's description he did not evoke any astonishment and simply proceeded to engage with the spirits.

The process of communication was tedious. Questions were written in pencil, the questioner not revealing them, so that no one but the questioner could know what was written. Answers were given by use of the alphabet. This was done by someone calling out

---

[XLIII] The specific location was revealed in a September 1851 letter of Harveysburg resident, James C. Brown

letters alphabetically until a rap was heard in the affirmative. And so on, through words and sentences.

"Is it you, my Son?" Orson wrote down his first question. The rapping followed and the answer was, *Yes!*

"Why have we not heard from you before?" Orson asked.

"I am your friend and Son, Carlos. It is not the first time."

"When before?"

"You ought to know."

"Can the remainder of these answers be given by the rappings at the other end of the table?"[XLIV]

"Yes. Do believe I have developed my presence in your room when you were writing for Capron. I will often be with you; and you will know me hereafter."

"May I be told why this peculiar form of manifestation is necessary?"

"I am done."

This frustrated the Murrays, but the Medium was staying with the Butterworths for several days, so the next night Catherine posed questions.

"Dear Mother: Do not doubt. I am here." the spirit of Carlos rapped out.

"Will you come to our house?"

"Yes—soon, Let me assure you I will communicate with you as soon as I can. You may feel contented and happy; for I am. Father must realize my presence; for I am a co-worker with him in all reforms."

"My dear Father and Mother—do be reconciled. You do not know how fully I enjoy your company; and I do not regret that I died."

[XLIV] Murray later insisted that he could not detect the origin of the rappings and insisted they could not have been produced by any motion of fingers or toes or working of any joints.

The spirit also answered that he had seen his two young sisters who had died and his maternal grandparents.

"I was at a loss to know what to think of the proceedings," Orson wrote. "What then is there of it? I do not know all there is of it. Am at a loss to know what else stands connected, out of the reach of our senses, with what comes within their reach. Am waiting for further evidence."[550]

In the August issue, Thomas Longshore of Philadelphia, a regular subscriber reported that Carlos had communicated to him the following message: "All are happy in this spirit home. We continually ascend nearer to the source of the divine Intelligence, and the harmony and love that is ours you cannot conceive of. O! Father: a spiritual existence is a blest reality."[551]

Orson expressed disbelief.

"I do not feel like saying much now in this connection. Know not what to say. Have nothing to suppress—and little to express. Am in a fix."[552]

In the September issue, there was a report of the rappings at the Harveysburg home of James C. Brown, one of whom attended the seances at the Butterworths. Orson had become less dubious and even said that he "formerly" thought they were "humbug" and mentioned the possibility of having "Carlos's writings renewed and continued in the Regenerator." But he concluded he still wanted more evidence: "my decision extends to the extent of evidence."[553]

Murray continued to report the manifestations with hopeful skepticism. One of them was a report by Marsena who was on a trip and visiting with Mediums.

"There may be more or less deception—humbug used in places," Marsena wrote. But in certain cases . . . I know there is none . . . Yet what is it? He tells of attending numerous seances. In one in Bethel, Vermont, he communicated with a spirit who claimed to be Carlos and then again in Argyle, New York.[554]

There were continuing reports of "Mysterious Manifestations," in *The Regenerator*, some exposing them as frauds. There was also another from Marsena, reporting on more Mediums whom he had visited. "The noises are heard," he wrote of the first, "the writings are witnessed, and these manifestations must be produced by some material thing. Certainly not by any trick or collusion of the medium—and if not of another state of existence, I cannot conceive of their source." On visiting a Medium in Woodstock, Vermont, a 15-year-old girl, who wrote down the answers from the alleged deceased, Marsena claimed that the Medium wrote the answers without looking at the paper on which she was writing. At another medium, he again encountered Carlos, who said he had visited the Murray household in Ohio. Marsena also asked questions about his grandfather about which no one else could've known the answer and they were answered correctly.[555] Orson remained skeptical:

> The evidence is yet to be found by me, or furnished to me, convincing me that there is any continued identical personal existence after death—whether such supposed existence is to be spiritual or material. I am yet to be shown or to know, that there are any such things in existence as spirits. At the same time, I have [manifested] a willingness and readiness to entertain and consider whatever may be offered as evidence to convince me of what may be supposed to be my error.[556]

Among the articles and letters about the spirit world appearing in *The Regenerator* came from Murray's old friend, Valentine Nicholson. "Let me say that I have investigated the subject of spiritual intercourse with earth's inhabitants, with some degree of diligence and care, for the past three years," He had found that there were many methods through which they communicated messages from the other side. Some used sound or vibrations, some used writing, others were clairvoyants. "And I am free to place upon record my firm conviction of the truth and reality of these things . .

. [without] harboring even a shadow of doubt as to their truth and to their great use and importance to mankind."[557]

More readers reported their accounts and firm convictions in the reality that the spirits of the dead were communicating to the living. But Murray was stubborn and had concluded otherwise:

[S]ince what I witnessed and published, the first time the rappings came under my own observation, I have never published, nor in any way expressed, nor entertained, the slightest doubt of the honesty, in this matter, of all those persons who honest in other things. On the contrary, I have published my confidence in their honesty. The difference between my spiritual friends and me. has been, that in reasoning from the known to the unknown I have not been carried to all the conclusions to which they have been.[558]

The reality of death continued to hover over his life with the passing of neighbor and former Ohio Governor, Jeremiah Morrow, who died on March 22, 1852, and described by Murray as "A model of magnanimity, peacefulness, and kindness . . . . Possessing the qualities in general which caused those who were acquainted with him to feel that he was eminently a man of goodness."[559]

Chapter 34

Extra! Extra! Read All About It!

The character whom we deem guilty of arrant hypocrisy, and far more than that phrase expresses, is somewhat widely known by the cognomen—Orson S. Murray, editor of a monthly newspaper called *The Regenerator* published at Fruit Hills, Warren Co., O. He has gained his notoriety principally by professing to believe in no God, Devil, Heaven, or Hell, or anything of the kind. By reformers in general and radicals in religious belief in particular, who know him, merely through this paper of his, he is thought to be the very acme of purity, the climax of perfection and goodness; but by those who are personally acquainted with him, he is known to be a man of very disreputable character, and one whose "preaching and practice" are sadly at variance.[560]

This was the beginning of a lengthy invective printed up as a pamphlet and mailed to Regenerator subscribers and Maineville residents on April 20, 1852. It was signed R. Peterson of Maineville, Ohio, on behalf of "many," who were not named.

Peterson had lived briefly in Fruit Hills. He had written Murray, asking to work for *The Regenerator*. He said he was a reformer and hoped that someday he could become a partner in publishing *The Regenerator*. Murray invited him to come on a trial basis. He thought Peterson could help Charles with the printing. They agreed on twelve dollars a month with room and board. Part of the agreement was that he also would work on the farm.

Unfortunately, Murray found his farm labors unproductive, and his work in the office inferior to his young son Charles. Murray tried to discuss improving his performance but Peterson was uncooperative. Finally, Murray terminated him. Peterson asked for another chance, but Murray only relented to give him time to make arrangements to leave. Finally, after a few days, Murray asked Peterson to leave, which he did on March 29.

However, he moved next door to stay with the Simonds. It wasn't too surprising because Peterson had met them prior to Murray when he arrived looking for directions to Fruit Hills. He stayed with them about three weeks and during that time three apple trees were uprooted, and fifteen dollars' worth of mill logs were rolled into the Little Miami and floated away. Murray had suspected that the Simonds had been behind the publication of the pamphlet and took advantage of the disgruntled Peterson. Such libelous charges could only have come from them. Murray believed that Peterson went to Cleveland to print the pamphlet and used the subscription list he had obtained while working in the office for the mailings.

Murray did not receive a copy of the pamphlet until one of the Regenerator's subscribers sent it to him. But Murray learned that neighbors had actually seen copies of it at the Simonds homestead before this. He published the June 1852 *Regenerator Extra* to answer the charges and mailed it out for free. In it he published both the pamphlet and rebuttal. He also published a letter from a man who worked at Fruit Hills along with Peterson. It read in part:

> This is to certify that I have lived in Orson S. Murray's family since the first of November last. R. Peterson and I lodged together while he was here. His published statements, prejudicial to O. S. Murray, so far as he makes them from an opportunity for personal knowledge of transactions and things while he was here, are grossly false throughout . . . Herbert R. Smith.

Murray also published a certificate attesting to his good character signed by 24 neighborhood residents, including the Morrows and Butterworths. In the July issue, C.D. Lewis who by his own testimony was the longest-tenured member of the Fruit Hills Community, wrote:

> I am sorry to learn that there are persons base enough to have put out a publication derogatory to your past life and present character, without, as I feel assured, the least grounds therefore. As I suppose you will meet the attack, and as I have had opportunity to know as much as anyone else—if not more — of your business transactions and private life, since your arrival in-Ohio, I take pleasure in being able to add my testimony to that of the many others you will easily procure.[561]

Things apparently settled down and Peterson did not return nor was he ever mentioned again.

All the stresses created by the death of Carlos and this new crisis weakened Murray. He did not publish the Regenerator in October or November, and on the front page of the December 1852 *Regenerator*, he wrote of his illness.

> (November 19) This frailty has confined me much of the time for upwards of two months. So, my old friends and associates in vegetable diet may now with propriety ask me what I have gained by returning to flesh eating. In my four years of experience in vegetable diet, I had nothing about me at any time like fever. Was prostrate only three days during that time—and that with diarrhea. I was, however, very much enfeebled, at different times.

> I have no doubt that my return to my former course of living has had to do with the suffering I have now been passing through. This suffering commenced with a malignant, bilious, intermittent fever, which lasted about two weeks. I "threw it

off," or cleansed it away, by abstinence and the use of water, principally. Began to feel better, went to work too soon, and fell into fever and ague. It was the first of my experience with this disease. I starved it out. But I have found it to be deceitful, as others had represented it to be. Have broken it up, gone to work, and brought it on again, now for the fourth time.

Yesterday, I had the severest shaking I have experienced of the kind. It continued from half past nine till about one—nearly or quite three hours and a half. The suffering, I will not attempt to describe . . . . I am little more than a skeleton. My family and friends have urged me to employ the doctors. I have not consented . . . . I have lived seven years and a half where I am. Every year there has been more or less of "chills and fever," as it is called, in the neighborhood. I have been through with the acclimation and kept clear of it up to the time of my present sickness. Do not believe I should have escaped thus if my diet for the first four or five years had been what it has been since. So safe did I feel, while dieting differently, I used to tell my neighbors humorously that I was proof against fever and ague. And so I proved myself to be, as long as I adhered to the diet . . . . The summing up of my case is simply this: I have had too much else to do to take care of myself— my own present personal welfare has been neglected in my struggles for something better in prospect for my family, myself, and others.

December 27. Have now just commenced recovering, the fifth time, after the fourth relapse, "Broke the chills," as the saying is here—recovered, or escaped, once more, from the ague and fever—by fasting. I have tried bitter decoctions—have, at the urgent request of family and friends, tried homeopathy, and a variety of other prescribed remedies; and all to little or no purpose. There is nothing like fasting to cleanse away and clear off this disease. It takes about three successive days of abstinence from food to stop the shaking. This will do more towards regulating the stomach and liver than all the calomel and quinine that can be administered . . . . The commencement with food should then be with moderation, having reference to quality and quantity. The exercise should also be moderate and with care. Here I have found difficulty, hitherto insurmountable, in my inexperience with the disease. After "stopping the chills" and beginning to gain strength, a little proper exercise, it is plain, would be promotive of strength and vigor. But to know what proper exercise is—that is the difficult thing. It can only be found out by experience, in the exercise of discernment and cautiousness.

I am at the bottom of a long, steep, rugged ascent. At the commencement of cold weather my vitality is exceedingly low—down near to zero. If the framework be in the main sound, there may yet be a building up that will last for a while. But if a few of the principal timbers prove rotten and give way at this crisis, my work is soon done.[562]

This latter description was reported and interpreted by three Vermont newspapers that Murray was near death.[563] Murray's symptoms suggested malaria which was common in the U.S. during this time and often deadly. But he soldiered on and in the next issue, he reported his health had "improved very much."[564]

Chapter 35

A Transition Period

Orson held on but the troubles in his life had taken a toll. In 1853, he published only eight issues of *The Regenerator*, suspending publication of it in March 1854, announcing there would be changes, including a name change. He would start up again in October 1854 as *Murray's Review*. Marsena took over the business operations of the latter, but after eighteen months suspended operations. Orson needed a break from his 20-year campaign to fix the problems of humanity. He then went into business selling potatoes with his 19-year-old son, Charles, and not much his heard from him until 1860, when his activism experienced a rejuvenation.

MURRAY'S REVIEW.

ORSON S. MURRAY, Editor.   *Ignorance the Evil—Knowledge the Remedy.*   CHAS. B. MURRAY, Printer.

VOLUME VII. No. 1.   FRUIT HILLS, Warren Co., Ohio, October, 1854.   Whole No. 177.

MURRAY'S REVIEW.

PUBLISHED MONTHLY—$1.00 A YEAR.

Our Post Office Address.
Fruit Hills, Twenty Miles Stand, Warren County, Ohio.

things visible and within the reach of knowledge, in order to being in the best relations to things invisible and beyond the reach of knowledge.

To prevent the sacrifice of the present to the past and the future.

To exalt humanity.

with my views of fidelity to freedom. Although, I was a Baptist, and, as I now see, a slave to religion, and in some degree to that peculiar form of religion, my tendencies were to larger liberty. My purchase of the paper was for the purpose—the avowed purpose—of making it freer than it had

One description of what life was like in his neighborhood at the time is captured in this depiction:

No factory whistles are ever heard in Maineville, consequently no tall chimneys are dark blots against the sky or pour forth clouds of thick black smoke to sully and begrime the many attractive homes. In some things the village is ahead of far larger towns, as was shown in the passing of an ordinance by the village council in the year 1855, forbidding the owners of certain animals known by the un-euphonious name of hogs, to permit them to use the village streets for promenading.[565]

Murray was busy on his farm and surely pleased with the ordinance prohibiting roaming hogs, as well as getting out the *Review*, preaching his reformist message of healthy living, hydropathy, vegetable diet, women's rights, antislavery, and of course, attacks on organized religion and the bible. But there was one noteworthy incident during that period in 1855 before suspension of the *Review*. The *Vermont Journal* had a condensed version of the antislavery meeting reporting Murray's part: "Orson S. Murray, once a Baptist clergyman in Vermont, and publisher of a Baptist newspaper in this State, has been disgusting the religious sense of community at Cincinnati by his ult abolitionism and infidelity."[566]

As Orson tells it, "Wm Wells Brown, colored Anti-Slavery agent and lecturer of some note[XLV] . . . while on his way to the Convention (Cincinnati Anti-Slavery Convention) had been lecturing in our neighborhood." Murray had heard one of Brown's topics was one of Orson's triggers, how Christianity did not support slavery. So, he "found it convenient to have some business in Cincinnati at the time and dropped in to take observation."[567]

It was the second day of the convention which ran for three days with morning, afternoon, and evening sessions. In addition to Wells Brown, another notable of the antislavery movement who attended was the Rev. John Rankin.[XLVI]

[XLV] William Wells Brown was, after Frederick Douglass, the foremost Black writer of the antebellum period. A fugitive slave, he first worked on Lake Erie boats and helped fugitive slaves escape. After his position as a literary figure was established, he confined his efforts to writing and lecturing.

[XLVI] John Rankin was among the most notable figures in the antislavery movement. His home in Ripley across the Ohio River was a widely used refuge for fugitive slaves. His renown and influence dated from

The morning started with the report of the Business Committee, which offered seven new resolutions in addition to the three from opening day. They included calling on Congress to abolish slavery in the District of Columbia and all Territories, forbid the transit of slaves between the States, and repeal all laws for the rendition of fugitive slaves; that the state legislature prohibit use of Ohio jails and law enforcement in the return of fugitive slaves, and make it a crime for anyone in Ohio to aid in their rendition; and make it a crime for slaveholders to pass through the state with their slaves. One of the earlier resolutions, however, was that in which Murray was most interested. It concerned the relationship between Christianity and slavery: "That American Slavery is antagonistic to the principles of Christianity and true Democracy; therefore, all attempts to reconcile them or to make them co-exist in harmony, under the same social, political and religious institutions - is an insult to God and an outrage upon man."[568] This was reinforced by a magazine that was handed out to attendees, which Murray described as presenting the idea that "slavery as it exists in this union, has no sanction either by precept or example in the Bible" that it "is repugnant to every principle developed in that blessed book."[569]

Murray was among the first to address the convention that morning. A report of the meeting disparaged his appearance as often was the case, saying that he was imitating the appearance of another renowned and disheveled lecturer, Charles C. Burleigh, with his long hair and beard and lack of a "cravat," calling him "Burleigh somewhat overdone."[570] Burleigh was a friend of Murray's from the

---

the serialization of his "Letters on American Slavery,' in *The Liberator* in 1832. They illustrated how slavery conflicted with the fundamental-principles of the Declaration of Independence and focused on the common humanity all races share with each other.

Vermont days, after whom son Charles was named. He at once went on the offensive and did not mince words as was his custom.

The Bible was proslavery and antislavery, Murray insisted. It took both sides; there was bad and good. The good was that it declared to do to others as you would have them do to you (the Golden Rule), but these words were spoken 400 years before Christ by Socrates, he said, even questioning whether Christ was a real person or just a myth. The Bible also sanctioned heinous acts of slavery, all in the name of the Christian God to whom obedience was absolute. It is time to face the truth and seek higher standards of behavior, "higher grounds," as Murray framed it, which elicited a response from the audience, "Give us your higher grounds," to which he replied, "It is that man is entitled to freedom, whether it is written in a book or not." There was applause. "Human rights first, and all books and makers of books afterwards." More applause.

But there was also unrest. "Some could not keep their seats and hear me through in the few words I had to utter," he later wrote. "I could not censure them, and cannot, for their disquietude and impatience." A member of the audience called out that he did not understand the purpose of such comments, and asked if Jesus Christ had ever said anything that was wrong, to which Murray replied, Yes, "he that believeth not shall be damned;" that is wrong and false.

There were angry cries and a committee member called for a point of order. Murray requested to speak a little longer, but then another person rose and shouted, "A few moments more of such indulgence would sink anti-slavery so deep in Cincinnati that it would never be dug up again." There was more tumult, and the committee decided to allow Murray to finish, but even as he left the podium to return to his seat, he continued to lecture.

Those who followed Murray agreed that there were strong elements of pro-slavery in the churches, but they could not agree that the Bible was pro-slavery. Another added that he could see no good resulting from continuing the discussion. Infidels never had benefited the antislavery cause. All reforms owed their origin to the influence of the churches. Finally, the Rev. Livermore expressed his belief that the New Testament did not sanction slavery, but it was the members of the church who did not live up to its standards. The morning session was over, but Murray was not done yet.

The afternoon's resolutions stated that the effort to prove human slavery was compatible with Christianity was the worst form of atheism, that it was the right of slaves to seek their freedom and to give them assistance and condemned those who attempted to seize a fugitive slave and return him to slavery.

Once again, Murray stepped up to the podium and criticized the first resolution for using the Bible as its justification for opposing slavery and began citing passages that showed it sanctioned murder, warfare, and polygamy in the Old Testament. A committee member rose and objected, saying that his line of discussion had nothing to do with the teachings of the bible related to slavery, and another said that the first resolution never used the word, Bible. It was then that Rev. Rankin rose to speak.

Rev. John Rankin

He addressed Murray directly.

"The gentleman is not alone in misunderstanding the Bible. No book in the world had ever been slandered as this, in regard to its teachings on slavery. And the gentleman who introduced the subject had been out of order—out of order in combing his hair during prayers." This snide remark drew laughter. Rankin then explained that there were three classes of law in the old Testament: judicial, which would not prohibit all wrongdoing, ceremonial, and moral law, which did prohibit all wrongdoing. He gave illustrations from the Bible of each, and insisted there was no slavery in the Bible, that Hebrew slavery was different from the chattel slavery than practiced in the South.

"The attempt to adduce slavery from the Bible, was a most perfect absurdity, just as though that man," he said, pointing at Murray, "had never read the Bible, at all."

There was applause.

Rankin added that "the clergy of Cincinnati did not join in these meetings because they could not come without meeting abuse and reproach, and seeing all the way sacred and dear to the held up to ridicule . . . He could not fellowship with the man who derided Him who spoke as never man spoke and he did not believe that man had sufficient love for his savior, who could."

There was more applause.

Murray attempted a retort, but the floor was taken by a Jewish man who claimed that the old Testament did indeed teach slavery. Following him, Murray rose, saying he needed to leave, but wished to discuss this matter another time.

In the next issue of *Murray's Review,* he gave his account of the proceedings and a detailed explanation of his reasoning. Taking the brunt of Murray's ire was Rankin: "John Rankin has grown grey in his bondage to his book." What followed next was Murray at his most annoying and prickly self:

> To John Rankin, I had been awfully irreverent, had been 'out of order,' not only in ' discussing the inspiration of the Bible,' but in 'combing my hair in prayer time.' The facts were these: The Bible subject had been introduced by the Convention

itself, through the action of its own Committee, appointed to report business for action. Furthermore, a large portion if not proportion, of the Convention were interested in the discussion. To these, nothing was more in order. And the chairman sustained me as being in order throughout, so far as I now recollect. As for the combing of my hair, it was . . . at the commencement of the morning session, while but few were yet in, a very sluggish, well-fed appearing man made a very indifferent prayer. Some stood, others sat, some with their heads up, others with their heads down, none manifesting much interest in what was going on. I occupied a seat on the outside of the collection, sitting by the side of my wife. Had left my pocket comb in my other vest at home. After purchasing a new one in the City, on my way to the Convention that morning, had not found a convenient opportunity for using it till then. Now if John Rankin had been in a devotional attitude how could he have seen what I was doing, or have been disturbed by it? I made no noise, took no position to attract attention. If John Rankin was among those who stood, why did he not bring his club down on the heads of those who sat, as having been out of order?

These were the large majority. What, in fact, was in order at that time, and what was not in order? Was John Rankin in order in gazing at me, instead of giving his attention to his idol; and then in the afternoon session giving me a flagellation before an audience, one fiftieth part of whom knew not the occasion for it? Really it is quite a matter of doubt with me whether five other persons besides John Rankin saw me combing my hair.

Murray believed in the Golden Rule, the "Higher Law," but not the one dictated to him by Rankin's God. It was one derived from human reason, from the self-evident compassion of human nature.

Blunt and sarcastic commentary like his rebuttal of Rankin was what made Murray a pariah. But that was Murray, a straight shooter who spoke the truth, didn't moderate his words, and never backed down, though it probably would've been to his advantage if he more easily admitted it when he was wrong. Likewise, he stuck to his position when it came to the spiritualist movement that had permeated America. No, he had not seen, heard, or read anything that had convinced him the people who were dead, including Carlos, were communicating with the living. But he was keeping his options open for that to happen.

Right up to the final issues of *Murray's Review*, there were articles, reports, and commentary on the "Mysterious and Spiritual Manifestations."[571] Up to the second-to-last issue of *Murray's Review*, he was still talking about Carlos. Perhaps the most interesting and insightful commentary he made about his views of the spiritual nature of existence and the actual manifestations in his life he thought indicative of it, were expressed in the following passage:

"I have often thought, since spiritualism has occupied so much of public attention, and my own views and opinion of it have been sought with so much urgency, that I would make known, some of my experience in things mysterious." He said it was impossible to remember when he had begun experiencing the incomprehensible, things that were marvelous and like poetry, especially those in the realm of superstition, things that were irrational, did not make sense. "Who has not had mysterious impressions, in connection with the approach of persons or things?"

He recalled the week before when he and Catherine visited another couple unannounced in Cincinnati. "They told me they had in the morning distinct and strong impressions that I should be there before night." But there was no reason for that expectation, and they ascribed it to something spiritual. They asked him how he could account for it. "The distance direct is not far from twenty miles," he speculated. "There is no doubt that living human beings may affect one another, under some circumstances in much greater distances than this. Cannons are heard very distinctly, at our place, from Cincinnati. The impressions from the cannon are not made on our eyes; but they are on our ears; and perhaps on our senses of feeling." He concluded that some sensitivity all humans share can connect us over very great distances.

"Animals have premonitions of storms. Geese and ducks flap their wings and fly about, in joyous anticipation of rain after a drought." He used the examples of storms when animals are able to sense their approach. "There is a mysterious sympathy among animals for the distressed and the diseased." He recalled an incident on his journey down the Alleghany River in 1844, after a strenuous day of rowing and having indigestion from dinner, awaking in the middle of the night, and having pain so severe that he thought he was having a heart attack. "While I was agonizing alone, a cat in the room came upon the bed and made noticeable and very remarkable expressions of sympathy."

He discussed the battle for his life during the storm on Lake Erie. "I had premonitions of that storm for several days. It was nothing definable or describable. It was an apprehension." He said it was difficult to describe but a feeling. People had been asking him when he expected to arrive in Ohio, and he would always reply "about the 20th of October, if I do not get into Lake Erie." He had begun to think about what he had said and wondered if he foresaw what had happened. His health hadn't been good, having gone back to eating meat and he wondered if that caused his premonition.

My son Carlos, then in Ohio, and in a like susceptible condition, and in very remarkable sympathy with me, was similarly premonished at the same time. He told me afterwards that he wrote me a letter to Buffalo, which, if I had received, would have kept me from the catastrophe. During that memorable and distressing night, while I was tossed on Lake Erie, he was disquieted, convulsed in bed.

On another occasion, Grandmother Rachel Butterworth, who lived next door and in good health but in the last stages of life, was home alone, her son away on business. Another son came by to check on her and Murray happened to talk with him, asking about his mother, whom he said was fine. The next morning, he was awakened by a nightmare that someone was dying. To his surprise, both Catherine and Carlos had the same dream. He surmised it meant Grandma Butterworth.

Four hours later, Catherine was told that Grandma Butterworth was about to die. She had called the family into her room and told them the end was near. Before the day had closed, she was no more. He had no explanation for these incidents, which he thought others might attribute to coincidence:

> Who has not felt the approach of others before they have been seen, or otherwise recognized by any of the five senses, so called often with doors and greater or less distance intervening? Who has not seen, for hours together, the effects of approaching storms, on the other animals and on human beings in peculiar conditions? Who has not witnessed the working of sympathy for the suffering? If these can go on at less distances, why not at greater? And who has not found himself and others to have been thinking of the same things at the same time, when no accompanying conditions recognizable by the recognized senses, could have produced the results or accounted for the facts?

Murray suggested a telepathic connection between himself and Carlos. At the same he did not believe it was caused by spiritual processes.

> There is more or less mystery investing, enshrouding them all. Let none be affected superstitiously, but all rationally, in contemplating these things. Such facts as have been related in

my experience, so far from making a spiritualist of me, have the contrary effect as before said; for if incomprehensible powers in incomprehensible natural elements, with which all living earthly existences stand in incomprehensible connection, are equal to such manifestations, why may it not be supposed they are equal to other manifestations, more profoundly mysterious and wonderfully wonderful?[572]

In the March 1856 issue of *Murray's Review*, there was a notice marked "Vacation." It stated that the Review was taking a break but would be back in July: "We are making important changes and a remove in part, of our home matters . . ."[573]

Murray moved to a house Marsena built for him across the river. Marsena had been doing well in his business, and by 1857 he was the owner of both his father's and the Simonds's properties.

But *Murray's Review* had published for the last time.

Chapter 36

Murray's Garden

"At the age of nineteen years," Charles Murray wrote, "I was allied with my father in agricultural and farm affairs, upon land to which he had removed in 1856, on the west side of the Little Miami River, near Foster's Crossings."

Little Miami River at Foster's Crossings Today

Now, Murray became a full-time farmer, or at least he didn't have the additional burden of publishing a newspaper for the first time in 20 years. He was fifty years old but had recovered from his bouts with illness. Farming was something he had done all his life concurrently with activism and writing. It was in his blood and his publications always included articles about farming. There were articles on potatoes, peaches, strawberries, watermelon, raspberries, cherries, corn, plowing, fertilizer, manure, seeds, pears, and apples from the *Albany Cultivator, Horticulturist, Country Gentleman, Working Farmer, Granite Farmer,* and *The Cultivator* among many others, as well as even more written by individuals probably surpassing in number those written about social, political, and religious topics, though on the back pages.

An interesting feature that was reprinted in the September 21, 1846, issue of *The Regenerator* was the story of Johnny Appleseed, who was a real person who lived in Ohio.[574] About the time of the survey of the lands in the United States military district, northwest of the river Ohio, the article explained, preparatory to the land issued by the government to the soldiers of the revolutionary war for their services, there came to the valley of the Muskingum, and its tributaries, the Tuscarawas and Mohican in eastern Ohio, a man whose real name, if ever known, is not remembered by its inhabitants, but who was commonly known all over the country by the name of Johnny Appleseed.

This man had imbibed so remarkable a passion for the rearing and cultivation of apple trees from seed and pursued it with so much zeal and perseverance to cause him to be regarded by settlers with a degree of almost superstitious admiration.

Immediately upon his advent, he commenced the raising of apple trees from the seed, at a time when there were not, perhaps, fifty while men within the forty miles square. He would clear a few rods of ground in an open part of the forest, girdle the trees standing on it, surround it with a brush fence, and plant his apple seeds. This done he would go off twenty miles or so, select another favorable spot, and again go through the same operation.

In this way, without family und without connection, he rambled from place to place, and employed his life. When the settlers began to flock in and open their clearings, old Appleseed was ready for them with his young trees. Thus, he proceeded, deriving a self-satisfaction amounting to delight, from the indulgence of his engrossing passion.

Such were the labors and life of Johnny Appleseed and such his unmingled enjoyments, till about fifteen years ago, when, probably feeling the encroachments of others upon his sphere, and desiring a new and more extended field of operations, he removed to the far West, there to enact over again the same career of humble but sublime usefulness.

This man, obscure and illiterate though he was, must have been born with the instinct of his theory. His usual practice was to gather his seeds from seedling trees, and to take them from as many different trees as were to be found within the range of his yearly autumnal rambles, and from those seedling trees affording the highest evidence in their fruit that the process of improving them was begun and was going on in them.

At first, his visits necessarily extended to the seedling orchards upon the Ohio and Monongahela rivers, in what were called the settlements, but when the orchards of his own planting began to bear, his wanderings, for the purpose of collecting seed, became more and more narrowed in their extent, till the time of his departure further westward.

Still true, however, to the instinct which first drew him to produce to new and improved varieties of apples, he has continued occasionally to return in the autumn to his beloved orchards hereabouts, to contemplate and ruminate upon the results of his labors, and of gathering seeds from his own seedling trees, to take with him, and carry on their reproduction in the West. Recently, his visits have been intermittent. Our hope, is, that he may yet live in the enjoyments of a green old age, happy in the multitude of its pleasing reminiscences.[575]

While there were all sorts of fruits and vegetables grown on Fruit Hills, the most prosperous for the Murray farming enterprise was the humble potato. According to Charles, the Murray farm developed a thriving sweet potato plant business, furnishing sweet potato plants sprouted from tubers in hot beds heated by wood fires.[576] During this time Marsena conceived "the idea of 'curing' sweet potatoes and invented a process of sweating and sterilizing them. In 1880, he moved to Tennessee where he found the sandy loam of the Chattanooga valley the perfect soil for the cultivation of his creation, the favorite sweet potato of Dixieland, "the Southern Queen." It made him famous and he became known as "Sweet Potato Murray."[577]

Numerous articles about potatoes, how to plant, reseed, preserve, and grow them appeared in the pages of *The Regenerator*. In one of them, which Murray also submitted to the *Albany Cultivator*, he talks about working along with Marsena in regenerating a crop of potatoes from small potatoes.

> During the past season I made an experiment with other potatoes, he wrote, using the kind, or variety, called the Neshannock, or Mercer. Side by side, treated alike, and of like quality, as far as it was possible, we planted large and small potatoes, separated from each other. Both planted, tilled, and harvested on the same days. The result is, quite as large an

amount, and quite as good quality, from the small potatoes used in planting. Our son, M. M., in my absence, dug an equal number of hills, in parallel rows, and called on me to decide between the heaps. I decided without hesitation, as to the amount and size. His mother was then called, and her decision agreed with mine. Our decision was in favor of those which he said were dug where the smaller were planted. We then went and dug the hole. The result agreed with the appearance of the heaps first dug.

Murray thought his reader might be skeptical of the procedure. "There is not the slightest doubt that any mistake has been made." If one can get equal or better potatoes from using smaller one as roots, then it is important that farmers know this. "If we can obtain as good a plant from the smaller tuber as from the larger one, it is what we all need to know."[578]

Charles also found success in the farming business during his association with Orson. One of his enterprises was cultivating seeds. "I had much experience in growing apple seedlings and in root grafting them, and in growing and budding peach seedlings." Another product he prospered from were "Wilson" strawberries, learning of them from advertisements. "I sent for some plants, and so far as I knew I was the first to grow this fruit in the state." One large grower came to try the Wilson berries and was very pleased. Charles claimed his strawberries were the best on the market. "Our house in strawberry time, with my mother's bread and butter, and abundance of good milk, was an attractive resort for visitors in that region. Raspberries and blackberries for home use were also grown."[579]

It was apparent that Murray loved trees. The anguish he felt when the Simonds cut down some of his favorites was felt in his *Regenerator Extra.* A fascinating article about large trees in New York State that he reprinted from the *Horticulturist* echoed his feelings:

It is much to be regretted that no work has ever been published with well engraved portraits of the finest specimens of our noble American forest trees, many of which are annually disappearing, either by old age, or by the process of "clearing up" the country. It is saddening to the heart of a lover of trees to see in many parts of the country the finest single specimens sacrificed by the wanton axe of the woodman, who sees only so much "cordwood" in what, to his descendants, would be valued "beyond rubies." Of course, new world forests must be cleared up, but it is difficult to understand what good reason the most practical common-sense man can have for despoiling the neighborhood of his own dwelling of stately single trees— that should be held sacred as the pride and glory of his home landscape.

The article marveled at the various large trees revealing their heights and the circumferences of their trunks. Among them was a white swamp oak in the Genesee Valley of western New York. At 20 feet its branches began, its trunk 27 feet in circumference and varied little in size as it ascended skyward. An elm cut down in central New York whose height was about 60 feet with a trunk circumference of 15 feet was found to be 300 years old based on its annular rings. Most of the trees, it said, were grown in valleys or ravines in rich soil with lots of organic material; it asked readers to send them descriptions of other large trees.[580]

Perhaps the following poem also affected his tender sensibilities because he had cut down so many trees himself.

> Woodman, spare that tree!
> Touch not a single bough,
> In youth it sheltered me,
> And I'll protect it now;
> 'Twas my forefather's hand

That placed it near his cot,
There, woodman, let it stand,
Thine axe shall harm it not
That old familiar tree,
Whose glory and renown
Are spread o'er land and sea,
And would'st thou hack it down,
Woodman, forbear thy stroke!
Cat not its earth-bound lies;
Oh! spare that aged oak,
Now towering to the skies!
When but an idle boy
I sought its grateful shade;
In all their gushing joy
Here, too, my sisters played.
My mother kissed me here;
My father press'd my hand—
Forgive this foolish tear;
But let that old oak stand!
My heart strings round thee cling
Close as thy bark, old friend!
Here shall the wild bird sing,
And still thy branches bend.
Old tree! the storm still brave!
And, woodman, leave the spot;
While I've a hand to save,
Thy axe shall harm it not.[581]

Before long, however, fate intervened, and Charles was put in charge of the farming operation.[582]

Chapter 37

The Struggle of the Hour

On May 18, 1860, Catherine Higgins Murray passed away. The *Western Star* notice reported that she died in Yellow Springs, which undoubtedly indicates she was being treated at the Glen Forest Water Cure facility. There is almost no information about her death, aside from the brief news report.[583] Charles Murray said her death was the "first real grief"[584] of his life. He said little more about her aside from complimenting for her bread and butter,[585] and her gentle manner of discipline in contrast to the firmness of Orson.[586] The death notice reports that her illness lasted six weeks and that there was a bone complaint. Perhaps it was cancer. We don't know and Orson never mentioned it in his writings, so far as we know.

The Glen Forest Water-Cure.

DEATHS.

—At Yellow Springs, on the 18th inst., Mrs. Maria Murray, wife of O. S. Murray, of this county.

We do know that Orson was in Buffalo four months later at a Philanthropic Convention and in New York five months later at an Infidel Convention.

"O.S. Murray them came forward," the report of the latter said, "He is a very old man with a massive head, and a length and volume of beard truly Aaronic."

It was fascinating because once again, as when Carlos died, he said he was dying and had not long to live because of consumption. He said he could not resist coming to the convention to speak in favor of the principle of infidelity.

"Resolved, That the saviors the world need are they who will save the world from the ignorance which keeps it in fear, and the fear which keeps it in ignorance—not pretenders to the supernatural or miraculous, but instructors in what is rational and real, natural and practical."[587]

In all, he read 54 reform resolutions, ending with the following, "That liberty and slavery are moral antagonisms, natural antipathies—the rights of the one being the wrongs of the other— love of the one, hatred of the other—life to the one, death to the other."[588]

The death of Catherine must've sparked a sense of renewal of his need to speak out to the world about his beliefs, his desire to make the world a better place and improve the welfare of humanity. Instead of dying, he began speaking publicly and writing.

On January 29, 1861, at the Thomas Paine celebration held at the Pike Opera House, he delivered a lengthy, bombastic attack on the political situation and the government's resistance to do anything about the Southern States that had begun seceding. He blasted the outgoing President Buchanan and Secretary of State William Seward, the latter who had made suggestions that to curtail the secessions, an Amendment to the Constitution should be passed that the Federal government could not interfere with slavery in the states where it was practiced. He wondered if Lincoln, who had not yet been inaugurated and was unable to act would take the same position because all that had so far been heard from Lincoln were words of conciliation. "While slavery exists, all the people of the Union must be slave holders," Murray said, during his harangue that continued for more than two hours.

No right to interfere with slavery in the States? But it interferes with us. It degrades labor. It inhibits speech. It suppresses intelligence. It corrupts our press. It debauches our pulpit. It makes our Constitution an iniquity. It makes the people of the North cowards and kidnappers. It makes pirates of our seamen. It makes mobocrats of our mayors, our merchants, and our manufacturers. It strikes down our senators. It assassinates our philanthropists. It murders our citizens. It carries bribery and intimidation into our legislative halls and our judicial and executive chambers. It emasculates our Websters and our Everetts; and makes traitors of our Buchanans and our Sewards. It makes misrule and anarchy.

The Constitution wisely and virtuously provides against legalizing religion. Religion enslaves — enthralls. It compels. It binds. It ties up. It puts us in fear. It keeps us in awe of arbitrary power. It educates into ignorance of nature — of natural rights and relations . . . . It is time for the people to know that their rights are not derived from Bibles and Constitutions. That Bibles and Constitutions are only the necessities of ignorance — things to be changed — to be outgrown and displaced by better things. Bibles and Constitutions are war-makers, bloodshedders, punishers, enslavers, destroyers. It is for men and women to be peacemakers, emancipators, and saviors.

So many of the ideas he had been professing for the last 25 years were embedded in this address. The struggles he was enduring also were being endured by the nation and now it was time to

294

overcome. "The struggle of the hour is between brute force and reason," he said, "between suppression and speech; between religion and righteousness; between money and humanity; between misanthropy and philanthropy; between ignorance and intelligence; between restraint and development."

Of the 68-page pamphlet that Murray published of the speech, William Lloyd Garrison who had been his nemesis for the last 20 years finally wrote something supportive:

> In the earliest and most trying period of the Anti-Slavery cause, Mr. Murray . . . was conspicuous in it, doing 'yeoman service,' both with his pen and voice. Since then, he has through various "dispensations;" but, however eccentric or divergent his course, or conflicting or startling his abstract speculations, he has always exhibited manly independence, a disposition to fearlessly to "prove all things," and a humane and loving spirit.[589]

In the next three years, Murray regularly contributed articles to *The Liberator* and to a new publication, *The New Republic*, based in Cleveland and published by radical reformer, Francis Barry. For the latter, they began listing him as a contributor. His articles to *The Liberator* concerned the war and slavery; his articles to *The New Republic* dealt with both the war and infidelity.

Murray's interest in the war first was shown in a series of articles in *The Liberator*. In one of the first, he said he had no faith in the war and because his friend Wendell Phillips had come out in support of it, he had decided to wait and see how things turned out. But the more he waited, the more discouraged he was becoming. He saw nothing good to come from the war, was worrying that the North, especially Seward, would appease the South by persuading Congress to pass an amendment to the Constitution that guaranteed the right to practice slavery in perpetuity if the Confederacy would surrender.[XLVII]

"The new Confederacy fights for freedom to take slavery out of the Union," he wrote. "The old Confederacy fights for freedom to keep slavery in the Union."

He was concerned that Lincoln might support such an agreement to end the war. As Lincoln had said, preserving the Union took precedence over ending slavery.

"It is the Union that restricts opposition to slavery in this country," Murray wrote: "It is the Union that is the guarantee against the full development here of the fearful and uncompromising hostility to slavery which pervades the world." Murray was worried because Seward had stated that John Brown, whom Murray admired, was justly hung and Murray distrusted Lincoln who he didn't view as a strong figure who would pursue a victory that ended slavery.[590] But as history has shown Murray's distrust was misplaced.

An incident for which Murray might best be remembered while in Ohio was when Wendell Phillips came to town. Prior to this, Murray had written several more letters to *The Liberator* critical of Lincoln, including criticism for offering financial incentives to those States which began gradual emancipation. In his memoir, Charles mentions mementos of that visit.

My father and Wendell Phillips were close friends. In writing to my father from Billerica, Massachusetts, under date August 15, 1859, he said: "Dear Brother: . . . You acted like yourself in that

---

[XLVII] The Amendment sometimes referred to as the Corwin Amendment was proposed by Senator Tom Corwin of Ohio, prior to the outbreak of the war as a solution to prevent it. It stated: "No amendment shall be made to the Constitution which will authorize or give to Congress the power to abolish or interfere, within any State, with the domestic institutions thereof, including that of persons held to labor or service by the laws of said State." It was signed by President Buchanan two days before leaving office and passed Congress but was never ratified.

nice sense of right which prompted you to enclose to me the contribution I made to your journal. I should have liked it full as well if you had notified me of your wish to apply it according to your own judgment, to some good purpose near yourself. But since you are willing it should go to our noble sister, 'the General,' [Harriet Tubman] as old John Brown of Osawatomie calls her, I will see that she has it, and knows from whose thoughtfulness it comes, for I must consider it your gift. I have read and reread your articles, specially the closest and most argumentative . . . Well, we don't agree, friend Murray, but I hold you in sincere regard and esteem, and whether you like it or not, must continue to consider you a much better Christian than nine-tenths of those about me, and far better perhaps than you would be willing to allow yourself to be . . . .

I possess a fine, large photograph of Mr. Phillips, framed, procured incident to his presence in Cincinnati, by my father, and a small, full-length photograph of him taken at the same time.[591]

Wendell Phillips Credit: fineartamerica.com

Phillips had been invited to speak about the war at the Pike Opera House in downtown Cincinnati.

There had been reports of possible trouble and the mayor had ordered police to stay clear of the area.[592] As a result, Phillips had been accompanied by six men: Murray; Samuel Reed, *Cincinnati Gazette* editor; Judge John Stallo; William Green; William Goodman; and John P. Foote. As he stepped on stage surrounded by his friends, there were hisses from those reported to be "liquored up,"[593] but there were also cheers. I am an abolitionist, he announced.

I have been invited to speak to you on the war—the convulsion which has divided the Union for a year and threatens, in the opinion of some, to divide it forever. No more serious subject can engage the attention of the American people, for I believe that within six months, perhaps within the coming hundred days, we, the people, are to decide what the future of these thirty-four States to be. Certainly, no question of deeper import can be presented to an American audience.

I believe that the war is no man's fault, that it is the work of neither section. [It is the] result of seventy years of struggle with one idea. It comes to us as a duty to which God lays upon this generation . . . How long will the war last? What will become of slavery? What will become of the Union? We are entering upon the great struggle which no people have ever avoided—a struggle between the few and the many—a struggle between aristocracy and democracy. The North represents a democracy, founded on industry, brains, and money; the South, an aristocracy whose right hand is negro slavery, and whose left is the ignorant white man.[594]

Suddenly, a heavy boulder was thrown from the third tier of boxes, crashing among the footlights like a cannon shot, just feet away from Phillips It was followed by a couple of rotten eggs, one of which struck him and there were yells and screams from the audience, "Down with the traitor," "Egg, the nigger Phillips," and more. Yet Phillips stood calm and silent waiting for the storm to pass.[595] Allow me one word more, he resumed.

I do not know what that fellow man meant who sent that stone, but I meant no insult to the non-slaveholding white man of the South. I sympathize with them, for they suffer from a despotism whose right hand is power and whose left hand is ignorance. If South Caroline ever sees the utmost exaltation of her masses, it will be when the stars and stripes guarantee freedom to every member of the thirty-four states. For thirty years I have been an Abolitionist, and nothing else.

Hisses drowned out Phillip's voice.

For sixteen years I have been a disunionist,[XLVIII] he resumed, the last word eliciting a volley of eggs. Nevertheless, he continued. "Whatever I may have thought of the Constitution as interpreted by the pro-slavery faction that has heretofore controlled the country, I am now the defender and supporter of the Constitution. It is to me a new instrument with guarantees for human freedom—not the nursing mother of human slavery. Whatever I may have thought of the propriety of maintaining the Union for the uses and purposes of man-sellers, I am, now that the Union promises to be the shield and protection of advancing liberty, a Union man![596]

A melee on the second balcony created increasing commotion. Cries and screams resounded. More eggs were hurled, one of which struck Murray, and there was a chorus of cries, "Lynch the Traitor, Hang the Nigger, Tar and Feather the Abolitionist," and some more profane. He struggled to continue. Rowdies rushed the stage. Fights erupted. Phillips was forced to stop. There were rumors of lynch mobs gathering and Phillips was put in disguise and hurriedly escorted out to safety. Long after he had left, the rowdies remained.[597]

In the next months, Murray continued to submit articles about his concern that Lincoln might still appease the South, notably his offer of financial considerations if they agreed to gradual emancipation and insisted that Lincoln had the power to declare emancipation. He mentioned an attempt by a group of Quakers from the Longwood Meeting in Chester County, PA, who met with

---

[XLVIII] Phillips was trying to explain that he no longer was a disunionist, that he supported the war effort to bring an end to slavery and the war. Because of the chaos that was occurring, there were some reports that he was still a disunionist.

Lincoln, requesting the President to do so.[598] This delegation met with the President on June 20,[599] and included Murray's former Vermont abolition colleague, Oliver Johnson, and noted abolitionist, Thomas Garrett, who claimed to have aided about 2,700 fugitive slaves[600] and infamously found guilty of violating the Fugitive Slave Law, which required him to pay a huge fine though unlike some others avoided jail time.

On July 17, Lincoln authorized the Confiscation Act of 1862 on July 17, 1862. It called for the seizure of land and property from Southerners who were loyal to the Confederacy as well as the emancipation of their slaves who would then be under control of the Union army.[601] In September, the bloody Battle of Antietam, one in which both sides suffered major casualties, compelled Lincoln to enact emancipation. Five days after the battle ended, Lincoln authorized the Emancipation Act of 1862, which freed all slaves in the Confederate States on January 1, 1863. However, the slaves of those border slave states that had remained neutral would remain in slavery.[602]

Two weeks prior to Lincoln's proclamation, Murray wrote an article for *The New Republic* discussing the need for better management of the war and the need to push the earlier Confiscation Act. He confided that his youngest son, Ichabod had enlisted, and that Charles and Marsena had enrolled, though Marsena now had three children and only did so reluctantly.[603]

The Emancipation Proclamation represented a victory for Murray and those who were pushing for the war to end slavery. It was with such satisfaction that he remarried: "On the 16th ult (October 16), in Chester county, Orson S. Murray, of Warren county Ohio, and Lydia P. Jacobs of the former place." Murray was 57 years old, the bride, 37. They refused to recognize any divine or legal authority. "Our promises are to ourselves and each other," they declared, "and not to others, but in ourselves and each other."[604]

Chapter 38

The Reunion of the Abolitionists

The marriage of Murray and Lydia P. Jacobs is a mystery. No one knows how long they were married, how and when they met, and why they even married. One local historian believes their marriage may have lasted only as short as a month.[605] It is not even listed in some genealogical records. One thing that is clear is that her family was among the staunchest of anti-slavery advocates. Her mother's brother, Dr. Bartholomew Fussell, was among the famed Underground Railroad conductors of the major Underground Railroad terminal in Kennett Square, Pennsylvania and a member of the radical Hicksite Quaker Longwood Meeting formed in 1853 in Kennett Square.

Dr. Fussell and his home in Kennett Square

It was the hub of a large and tightly connected Underground Railroad in southeastern Pennsylvania. Less than three miles from the Delaware border, it had a close relationship with Thomas Garrett in Wilmington, Delaware, about 10 miles away. Among its foremost conductors were John and Hannah Cox; Isaac and Dinah Mendenhall; the Barnard brothers, Simon and Eusebius; and Uncle Fussell.[606] They were part of a large Quaker network that collaborated with a smaller number of free black conductors. Recent scholarship has identified 132 known Underground Railroad agents in Chester County alone that included 82 Quakers and 31 blacks.[607]

Charles C. Burleigh, Murray's good friend when he was in Vermont and after whom Murray named son Charles Burleigh Murray, was well-known there for helping to abolitionize the community with his lectures in the 1830s.[608]

And Uncle Bartholomew may have assisted as many as 2,000 fugitive slaves, according to Underground Railroad historian Robert Smedley. His home, known as "the Pines," was one of Kennett's earliest refuges for fugitive slaves.[609]

Whatever may have happened their marriage or whether they moved to Ohio or Murray stayed for a time in Pennsylvania is not known. We do know that during this time Murray sent a series of letters to *The Liberator*, in which he questioned the efficacy and motives of the Emancipation Proclamation, criticized the conduct of the war and called for new commanders, commented on the villainy of Seward, Weed, and Greeley, and questioned why Congress had not repealed the Fugitive Slave Law. He also sent a letter praising the antislavery positions of Indiana Congressman, George Washington Julian, who had attempted to present a bill for the repeal of the Fugitive Slave Law.[610]

Then came the announcement of the Three Decades Meeting celebrating the founding of the American Anti-Slavery Society at which he was present and a founding member. He could not resist the urge to go, renew old friendships, relive the mighty moment of which he was a part. He also was wary. He had often attacked Garrison in *The Regenerator* and their falling out had lasted almost 20 years until a recent thaw had allowed for publication of his letters and articles. Equally troubling was that many of his abolitionist colleagues believed in the Christian God, which he had been attacking for nearly 20 years.

"I prepared a brief, condensed expression of sentiments, in the form of resolutions," he wrote, "was constantly on my guard against any utterance that could wound the feelings or excite the apprehensions, of my friends disagreeing with me in affairs of religious belief."[611]

The "Three Decades Meeting" was a significant event for the abolitionists. Slavery appeared to be on the brink of ending and it was time for celebration. The elaborate decorations and banners hung throughout Concert Hall illustrated this. Among them were banners inscribed with the words of Whittier and Washington, the latter expressing hope that someday slavery would be abolished. There were American flags at the rear of speakers' platform draped around a picture of John Brown and above it a banner with the phrase "Liberty and Union."[612]

The Hall was quickly filled, and much time was spent greeting and congratulating those who had come from different parts of the country. They shared a feeling of hopefulness and thanksgiving for what they anticipated would finally be the accomplishment of the great mission to which they had devoted their lives, the end of slavery.

Those who had seats on the speakers' platform were among the most notable abolitionists of the time: Garrison, Oliver Johnson, J. Miller McKim, Charles C. Burleigh, Abby Kelley Foster, Stephen S. Foster, Lucy Stone, Susan B. Anthony. Frederick Douglass, Rev. William Furness, Rev. Samuel J. May, Samuel May, Jr. (yes, two different individuals), Thomas Garrett, and others.[613]

Charles C. Burleigh

Murray did not arrive until the evening session of the first day. Prior to his arrival, letters from illustrious abolitionists unable to attend had been read by Garrison: from Arthur Tappan, the first president of the society; from Theodore and Angelina Grimke Weld, and her sister, Sarah; from John Greenleaf Whittier; from the Rev. John Rankin; and the dying Owen Lovejoy, among others. After a speech by Rev. William Furness, Garrison took the podium.

Thirty years ago, he declared, the Declaration to which you have just listened was issued by a small body assembled in this city, and the signatures of the members present were appended to the instrument. The result was, the immediate formation of the American Anti-Slavery Society, which adopted the Declaration as the basis upon which all its action should rest. Has the Society been true to its principles and sentiments? I

305

feel I can truly say that it has been faithful and uncompromising from the beginning till now; that we have not yielded one jot or tittle of any of our demands; that in all trials, in all discouragements, in the hottest persecution, we have been faithful to our cause, and to the victims whose advocates we profess to be.[614]

But John Greenleaf Whittier may have best captured the historic magnitude of the event in his letter:

I am not insensible to literary reputation. I love, perhaps too well, the praise and goodwill of my fellowmen; but I set a higher value on my name as appended to the Anti-Slavery Declaration of 1833, than on the titlepage of any book. Looking over a life marked by many errors and shortcomings, I rejoice that I have been able to maintain the pledge of that signature; and that, in the long intervening years.[615]

John Greenleaf Whittier

Of course, this was not lost on Murray and why he wanted to be there, for it was one of the most important events in his life, something he himself had been part of in the beginning and which he had fought for all his life—for many years it had taken a back seat to infidelity, vegetarianism, and hydrotherapy. Nevertheless, he was the sole representative from Vermont at the founders meeting, and the organizer of the state's antislavery society. Whittier would recall him in his 1874 essay about the 1833 organizational meeting: "Vermont sent down from her mountains Orson S. Murray, a man terribly earnest, with a zeal that bordered on fanaticism, and who was none the more genial for the mob violence to which he had been subjected."[616]

He had risked his life for the cause and it must've filled him with some pride when Garrison called for those who had been among the original signers of the Declaration of Sentiments at the organizational and who were present to rise and be recognized: Isaac Winslow, Orson S. Murray, William Lloyd Garrison, Robert Purvis, Uncle Bartholomew Fussell, Enoch Mack, James Miller McKim, Thomas Whitson, James Mott, James McCrummell, and Samuel Joseph May.[617]

J. Miller McKim

But this moment of commemoration would turn into disappointment. Murray later wrote of this. He had arrived early that evening and had been greeted cordially by Lucretia Mott who had attended the organizational meeting as an observer because women were then not allowed to be members of male antislavery societies. Then he saw his Vermont brother Oliver Johnson, who had long since become one of the nation's leading abolitionists as editor of both the *Pennsylvania Freeman* and *National Anti-Slavery Standard*, and Garrison's closest associate. Murray described the meeting as icy. It was as if, Murray wrote, he was telling me that he wished I hadn't come. Garrison who arrived shortly after was only a little more cordial. Though Garrison recently had been publishing his articles, the animosity that had built up over the years apparently remained.

The next morning when Murray expected to be given time for remarks, he handed a note to McKim, who was moderating the event that morning and asked permission to read his resolutions. He asked for 25-to-30 minutes. Unknown to Murray, however, a rule had been established to limit the day's speakers to 15 minutes. Before he spoke, time was given to Henry Ward Beecher, who had been the subject of many scathing attacks by Murray, deprecating his religion and his wealth. Murray resented that he went on so long, apparently longer than 15 minutes. Finally, when Murray was given his opportunity to speak, he was cut off at exactly 15 minutes, well before he was finished.

The official report of the meeting stated: "Orson S. Murray, of Ohio, one of the signers of the Declaration of Sentiments, occupied fifteen minutes in reading part of a series of resolutions, written by himself, upon which he said he neither asked nor deprecated the action of the meeting. No action was taken upon them."[618]

Murray did not return for the evening session when Frederick Douglass electrified the audience with his concluding remarks, talking of his private meeting with Lincoln, whom he called "Abraham the Eloquent" and described as "wise and great."

Frederick Douglass

But we are not to be saved by Abraham Lincoln, but by that power behind the throne, greater than the throne itself. You and I and all of us have this matter in hand. Men talk about saving the Union, and restoring the Union as it was. They delude themselves with the miserable idea that that old Union

309

can be brought to life again. That old Union, whose canonized bones we so quietly inurned under the shattered walls of Sumter, can never come to life again. It is dead, and you cannot put life in it . . . What business, then, have we to fight for the old Union ? We are not fighting for it. We are fighting for something incomparably better than the old Union. We are fighting for unity ; unity of idea, unity of sentiment, unity of object, unity of institutions, in which there shall be no North, no South, no East, no West, no black, no white, but a solidarity of the nation, making every slave free, and every free man a voter.[619]

The audience erupted into applause.

Murray stayed away and wrote a bitter letter to *The Liberator*, describing the hurt he felt, that while others were permitted to exceed the time limit, he was cut off:

On my way home to Vermont, from this place, thirty years ago, when I reached Bennington, the battleground where Stark met Freedom's foes, my utterance before an audience was forbidden and prevented by the servitors and conservators of slavery and colonization. At this time thirty years afterwards my utterance before an utterance in Concert Hall was prevented by the servitors and conservators of religion and politics. The former was a mob. Call the latter what you please. Both were conspiracies against speech.[620]

Surprisingly, there was scant and derogatory coverage of the event by the nation's newspapers, some northern newspapers even mocking Douglass, and characterizing Lincoln as a tool of the abolitionists.[621] But it surely was a monumental day for them, probably eclipsed only by the passage of the Thirteenth Amendment that proclaimed: "Neither slavery nor involuntary servitude, except as a punishment for crime whereof the party shall have been duly convicted, shall exist within the United States, or any place subject to their jurisdiction."

Murray never again published in *The Liberator*. He felt humiliated by the very individual who once had called him "the Clarkson of Vermont," though Garrison insisted that there had been no slight of Murray, that they were just following rules that had been established for speakers that day.[622]

Chapter 39

Grandpa Orson

On October 2, 1865, Murray married Ianthe Poore, the daughter of a prosperous farmer in Fosters Crossings, a short distance from Fruit Hills. It would be a marriage of families as Murray's son, Ichabod would marry Ianthe's younger sister, Lucy; his daughter, Rachel, Lucy's brother, William Henry; and his daughter Roselinda, William's business partner, Henry B. Kelley. His daughters' husbands were quite prosperous as they created a new method of corn drying.[623]

Murray had moved around Fruit Hills between a couple residences from 1856, to properties of Marsena, who was doing well selling potatoes. It's a bit hard to keep track. He ended up on property near the Poore family farm not far from Foster's Crossings.

Poore and Kelley's Fruit Farm, Courtesy Karen Dinsmore

Poore and Kelley's Corn Drying Factory, courtesy Karen Dinsmore

After settling into his marriage, he and Ianthe briefly became involved in a Woman's Emancipation Society, in 1873. He was listed as the President of the organizational meeting, whose principal sponsor was free-love advocate, Francis Barry, the former editor of the *New Republic* for which Murray had done some writing during the early 1860s. The Convention roster also shows Ianthe as a member. They likely took the train to get to Ravenna, the site of the convention, about 40 miles south of Cleveland.

EMANCIPATION CONVENTION.

We invite all who desire the emancipation of woman from the slavery of all institutions, laws or customs which interfere in any manner or degree with her absolute freedom in any department of life, or in any sphere of activity, to meet at Ravenna, O., on Sunday, December 7, 1873, to organize an American Woman's Emancipation Society.

Seward Mitchell, Maine.	Helen Nash, Ohio.
Parma W. Olmsted, Vt.	Orson S. Murray, Ohio.
E. H. Heywood, Mass.	Ianthe P. Murray, Ohio.
Angela T. Heywood, Mass.	Wm. A. Poor, Ohio.
Benj. R. Tucker, Mass.	L. M. R. Pool, Ohio.
Moses Hull, Mass.	A. Bailey, Ohio.
Anna M. Middlebrook, Ct.	Sarah M. Day, Ohio.
C. S. Middlebrook, Ct.	Ann B. Spink, Ohio.
Joseph Treat, N. Y.	Francis P. Sutliff, Ohio.
Austin Kent, N. Y.	Francis Barry, Ohio.
Anthony Higgins, N. J.	Addie L. Ballou, Ind.
Elvira Hull, N. J.	Sada Bailey, Ill.
Annie E. Rigby, Pa.	J. W. Evarts, Ill.
Lewis Morris, Md.	Franc P. Evarts, Ill.
Sarah L. Tibbals, Va.	J. F. Hollister, Ill.
J. Q. Henck, Va.	Jonathan Walker, Mich.
Mary H. Henck, Va.	George Roberts, Mich.
G. W. Gore, Va.	Julia H. Severance, Wis.
C. M. Overton, Ohio.	C. L. James, Wis.
Mary Overton, Ohio.	Warren Chase, Mo.
Oliver Stevens, Ohio.	J. H. Cook, Kan.
V. F. Stevens, Ohio.	Francis Rose Mackinley, Cal.
J. H. Philleo, Ohio.	Eleanor L. Lindsay, Cal.

313

Murray had always supported women's rights, printed articles by Elizabeth Cady Stanton and Sarah Grimke. Among the convention's resolutions were:

Resolved, That human rights inhere in human nature; that every human being is endowed with his or her rights by virtue of his or her individuality, and that gods and governments are alike impotent as authors or bestowers of rights.

Resolved, That rights are inalienable, and that when government attempts to abrogate or control any human right, it becomes a tyrant and usurper, a power to be resisted, a nuisance to be abated.

Resolved, That the United States government, professedly republican, and yet owing its existence to power usurped by a minority and ignoring the rights of one half of society on account of their sex, is a fraud and a conspiracy, and worthy only to be disobeyed and superseded.

Resolved, That the question of woman's freedom and equality exceeds in importance all other questions of the hour, and that only on the recognition of this principle as a basis can any other question be settled, or even intelligently discussed.

Resolved, That woman's right to freedom and equality implies her right to vote, her right to choose her own vocation, her right to dress according to her own taste or fancy, her right to love, and especially her right to the absolute and unlimited control of her maternal nature according to her own highest aspirations, her own best judgment and her own, strongest and purest attractions.[624]

Among interesting remnants from this latter-day period was a letter to Rowland T. Robinson dated November 21, 1875.[625]

To Rowland T. Robinson – if living:

One week ago, I had a visit from our good friend, John Orvis. Among my first and particular inquires, as to his knowledge of existing persons and things in Vermont, was to know if our old and excellent Brother and patron, Rowland T. Robinson, is still living. He said you were living, six months ago; and thought it would have come to his knowledge if you had since died – unless quite recently. So, I write to let you know, if living, that I am also living, and that I hold in grateful remembrance the experience I had in making your acquaintance and enjoying your society. The remembrance of those experiences of long years ago, and of your many loving kindnesses, will be cherished while I live and retain the power of memory.

It is thirty-one years, to-day, since I passed over the ground I now occupy. During this time, the changes have been great and innumerable, within your knowledge and mine. I am now in my seventieth year, quite comfortably situated on the soil, with children and grandchildren around me. Have five living children, out of nine; and nineteen living grandchildren out of twenty-one.

As in relation to material means for enjoyment in life, mine is much the situation of the one who prayed to have "neither poverty nor riches." Am seven years older than Henry Ward Beecher; have been diligent and frugal throughout life; and have never at any one time had as much money at my control as he carried home from the West but two years ago, for twelve evenings of self-display on the stage, demoralizing and debauching thousands who came stricken and taken by his rhetoric and magnetism, and for which he carried off twelve thousand dollars, to do his corrupt work with in Brooklyn.

I know not your views of Beecher; but you will, by this time, apprehend some of mine. It is fifteen years since I was constrained to think and pronounce him a heartless hypocrite and a corrupter of the public morals; and during all this time I have never been able to find the least evidence relieving me of this conviction – reversing this conclusion. In my estimation, those such as Tweed are small demoralizers compared with Beecher. He preaches, affects to teach, a "law of equivalents;" and pockets for his vile, vicious, villainous purposes five hundred dollars an hour, while he is making the moral atmosphere corrupt and contagious with his pestilential breath. Tweed steals only money. In addition to money, Beecher steals brains. "What is the chaff to the wheat?"

Imagine, Murray had not given up his hatred of Beecher, after more than thirty years.

Be your own views of this matter what they may be, you will know how to treat expressions from your old fellow worker for human welfare . . . It would be greatly gratifying to me to see you all – and others in Vermont – once more. But rail-road riding – always disagreeable to me when continued beyond a few hours – grows more so as I grow older.

I have but one sister – Harriet Dean, of West Cornwall, and some cousins – in addition to such friends as I have now spoken to and of – left in Vermont to attract me – besides the attractions of the mountains, the hills and valleys, the lakes, and views of my native State.

If alive, I hope that you will write and let me know that you have received this.

Remember me to all the living of your family, and any friends who would care to know of my welfare.

My health is excellent. You will see that my nerves are not very unsteady. I look forward to some more years and yet of life to enjoy.

Affectionately, Fraternally, Orson S. Murray

Possibly Murray's last home, no longer existing, courtesy Karen Dinsmore

So, what else was occupying Murray then, nineteen grandkids? Was he still on his vegetarian diet; he certainly had enough corn to eat, as well as oatmeal and berries, bread sure, milk, butter who knows. Charles said he sometimes still chopped wood for exercise in his later years.[626] And while he was not rich, he was relatively comfortable, and his boys also were doing well in their businesses. The tragedies of his life had some time to pass, though of course, no one ever completely recovers from them.

317

Chapter 40

Deathbed Thoughts

Ignorance the Evil — Knowledge the Remedy

Orson S. Murray.

It was not revealed whether it was a long or short illness, whether he was applying the water cure treatment or immersing himself in cold water. But tough, old Orson, whom people had called an old man for 30 years, finally succumbed to his humanity.

At his funeral, the door to his farmhouse was open, revealing his body in an ice chest. According to his wishes, he was to be cremated and there were no crematoriums yet in Ohio, so his body had to be put on ice for the four-day trip by rail to the crematorium in Lancaster, Pennsylvania.

Family and friends sat on the grass in a semi-circle in front of the farmhouse. It was a June Sunday, temperature in the low-70s, a haze of clouds occasionally letting the sun peek through. The flowing water from Governor Morrow's mill could be heard in the distance and the hillsides were green and blooming with flowers. Friends had prepared remarks, but the principal eulogy had been prepared by Murray himself. It followed the remarks of Murray's son, Charles, and was read by Herman Marckworth, a Cincinnati attorney and German immigrant.

Charles Burleigh Murray

Like his father, Charles had become a journalist, albeit more conventional, and an international authority on the pork packing business through his weekly, *Cincinnati Price Current*. He addressed the mourners:

"It may be proper to say that to conform to the view, practices and wishes of the deceased, these ceremonies cannot be conducted in the usual manner, through the ministration of a minister of the Gospel."[627]

Charles paused and looked out over the gathering.

"Perhaps no one present is unfamiliar with the convictions of Orson S. Murray with reference to the duties of life and what the termination of life, or existence, implies. His belief was that with death the individual existence completely ended."[628]

There was silence and only the coos of nature could be heard.

Charles stressed how important it was to grant his father's wishes and have him cremated though few agreed. Among the most outspoken reformers of his time, Orson Murray grew more infamous over time. One description of him from contemporary sources described him as "a tall raw-boned person with [shoulder-length] hair and beard a foot long, and with eyes of remarkable intensity that conveyed an impression of insanity that made him a terror to children."[629] Standing over six-feet tall, he was an imposing figure, and some compared his appearance to Moses in the Bible, and there was no doubt that he looked like one of the prophets or John Brown calling on the slaves to fight with him to end slavery.

Charles explained that he would accompany the body on the train that would take them eventually to the crematorium. He would return with the ashes which would be buried next to his mother, Catherine Higgins Murray, Orson's first wife. He sat and Marckworth rose to address the mourners. A successful lawyer and friend of the family, he was part of the huge wave of German immigrants who had contributed so much to the growth of Cincinnati.

"It is my honor to address you on this sad day for us all and to read the words of our friend, Orson," he said in his heavy accent, "his 'Deathbed Thoughts.' "[630]

Marckworth paused and cleared his throat. There was a slight rustle among the mourners and the hum of the mill became more apparent. He began: "On these occasions of disposition of the dead, it is the practice of Christendom to have speaking done exclusively by those who claim to be superhumanly appointed and qualified. They claim to be 'a chosen generation,' a 'royal priesthood.' On this occasion no such assumption will be tolerated."[631]

Marckworth's tone was grave.

"The speaking will be of death; deathbed thoughts of him who now lies before you, and whose thinking is now at an end. The chief efforts made by other speakers are to impress the living with fear. Fear is a demoralizing force. It comes of ignorance and underdevelopment. The inculcation of it is not worthy of thinking, reasoning beings."[632]

Marckworth hesitated and a bird called in the distance. He looked over the audience.

"The philosophy which assures me of rest and peace, includes the thought, the full abiding conviction in the perpetual motion and universal change of all things; that in the relation of things this is inevitable; that in these processes all forms have their beginnings, their periods, terms, and terminations of existence; that no form is or can be the same thing two moments of time during its existence, and never again the same existence; that this pertains to all forms - whatever have been, are, or can be."[633]

There was silence and a dark cloud eerily passed like a ghost over Fruit Hills.

He had always been a champion of the less fortunate, a part of the Underground Railroad, a defender of human rights. But he also was abrasive. And because of this, his unpopularity grew with the years, especially as he evolved into an Infidel, an atheist, a non-believer in a higher power, a deity who controlled the destiny of human life. Many of his closest abolitionist friends had lost faith in him. Nevertheless, he was well respected by those closest to him, here in Ohio, and that day they followed his eulogy with words of praise.

There were neighbors Benjamin Butterworth and Benjamin Carman; Richard Wales, the nephew of neighbor Nancy Butterworth; Christian Lotze., the proprietor of Cincinnati's first crematorium then in construction, and Valentine Nicholson.

Valentine Nicholson
Credit: Indiana Historical Society

Nicholson, who welcomed Murray to Ohio forty years earlier said that he loved Murray like a brother and had the highest respect for him even though they disagreed about belief in a divine creator.

Carman spoke of Murray's humanity and the compassion he showed when Carman's wife died.

Butterworth, who grew up with Charles referred to Orson as Father Murray and acknowledged the antagonism that he faced because of his opinions. But at the same time said his life was exemplified by politeness and kindness.[634] Lotze spoke with admiration for Murray:

His life was almost an ideal one and were all men here to live such a life there would be no need of laws and reforms. His whole being seemed taken up with the idea of doing good, and he believed one of the best ways to do good, was to dispel by persuasion the superstition that held the human race in ignorance. He had succeeded in harmonizing his life with his belief; had lived as he thought without regard to self-interest, and had succeeded in all he had undertaken . . . [635]

The *Boston Investigator*, the long-time reformist periodical whose articles were often reprinted by Murray, said:

Mr. Murray was the friend of truth, the advocate of the equal rights of men and women, and the firm and unyielding opponent of every species of tyranny over the human mind. We hardly know where to look to find, in the history of any public man for the last fifty years, a greater degree of moral courage in the maintenance of what he believed to be true, right, and just, no matter what the amount of opposition arrayed against him, than was exhibited in the life of Orson S. Murray.[636]

Orson S. Murray devoted his life to a search for truth, to a "Higher Law," a law not dictated by a higher power but that resides within us all, a law that is self-evident. "[If] it begins with making the god the 'supreme lawgiver,' he wrote, "it leaves off making man's conscience the supreme and final arbiter." [637]

His conscience, his rational powers, his search for the best ways of human living – this was his "Higher Law." Gods, governments, rules that required absolute obedience had no place in his life. He was a questioner, a gadfly, a "troublemaker" who disturbed the peace and comfort of established ways and accepted truths. For Murray, there was no such thing as an accepted truth. There was always finding a better way, an even higher law.

Chapter 41

Ashes to Ashes, Dust to Dust

A pamphlet promoting the virtues of cremation published the year of Murray's death included such nuggets of information as those below for those who thought it unthinkable:

Every grave and every tomb—and it matters not how air-tight the corpse may have been encased—in course of time exhales poisonous gases.

[For instance] Hannibal died, along with a vast number of his army, of a pestilence caused by the destruction of tombs. The death of the vandals who violated the coffin of Francis I., in the French revolution, is a similar case. The London cholera, of 1854, is believed to have had its origin in the upturning of the earth where victims of the disease in 1685 were buried; and the London Board of Health, in 1849, said cholera was especially prevalent in the vicinity of graveyards.[638]

MODERN CREMATION

SHOULD REPLACE

EARTH-BURIAL.

AN EXPOSÉ OF THE DANGERS CAUSED BY INHUMATION

AND

AN EXPLANATION OF THE SUPERIOR MERITS OF INCINERATION UPON NEW AND SCIENTIFIC PRINCIPLES.

Contributed and Compiled by Max Levy, Esq., Secretary of the San Francisco Cremation Company, under the supervision of the Board of Directors.

SAN FRANCISCO: BACON & COMPANY, BOOK AND JOB PRINTERS, Corner of Clay and Sansome Streets. 1885.

Cremation was a revolutionary idea in 1885. The crematorium where Murray's body was being taken was only the second one completed in the United States. His body arrived ahead of the party accompanying it: Charles B. Murray; Major Henry Oliver, Superintendent of the House of Refuge and Treasurer of the Cincinnati Cremation Society; C.M. Lotz, Society Attorney; and Albert Meininger, Secretary of the Society. An officer of the Lancaster Cremation society placed the corpse in the reception room The ceremony had been made public to honor the wishes of the Murray family, and 100 men and women had gathered in the auditorium awaiting them.[639]

After some conversation, the gathering was led into the crematorium. The officers of both cremation societies formed a semi-circle in front of the furnace, with the son of the deceased in the center. There was a knock at the door and the table carrying the remains was rolled in front of the furnace. It was covered with a heavy dark cloth. The cloth was removed and revealed the corpse, enveloped in a large white muslin sheet, soaked in alum water. There was a murmur then silence in the room. The door of the furnace swung open and the rosy light inside filled the room with heat. No fire was visible. Simply incandescent light thrown by the heat, akin to that of the setting sun. The iron cradle upon which lay the body was rolled into the furnace and disappeared in the light. The door closed. No noise, no fire, no burning, nothing of an unpleasant nature marred the operation. No sound at all.

After the spectators left, Charles and the cremation society officials remained. A small opening, two inches in diameter, was made by pressing a small knob in the wall, and the incineration was seen. The cradle was plainly visible, and the body lay still covered by its sheet, appearing unscathed, though a pure white color. It was resolving into its natural elements, being converted into vapor and

326

gas, and powdery ashes sifting into dust. Charles and the others departed until the next day.

At 7 a.m. the door to the furnace was opened and a small heap of ashes was visible. These were carefully removed by means of a wire brush from the bottom of the retort, or cremation chamber, and placed in a small six-by-six-inch metal case. They were found to weigh four pounds and one ounce. Some small bone fragments were among them. The work was complete. Murray was now only white dust.[640]

While he would refuse to believe it, the spirit of Orson S. Murray still sifts through the wind at Fruit Hills. You can hear it in the birds along the Little Miami Bike Trail, in the parlor of the old house where ancestors of the Butterworths spend their relaxing summer nights, and in the laughter at the Monkey Bar that now sits alongside the land where he once reflected, along the gentle river where people had dreams of a community long forgotten.

Index

Adams, John Quincy, 81
Addison County Baptist
    Association Meeting, 162
Ague (malaria), 272
Albany Liberty Party
    convention, 128
Albany Cultivator, 288
Alcohol, 74, 182, 198, 255-
    256
Allegheny Anti-Slavery
    Society, 130
Allen, Abram, 172, 194,
    211, 215
Allen, Richard, 12
Alton, 53, 86–92, 145
American Advocate for
Peace 68
American and Foreign Anti-
    Slavery Society, 131
American and Foreign Bible
    Society, 118, 162
American Anti-Slavery
    Society, 18, 34–36, 51,
    57–58, 73, 95, 97, 111,
    115, 124
    annual meetings 82, 93,
    121, 125, 129, 303-305
    Declaration of
    Sentiments, 22, 132, 305-
    306

first woman participants,
    129-131
    petition drive, 48
American Baptist Anti-
    Slavery Convention, 127-
    129
American Baptist
    convention, 132
American Colonization
    Society, 11-12, 85, 135-
    141
    Founders, 11
American Convention of
    Women, 102
American Indians, 134, 259
American Methodist
    Episcopal Zion (AMEZ),
    12
American Peace Society, 68
American pro-slavery
    atrocities, 99
Andover Seminary, 38
Angier, Aaron, 66
Animals, cruelty to, 207,
    217, 230, 231, 252-253
    domestic abuse, 219, 228
    premonitions, 282-283
Anthony, Susan B., 304
Anti-abolitionists, 34, 38,
    56-57, 87, 89, 101, 137,
    162
Antietam, 301
Anti-Slavery Bugle, 56

Antislavery lecturers
  recruited by Weld, 57-58
  "The Seventy," 83
Antislavery movement split,
  126
Antislavery / anti-slavery
  societies, 22, 32-33, 35,
  37, 44, 50, 85, 116, 117,
  126, 128
  nation's first state society
    formed in Vermont, 33
Apostle Paul, 125
Apples, 175, 196, 206, 211,
  259, 265
  seedlings, 289
Appleseed, Johnny, 176,
  286-288
Argyle, N.Y. 46, 270
Arms, broken, 245, 260
Arthur, Rev. William, 41–42,
  45, 170
Arthur, Chester, 45, 170
Ascension Rock, 157
Attitude of Free Negroes to
  Colonization, 12
Attleboro PA, 246
Auburn, N.Y., 249, 258
Ballou, Eli, 147
Baltimore Sun, 155
Baptist Conventions,
  Anti-Slavery, 121, 127,
  142, 163
  American Baptist, 132
  State Baptist, 143
Baptist Church, 6, 10, 25,
  29, 41, 43, 61, 66, 85,
  123-124, 128, 135, 167

Bottskill, 45, 61, 85
Brandon, 43
Charlotte, 168
Dresden, 25
Freewill Baptists, 10
Murray: sever ties with
  pro-slavery Baptists, 129
Orwell, 6, 25, 66, 147
  Orson loss of support
  for the *Telegraph*, 162
Shoreham, 66

Baptist General Tract
  Society, 47
Baptist newspapers, 128
Baptist Register, 128
Baptists, 167
  and women, 123
  antislavery convention,
  129-131
Bascom, Roselinda, Orson's
  mother, 5
Bascom, Elisha, Orson's
  uncle, 33
Barry, Francis, 295-313
Bateman, Jacob, 211
Bateman, Warner M., 195
Bates, Joseph, 150
Beecher, Austin, 110, 115
Beecher, Henry Ward, 308,
  315-316
Beecher, Lyman, 44, 55
Beer's History, 217
Bennington VT, 13, 16, 22,
  35, 155, 310

Bible,
    American and Foreign
        Bible Society is neutral
        re slavery, 118
    and slavery, 278-280
    Miller,
        using bible to predict
            2nd Coming, 24-26, 28
        knowledge of bible,
            148
        obsession w/bible, 60
        sales of bibles, 150
    Murray,
        Antislavery or Pro-
            Slavery, 250, 277-281
        bible not divine work,
            161, 166
        would not swear on
            bible, 236, 242
        errors in, 251
        hinders human
            progress, 251
        promotes war, 294
        southern clergy claim
            bible is pro-slavery, 84
    Women's rights and the
        bible, 122-125
Billerica MA, 296
Birney, James, 13, 50, 54,
    80, 83, 96-97, 126-127
Blanchard, Jonathan, 58
blast furnaces, 6, 76
Borton, Elizabeth, 172
Boston Daily Advocate, 135
Boston Investigator, 323

Boston Mercantile Journal,
    46
Boston Peace Society, 72
Brainerd, Laurence, 115
Braintree MA, 161
Brandon VT, 6, 20, 42, 43,
    68, 72-73, 76-77, 82, 98,
    110, 114, 118, 138, 140,
    159, 163, 167-169, 250
Brandon Anti-Slavery
    Society, 76
Brandon Congregational
    Church, 72, 138
Bread, 94
    bread making, 182-184
Broadway Tabernacle, 95,
    97
Brooke brothers, 211
Brooke, Abram, 172, 181,
    185, 195, 214, 219
    description of, 193
    rejection of money, 193-
        194
    slave rescue, 211
Brooklyn, 175–178, 241
Brown, Rev. George, 137,
    140
Brown, John, 91, 296, 297,
    304, 320
Brown, William Wells, 275
Buffalo N.Y., 184, 282, 293
Burleigh, Charles C., 58, 98,
    100, 131, 155, 167, 303,
    304–305, 311
Burleigh, William H., 180
Burned-Over District, 60

Butterworths, 230
  séance, 264-266
  Underground Railroad,
    195, 212-215
Butterworth, Benjamin,
  322-323
Butterworth, Henry T, 192,
  210
Butterworth, Nancy, 212
Butterworth, Rachel, death,
  283
Butterworth, William, 195,
  201, 204, 210, 245
Caesar's Creek, 214
California Gold Rush, 259
Campbell, William, 88
Canada, 9, 26
  fugitive slaves, 105, 107–
    110, 216
  Patriot War. 69-70, 107
Canterbury CT, 120
Capron, E.W., 249-250, 254,
  258, 262, 265
Carman, Benjamin, 322
Carmine Presbyterian
  Church, 130
Carroll, Robert, 214
Castleton, 18, 35
  seminary, 10
Champlain Canal, 98
Chaplin, William L., 131
Cheese, resumed eating,
  256-257
Chester County, PA, 172,
  300, 301
Chestertown, N.Y., 140–141

Cheyne, Robert, 205, 226,
  243, 248-255
Chittenden County VT Anti-
  Slavery Society, 110, 115
Christ, 7, 63, 71, 72, 79,
  129, 228, 258
  Miller predicts His Second
    Coming, 153
  Murray scorns Christian
    hypocrisy, 198,
    Second Coming, 7-8,
    24-28, 66, 147-148,
    150-151
  Murray's thoughts on
    Second Coming, 65-67
Christian apologists of
  slavery, 141
Christian Reflector, 128
Christianity, 8
  Garrison, slavery
    inconsistent with
    Christianity, 63
  Murray, hypocrisy of
    Colonization minister
    killing Africans, 137-140
  Murray
    debate with Rankin re
      Christianity sanctions
      slavery, 277-281
    disbelief in divinity of
      Jesus Christ, 254
Christians, hypocrisy re
  violence & warfare, 33,
  68, 72,
  no union w/slavery, 140,

143
Churches
  come-outer, 85
  Murray battles with the
    Church, 134–146
Cincinnati,
  Anti-Slavery Convention
    1855, 275-280
  Lane Debates, 50
  Lane Rebels, 34, 55-56
  UGRR, route from, 195,
    211
Cincinnati Cremation
  Society, 326
Cincinnati *Price Current*,
  320
Circuit riders, 8, 17
Clay, Senator Henry, 11
Clerics, slaveholding, 63,
  140
Clinton County, OH, UGRR
  215–216
Coddington, David, 213–14
Coffee, 182, 198, 231, 255
Colver, Nathaniel, 45, 47,
  58, 61, 85, 128, 145
Comet, 156–157
Community Movement,
  181-182, 208, 210
  Fruit Hills, 187, 196-197,
    201, 204, 207
    Expense to Murrays,
      209
    Members, 205-206
  Prairie Home, 181, 182,
    195-196, 205
    description of, 184-185

Conant, John, 42-43, 76-77,
  143, 250
Conant Stove, 77
Concert Hall, Philadelphia,
  304, 310
Concord NH, 38
Confiscation Act, 301
Confucius, 223
Congress
  power to limit abolish
    slavery, 96
    Gag Rule, 48, 81, 82
    VT Assembly votes that
      Congress should have
      power to abolish
      slavery, 80
Connecticut, 5, 28, 120
Constitution, U.S., 48-51,
  96, 101, 132, 295, 300
Consumption, see
  Tuberculosis,
  Carlos, 240-241
  Orson, 293
Cooper, Griffith, 190, 196
Corliss, Hiram, 85
Corn, 237, 312
Cornish, Samuel, 58
Corwin, Robert G., UGRR,
  216
Corwin, Senator Thomas,
  236, 296
Cox, Hannah, 303
Cremation, 325-326
crematorium, 319, 320,
  322, 326
Cross, John, 58
Cross, Whitney, 60

Culver, Erastus, 45-47, 60, 62

Curtis, Harvey, 72, 138-139

Dakin, George, 215

Dakin, Perry, 215

Danville VT, 161–62, 168

Davis, Andrew, 213

Davis, Isaac, 211

Davis, Joel P., 206, UGRR, 210-212

debts, 168

Declaration of Independence, 33, 74, 127

Denison, Charles W., 131

Dickens, 259

Douglass, 315

Douglass, Frederick, 304, 309–10

Dow, Lorenzo, 7, 54, 250

Dresden, N.Y., 25

Dresser, Amos, 34, 58

Dugdale, Sara, 172, 212

Dunleavy, A.H., 218

Dyer, Benjamin W., 161-164

Emancipated slaves, 58, 61, 83, 84

Emancipation Proclamation, 301, 303

Erie Canal, 184, 197

Farr, Franklin, 211

Female Anti-Slavery Society, 38, 101, 124-125

Ferrisburgh VT, 78, 166

Ferrisburgh Anti-Slavery Society, 81

Finney, Charles, 7, 43, 54, 60

First Great Awakening, 25

Fisher, William, 6

Foods, stimulating, 182, 221, 232, 257, 258 uncooked, 182

Foote, John P., 298

Fort Ticonderoga, 5

Foster, Abby Kelley, 100, 131, 304

Foster, Stephen S., 304

Fosters Crossings, 195

Foster's Crossings toll bridge, 213, 214

Fox, George, 250

Free paper, 187, 190, 193, 209, 217, 225

Freewill Baptist Church, 10

Friend of Man, 63, 108, 127, 136

Fruit Hills Community, See Community

Fugitive Slave Law, 81, 114, 216, 261, 301, 303

Fugitive slave missionary, See Hiram Wilson

Fugitive slaves, 22, 45, 51, 78, 105-116, 195, 210-211, 213, 215-216, 276, 301, 303

Furness, William, 304–305

Fussell, Dr. Bartholomew, 20, 172, 302-303, 307

Fussell, Edwin, 172

Gag Rule, see Congress

Galusha, Elon, 129, 151
Gardiner, Charles W., 131
Garrett, Thomas, 301, 302, 304
Garrison, William Lloyd, 11, 16, 17, 18, 19, 78
AAS organizational meeting, 20
anti-Colonization, 13-14
attacked by mob, 39-40
battles clerics 63, 126
Decades meeting, 303-305, 307
invites Thompson, 34
Pennsylvania Hall, 101-103
praises Murray, 32
opposes political action. 127-129, 132
supports female participation in abolition mvt, 129-131
Genesee Valley, 290
Ghosts, 249. 263
Glen Forest Water Cure facility, 292
God
Murray disbelief, 161, 166, 224, 251, 254, 293
Goodell, William, 20, 56, 60, 127
Goodman, William, 298
Graham, Sylvester, 10, 182, 221
Grant, Elder William, 61

Granville VT, 30, 32, 34
Granville, N.Y., 93
Greeley, Horace, 180, 205, 303
Green Mountain Gem, 234
Green Plain, 172, 212
Green, Beriah, 20, 58, 94
Green, Shadrach, 84
Green, William, 298
Greene County, OH, UGRR, 211, 212, 216
Gregory, Joseph, 206. 208, 216
Grimke, Angelina, 58, 83, 100, 101, 305
Grimke, Sarah, 83, 305, 314
Guilford, CT, 5
Hale, Ezekiel, 151
Halley's Comet, 156
Hamilton College, 77
Hancock VT, 30, 32, 34
Hannibal, 325
Harrington, Judge Theophilus, Clarendon, Vermont Supreme Court Judge, 108
Hartland VT, 31
Harveysburg, OH, 172, 181, 192, 194
UGRR, 211–15
Hayden, Judge Chester, 37
Hemenway's Gazetteer, 77
Henson, Josiah, 70
Higher Law, 280, 323-324
Himes, Joshua, 149-151, 157-158, 187

Holcomb, 73–76, 110–12, 113, 115, 122, 167
editor, *Voice of Freedom*, 175
Hurford, Aquila, 231
Hurford, John, 206, 231
Hurlbut, Pastor, 165
Hutchinson, Judge, 31
Infidel Convention, 293
Infidelity, 139, 210, 224, 250, 251, 253, 275, 293
Murray denies praying during near-death experience, 210
Jackson, Francis, VP of AAS, 130
Jacobs, Lydia P., 301-302
Johnson, Oliver, 16, 56, 78, 108, 124, 129, 301, 304, 308
Johnson, Simeon, 212
Jones, Henry, 26, 150
Julian, George Washington, 303
Kelley, Henry B., 312
Kelley's Corn Drying Factory, 313
Kelley's Fruit Farm, 312
Kennett Square, 302-303
Key, Francis Scott, 11
Kimmey, Edgar, 103
Kingston VT, 30
Kirk, Edward, 151
Knapp, Chauncey, 109, 115
Knapp, Elder Jacob, 150-151

Ladies Anti-Slavery Fair in Boston, 81
Lake Champlain, 5, 10, 114
Lake Erie, 188, 191, 197, 204, 282, 283
Lebanon, OH, 211, 216, 218
Lemmon fugitive slaves, 45
Lemmon, Jonathan, *45*
Lewis, C.D., 206, 208-209, 271
Liberator, The 11, 13, 14, 16, 32, 57, 127, 132, 145, 172, 250
Murray letters, 295, 296, 303, 310, 311
Liberator wagon, 173, 174, 194, 211
Liberia, 11, 15, 137, 139–40
Liberty Party, 127, 131, 166
Lincoln, President, 293, 294, 296, 300, 301, 309, 310
Little Miami Railroad, 204-205
Little Miami River, 203, 204, 270, 285
Longwood Meeting, 300, 302
Lotze, Christian, 322, 323
Lovejoy, Owen, 91, 305
Lovejoy, Elijah, 51–53, 86–92, 145
shot that killed rioter, 91
Low Hampton, N.Y., 24
Lybrand, Jacob, 225
MacDonald, A.J., 184, 193, 205

Madison County IL Anti-Slavery Society, 87
Manhattan (NYC), 177–178
Manifestations, 47, 258, 259, 264, 266, 267, 281, 284
Marckworth, 319–321
Marshall, Chief Justice John, 11
Massachusetts Abolition Society, 126
May, Samuel J, 19–20, 22, 36, 56, 304, 307
May Jr, Samuel, 304
Mcintosh, 52, 53
McKim, James Miller, 20, 58, 304, 307
Mendenhall, Dinah, 303
Middlebury Argus, 18
Miller, Colonel Jonathan P., 37, 115
Miller, William, 7, 24–26, 28, 60, 62, 67, 148, 150 152-153, 165, 189
  2nd Coming Theory, 25-26, 60-62
  43 Baptist clerics support Miller, 29
  Angier's response to Miller, 66
  description of the coming in 1843, 155
  knowledge of bible, 148
  lecture, Bennington, 155
  obsession with bible, 60
  Miller revival, 152-153
  sales, bibles & Miller, 150
  the day of the failed 2nd Coming, 153-159
  Murray's opinion of Miller in 1837, 65
  Murray: re the failure of 2nd Coming, 158-159
  Women kissing him, 153
Mob violence, 17, 18, 30, 31, 35, 44-46, 50-53, 56-58
  Alton, 86-92
  Garrison near lynching 38-39
  Noyes Academy riot, 35
  Pennsylvania Hall riot, 101-102
  Phillips riot, 298-300
Monkey Bar, 214, 327
Monroe, James, 11
Montpelier VT, 16, 36, 44, 66, 148, 175
Moriah, N.Y., 61, 245
Mormonism, 7
Morris, Thomas, 100
Morrow, Jeremiah, 204–205, 226
  Obit, 268
Morrow, Josiah, 236, 356, 370
Morrow, OH, 204, 205, 215
Mott, Lucretia, 20, 100, 101, 102, 132, 307
Mott, Lydia, 221
Mowry, William H., 85
Murray, Asahel, 43

Murray, Carlos Orson, 10, 98, 219, 228-230, 232-235, 240
  burial, 242
  death, 241-249
  health, 232, 240
  spirit speaks from the dead, 264-267
  desire to speak to Carlos, 254, 256, 258, 271, 281, 283, 293

Murray, Catherine Lucretia, 120

Murray, Catherine "Maria" Higgins, 10, 180, 184, 242, 251, 265, 281, 283
  re: atheism, 223

Murray, Charles B., 178, 184, 205, 219, 276, 285, 289, 291, 292, 296, 301, 303, 309, 319-320, 326
  grief at death of mother, 292
  in farm business with father, 285

Murray, David, brother, 76
  printer, *Voice of Freedom*, 177

Murray, Eber, 6, 25

Murray, Harriet, 117-118, 121

Murray, Ichabod, 184, 301, 312

Murray, Jonathan, 5, 219-220

Murray, Marsena, 10, 117, 219, 228, 240, 256, 266, 267, 274, 284, 288, 301, 312
  Sweet Potato Murray, 292

Murray, Orson S.
  atheism, 210, 223–227, 251, 294
  attacks Garrison, 223, 310
  court appearance, 236-240
  death, 319
  denounced, 18, 19, 135
  courage 30-33
  diet, 10, 164, 193, 208, 232, 240, 255, 257, 271-272
  disagreement with peace societies, 68, 69, 71
  disfellowshipped, 145
  distrust of Lincoln, 296, 300
  evangelical roots, 6, 43
  fasting, 272
  favorite meal, 94
  illness, 271-273
  lecturer, New England A-S Society, 42
  long hair and beard, 179-180
  loss of religious faith, 141
  marries Ianthe Poore, 312
  marries Lydia Jacobs, 301-302

obit, 323
obstinacy, 135
proficient with ax, 6
rail travel, 316
thoughts on spirits, 285
Underground Railroad,
105-116
Murray, Rachel, 188, 312
Murray, Roselinda,
daughter, 191, 312
Mysterious Spiritual
Manifestations, Noises,
Knockings, 151, 258-259,
264, 266-267, 281, 284
Nashville TN, 34
Nat Turner, 11, 82, 119
National Anti-Slavery
Standard, 110, 172, 308
Negro pew, 128
Nelson, David, 51
Nelson, Robert, 246
Neshobe River, 43
New Brighton PA, 192
New England Anti-Slavery
Convention, 49, 133, 135
New England Anti-Slavery
Society, 14, 17, 42, 124
New England Non-
Resistance Society, 71
New Hampshire, 5, 35, 38,
56, 120, 152, 252
New Republic, 295, 301,
313
New Testament, 28, 68,
122, 278

New York Baptist Register,
144
New York City, 19, 45, 57–
58, 95, 126-127, 175-177,
182, 252
New York City Anti-Slavery
Society, 126
New York Evening Post, 137
New York Observer, 71
New York State Anti-Slavery
Society, 37, 111
New York Tribune, 179, 205,
241, 258, 262
Newport NH, 5
Nichols, Rebecca, 172
Nicholson, Valentine, 172,
181, 192-193, 203, 212,
264, 267, 322
autobiography, 185
Underground Railroad,
195, 215
Nickerson, Artemas, 211
Non-resistance, 71–72, 126,
133, 134, 138, 161
Non-Resistance Society, 71
North Star, 106, 110, 195,
210
Noyes Academy, 35, 120
Oakland OH, 171–72, 181,
185, 192
UGRR, 211, 215
Oberlin OH, 56, 111
Observer, Alton, 86-89
Ohio jails and law
enforcement, 280
Ohio River, 50, 90, 192, 275

Old Testament, 122, 160,
278-279
Oneida Institute, 20
Orvis, John, 78, 166, 315
Orwell, 5–6, 23, 42, 99, 182
Osborn, William, 212
Paintersville, OH
UGRR, 211-212
Petersen pamphlet, 269-
271
Passumpsic VT, 161
Patriot War, 70, 107
Peacham VT, 16
Peck, John, 145
Pendleton, Indiana, 172
Pennsylvania Anti-Slavery
Society, 99
Pennsylvania Freeman, 99,
308
Pennsylvania Hall, 99-104
Peterboro, 38
Peterson, 269-271
Phelps, Amos, 131
Phelps, Elnathan, 25
Philadelphia, 12, 14, 18, 19–
20, 99–100, 103, 156,
269
Phillips, Wendell, 96, 295-
300
Pierce, James, 241
Pike Opera House, 293, 298
Pinckney Resolutions, 49
Pinckney, Henry, 48
Pittsburgh PA, 52, 190-192
Pittsburgh and Allegheny
Anti-Slavery Society, 130
Pittsford Iron Works, 76

Pittsford VT, 117
Plattsburgh N.Y., 25
Poore, William Henry, 312
Poore and Kelley's Fruit
Farm, 312
Poore family, 312
potatoes, 6, 196, 232, 289,
292–93
sweet, 288
planting, 263
selling, 278, 317
Potatoes, Neshannock, 288
Potts, John, UGRR, 197
Pratt, Henry, 182
President Buchanan, 293-
294
President Chester Arthur,
41, 45
President Taylor, 258-259
Princeton Theological
School, 51
Prindle, Cyrus, 115
Pro-slavery, 47, 99, 125-
126, 136, 144, 213, 277,
300
Pro-slavery editors, 136-137
Pro-Slavery in Church and
State, 47
Prosser, Gabriel, 11, 83
Prudence Crandall, 120
Punishment, capital, 134
Purvis, Robert, 20, 307
Pusey, Pennock, 206, 243
Quakers, 78, 184, 194, 216,
303
Quebec, 26
Quincy IL, 89

Randolph, 30
Rankin, Rev. John, 60, 275–280, 305
Rappings, see Manifestations
Ravenna, OH, 313
Ray, Charles, 137
Reddington, David, 244–245
Reed, Samuel, 298
Reformers, 7–8, 100, 171, 181, 269
Regenerator Extra of 1845 195-201
Regenerator Extra of 1852 269-271
Regenerator's subscribers, 93, 160, 169, 178, 179
  delinquent, 93, 169, 217, 225
  List, 178
  soliciting, 161
  UGRR 215
Religious newspapers, 41, 128, 134, 143
Revivals, 7, 43, 60–61, 67, 148
Rhode Island, 56, 130
Richmond Whig, 81, 136
rights
Rioters, see Mob Violence
Ripley OH, 275
Ritner, Governor Joseph, 103
Robert Fulton steamer, 187, 190

Robinson, Marius,56
Robinson, Rowland T., 69, 78, 81, 108, 122, 131, 166-167, 315
  Rokeby home, 108-109
  UGRR, decline of
    activity after 1850, 78
Rochester OH, 215
Rochester VT, 30, 32, 35
Rollings, G. W., 206
Roselinda Bascom, 5
Royal Weller, 91
Rupert VT, 23, 32
Rutland VT, 18, 35
Rutland Herald, 14
Rutland Weekly, 156
Sabin, Alvah, 115
Salt, 182, 183, 198, 208, 201, 210, 255, 257
Sandusky, 184, 187–88, 198, 204
  UGRR, 216
Saratoga Springs, 156
Scotland, 193, 206, 248
Scott, Orange, 84, 96
Scripture, 9, 28, 65, 74–76, 119, 120, 124, 125, 149, 160, 166, 223
seances, 266
Seaver, E., 246
Second Great Awakening, 60
Seeds, 286-289
Seventh Day Adventists, 158, 187
Seward, William, 293–96, 303

Sexual abstinence, 20, 182
Sexton, Pliny, 190, 196
Shaving, 179–180
Shew, Dr. Joel, 221-222, 240
    Water Cure Treatment, 222
Shipwreck, 188-190, 195,
    Denies praying, 210
Shooting Star Spectacle, 26
    Olmstead, 27
Shoreham Academy, 10
Siebert, Wilbur, 114, 204, 212–213, 215–16
Simonds, 245–46, 251-252, 270
Simonds property, 284
Simonds, Anna, 251
Simonds, Thomas, 245
Slaughterhouses, 230
Slave escaping, 194
Slave Patrols, 82
Slave population, 15, 83
Slave trade, 32, 80, 97
    domestic, 21
    international, 12, 15
Slavecatchers / Slave-hunters, 81, 114, 216
Slavery
    prevent discussion of, 49, 51, 63
    sanction of, 63, 69, 71, 76, 276-278
Slaves, 96,
    Auction of, 21
    Emancipated, 83-84
    Law to prevent transit

    by owners in free states
    Obligation to free, 20
    Reluctance to free, 12
    Teach to read, 119
Smedley, Robert, 303
Smith, Gerrit, 13, 37–38, 94–97, 126, 127
Smith, Herbert R., 270
Smith, Joseph, 7
Snow, Samuel, 151
Society for Universal Inquiry and Reform, 181
Socrates, 223, 277
Soffe, Henry, 225
Soil, 184, 208, 290
Soil, the, 197, 202, 203, 209, 217, 220, 229, 230
Southard, Nathaniel, 151
Spear, Jacob, 164
Spirits, spiritual world, see Manifestations
Sprague, Nathan T., 43
Springboro, UGRR, 197, 214, 218
Springfield OH, 207
Springville N.Y. 190
St. Lawrence Valley, 29
St. Louis Observer, 51
Stallo, Judge John, 302
Stanton, Elizabeth Cady, 56, 314
Stanton, Henry B., 56-58, 95, 97, 126
Starksboro VT, 165
    antislavery society, 48
Starkweather, John, 151

Stars, see shooting star
States
    slaveholding, 33, 163
steamboats, 19, 130, 175,
    184, 188, 190, 192
Stewart, Alvan, 37, 96–97,
    100, 127
Stewart's argument for
    Congress, 96
Stone, Lucy, 304
Storrs, George, 151
Stowe, Harriet Beecher, 44
Stuart, Charles, 48. 128, 136
Sudbury VT, 93
Sumner, H.A., 120–21, 132
Supreme Court, 81, (VT),
    108
Swallow, The, 94, 98
Syracuse, N.Y., 258
Tappan, Arthur, 13, 34, 54-
    55, 97, 132, 305
Tappan, Lewis, 13, 20, 37,
    57, 58, 97, 126, 127, 128,
    131
Taylor, President Zachary,
    259
Temperance, 8, 10, 50, 73,
    122, 150–51, 198
    Safford's Tavern, 94
Tennessee, 112, 288
Texas, 83, 97
*The Cultivato*r, 288
Thirteenth Amendment,
    310
Thomas Paine celebration,
    293
Thomas, David, 205

Thompson, George, 34, 38–
    39, 49–50, 69, 83, 171
Thompson, H.D., 211
Thorburn, Robert T., 205
Three Decades Meeting,
    303-304
Tiffin, OH, 184
Todd's Fork, 215
Tracy, Ebenezer Carter, 31-
    32, 135-137
Tracy, Joseph, 135
Trains, see Rail travel, 19,
    172, 192, 204, 205
    Transporting mail, 216,
    319
Trees, 6, 251, 261, 286, 52,
    289-290
290
    large, 293–94
    loved, 293
    seedling, 291–92
Tremont Temple, 45
Troy, N.Y., 57, 98, 171
Tuberculosis,
    Carlos, 240-241
    Orson, 293
Tubers, 288
Tubman, Harriet, 297
Turner Welch, 216
UGRR. *See* Underground
    Railroad.
Ultraism, 60, 65, 69, 141-
    142
Underground Railroad
    (UGRR), 47, 55, 60, 70,
    78, 105-116, 137, 172,

193, 194, 210-216, 302-303

Ullery, Jacob,108

Underground Railroad in Ohio, 210-216

Underground Railroad in Vermont, 105-116

Union Village NY, 45, 60, 85, 170

Universalist Watchmen, 66, 147

Upper Canada, 111

Urner, Benjamin, 194

Utica, N.Y., 36-38, 44, 94

Utica Anti-Slavery Society, 37

Utica Standard, 38

Van Zandt, John, UGRR, 211

VBJ (Vermont Baptist Journal), 144–45, 162

Vegetarianism, 10, See, Orson S. Murray, diet

Vermont Anti-Slavery Baptist conventions, 145

Vermont Antislavery Society, 36, 73, 82, 141, 166

Vermont Anti-Slavery Society, 73, 82, 141, 167

Vermont Baptist Anti-Slavery convention, 142

Vermont Baptist Anti-Slavery Society, 163

Vermont blast furnace, 6, 76

Vermont Chronicle, 30, 32, 75, 118, 135, 136, 138, 144

Vermont delegates to Amn Anti-Slavery meeting, 115

Vermont General Assembly decree on slavery, 80

Vermont Journal, 275

Vermont Mercury, 156

Vermont Observer, 163, 210

Vermont Peace Society, 69

Vermont Religious Observer, 163

Vermont State Anti-Slavery Society's Executive Committee, 115

Harrington, Judge Theophilus, Clarendon, Vermont Supreme Court Judge, 108

Vindicator, Baptist, 128,

Virginia, 11, 18, **45**, 83, 119

Virginia Governor McDuffie, 81

Wales family, 212, UGRR, 213

Wales, Richard, 322

Ward, Henry Dana, 151

Warfare, 140, 251, 278

Water Cure Treatment, 221-222, 240-241

Water Cure Journal, 222

Waterbury VT 142

Watermelons, 203, 286

Wattles, John, 171, 172, 181, 206
poetic escription of Prairie Home, 186
Way, Robert, 213
Waynesville, OH, 175
Welch, Turner, UGRR, 213
Weld, Angelina Grimke 58, 83, 100-101, 305, 314
Weld, Theodore, 50, 54–58, 101, 305
Weld's objectives, 55
Weld training session, 57-58
Lecturers there, 58
Welsh, Amos, UGRR, 172
Wesley, John, 94
West Brookfield VT, 164
West Cornwall VT, 316
West Indies, 9
West Liberty OH, 184, 196
Western Star newspaper in Lebanon, 296
Whipple, George, 56
Whipple, S., 218–219
White, James, 151
White, John, 207, 221
Whitney, Joseph, 213
Whitney, William, 215
Whitson, Thomas, 307
Whittier, John Greenleaf, 18-20, 100, 103, 152, 304-307

describes Murray, 307
William Wells Brown, 275
Williamstown VT, 161
Williston, VT, 164–65
Wilmington DE, 302
Wilson strawberries, 289
Wilson, Hiram, 56, 110-112
Windsor VT, 30, 31–32, 112, 135
Winslow, Isaac, 307
Winthrop Gilman, 89-91
Wisconsin Territory, 225
Woman's Emancipation Society, 313
Women, 73, 78, 153, 166, 308, 313
Rights 122–26, 130–32, Convention of, 102
Woodstock, VT, 30–32, 267
Worcester MA, 128
Working Farmer, 286
World Anti-Slavery Convention, London, 127-128
Wright, Elizur, 20, 58
Wright, Henry C., 58
Yaeger, Samuel, 103
Yale College, 27
Yellow Springs OH, 292
Zanesville OH, 56
Zion's Watchman, 128
Zion's Watchtower, 128

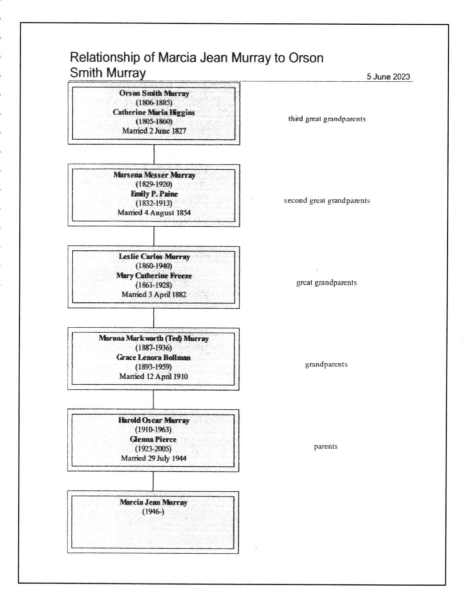

Relationship of Marcia Jean Murray to Orson Smith Murray

5 June 2023

Orson Smith Murray
(1806-1885)
Catherine Maria Higgins
(1805-1860)
Married 2 June 1827

third great grandparents

Marsena Messer Murray
(1829-1920)
Emily P. Paine
(1832-1913)
Married 4 August 1854

second great grandparents

Leslie Carlos Murray
(1860-1940)
Mary Catherine Freeze
(1861-1928)
Married 3 April 1882

great grandparents

Maruna Markworth (Ted) Murray
(1887-1936)
Grace Lenora Bollman
(1893-1959)
Married 12 April 1910

grandparents

Harold Oscar Murray
(1910-1963)
Glenna Pierce
(1923-2005)
Married 29 July 1944

parents

Marcia Jean Murray
(1946-)

Genealogy Compiled by Marcia Jean Murray Holstrum

Father Orson Smith MURRAY

Birth	23 Sep 1806	Orwell, Addison, Vermont
Census	1830	Shoreham, Addison County, Vermont
Census	1850	Hamilton Township, Warren County, Ohio
Census	1860	Post Office 20 Mile Stand, Deerfield, Warren County, Ohio
Death	14 Jun 1885	Warren Co. Ohio
Description	1886	Rutland County, Vermont
Burial		Sycamore Grave-Yard, Twenty-Mile Stand, Warren County, Ohio
Description		Portraits of American Abolitionists
Occupation		
Occupation		
Misc		
Death		
Marriage	2 Jun 1827	
Father	Jonathan MURRAY (1781-1846)	
Mother	Roselinda BASCOM (1784-1868)	
Other spouse	Thurza Ianthe POORE (1834-)	
Marriage	8 Oct 1865	
Other spouse	Lydia P. JACOBS (-)	
Marriage	Nov 1862	Chester County, Pennsylvania

Mother Catherine Maria HIGGINS

Birth	3 Jun 1805	Benson, Rutland County, Vermont
Death	18 May 1860	Warren Co. Ohio
Father	Ichabod HIGGINS (1771-1844)	
Mother	Catherine NOBLE (1835)	

Children

F Betsy MURRAY

Birth	29 Oct 1826	Rutland County, Vermont
Death	20 Jan 1833	Rutland County, Vermont

M Carlos Orson MURRAY[18]

Birth	2 Mar 1828	Vermont
Death	19 Apr 1849	

M Marsena Messer MURRAY

Birth	12 Aug 1829	Orwell, Vermont
Census	1860	Post Office: Fosters Crossings, Hamilton, Warren County, Ohio
Residence	1890-91	Chattanooga, Hamilton Co., Tennessee
Death	10 Sep 1920	Chattanooga, Hamilton Co., Tennessee
Burial	11 Sep 1920	Forest Hills Cemetery, Hamilton Co., Tennessee
Will	13 Sep 1920	Hamilton County, Tennessee
Spouse	Emma ST. GEORGE (-1895)	
Spouse	Carrie E. LITTLE (1845-)	
Marriage	25 Nov 1896	
Spouse	Emily P. PAINE (1832-1913)	
Marriage	4 Aug 1854	Randolph, Vermont

F Ruth MURRAY

Birth	6 Apr 1831	
Death	19 Feb 1832	

F Harriet Maria MURRAY[18]

Birth	9 Jul 1833	Vermont
Death	13 Aug 1839	Brandon, Rutland Co., Vermont

Father Orson Smith MURRAY	
Mother Catherine Maria HIGGINS	
Children	

	Harriet Maria MURRAY (continued)	
	Burial	The Old One (Cemetery), Brandon, Rutland Co., Vermont

F	Catherine Lucretia MURRAY[18]	
	Birth	14 Nov 1835 Vermont
	Death	23 Jan 1840
	Burial	The Old One (Cemetery), Brandon, Rutland Co., Vermont[19]

M	Charles Burleigh MURRAY	
	Birth	10 Jun 1837 Brandon, Rutland Co., Vermont
	Death	5 Mar 1918 Cincinnati, Hamilton Co., Ohio
	Spouse	Sallie M. POWELL (-)

F	Rachel Robinson MURRAY	
	Birth	3 May 1839 Vermont
	Death	27 Jan 1916
	Burial	aft 27 Jan 1916 Union Cemetery, Warren County, Ohio
	Spouse	William H. POORE (-)
	Marriage	

F	Rosalinda Bascom MURRAY	
	Birth	17 Dec 1840 Vermont
	Burial	1883 Union Cemetery, Warren County, Ohio
	Death	30 Mar 1883
	Spouse	I. N. SHORT (-)
	Marriage	
	Spouse	Henry B. KELLEY (1844-)
	Marriage	1867

M	Ichabod MURRAY	
	Birth	1844 Vermont
	Death	5 Nov 1921 Winlock, Lewis, Washington

Preparer	Comments
Marcia Murray Holstrom	
marciaholstrom@gmail.com	

FAMILY NOTES

General: Orson and Catherine had a daughter, Catherine Lucretia Murray, who died on January 23, 1840, and the age of 4, according to the death record from Brandon, Vermont. Her birth date is not given on the death record. She is buried in "The Old One" cemetery according to the death record, signed by Winifred C. Jones, Assistant Town Clerk of Brandon, Vermont.

FATHER NOTES: Orson Smith MURRAY

Census (1830): Males under 5 years old: 2
Males 20-30: 1
Females 20-30: 1
Census (1850): Also in household with Murray name: Catherine, 45; Marsena M., 21; Charles B., 13; Rachel R., 11; Rosalinda, 9; Ichabod, 6. All born in Vermont.
Census (1860): On Census: 53 years old, born abt. 1807 in Vermont. Also in household: C. B. Murray, 23; Rachel R. Murray, 21; Rosa B. Murray, 19; Ichabod H. Murray, 16; and 5 Farm Workers.
Death (14 June 1885): Lebanon Gazette, 20 June 1885
Death of "Warren's Iconoclast."

Orson S. Murray, "Warren's Iconoclast," as he has repeatedly been termed, died at his home, ear Foster's, last Sunday evening, at the age of seventy-eight years. Ever since February he has been suffering with combined liver and stomach trouble, and it was this that finally ended the career of a man who, years ago, was one of the most noted anti-slavery men of the country.

Orson S. Murray was a native of Vermont. He was educated for the Baptist ministry, and he was an earnest, hard-working pastor for some years. Then, losing his church, he became the publisher of a Baptist paper of anti-slavery tendencies (the Telegraph), and in this enterprise he was aided by ex-President Arthur's father. While conducting the paper he worked into the strong, terse,forcible style that

Ahnentafel of Marcia Jean Murray

Generation 1

1. **Marcia Jean MURRAY**: born 24 Sep 1946 in Dayton, Montgomery Co., Ohio.

Generation 2

2. **Harold Oscar "Bub" MURRAY**: born 15 Nov 1910 in Xenia, Greene Co., Ohio; married 29 Jul 1944 in Spring Valley, Montgomery Co., Ohio; died 22 Feb 1963 in Dayton, Montgomery Co., Ohio.

3. **Glenna PIERCE**: born 24 Jan 1923 in Coolville, Troy Twp., Athens Co., Ohio; died 2 Jan 2005 in Defiance, Defiance Co., Ohio.

Generation 3

4. **Maruna Markworth (Ted) MURRAY**: born 6 Jan 1887 in Hamilton Twp., Warren Co., Ohio; married 12 Apr 1910 in Campbell County, Kentucky; died 29 Jan 1936 in Goes Station, Greene Co., Ohio.

5. **Grace Lenora BOLLMAN**: born 12 Dec 1893 in Hopewell, Bedford Co., Pennsylvania; died 10 Mar 1959 in Everett, Bedford Co., Pennsylvania.

6. **Carl Glen Edwin PIERCE**: born 26 Feb 1886 in Wirt Co., West Virginia; married 14 Feb 1907 in Wood Co., West Virginia; died 11 Nov 1979 in Mark Rest Center, McConnelsville, Morgan Co., Ohio.

7. **Loia Ellen MORRIS**: born 4 Aug 1884 in Odaville, Jackson Co., West Virginia; died 12 Feb 1955 in Parkersburg, Wood County, West Virginia.

Generation 4

8. **Leslie Carlos MURRAY**: born 6 Jan 1860 in Fosters, Warren Co., Ohio; married 3 Apr 1882; died 11 Feb 1940 in at home, 4128 North Avenue, Silverton, Hamilton Co., Ohio.

9. **Mary Catherine FREEZE**: born 11 Feb 1861 in Warren Co., Ohio; died 5 Dec 1928 in Hamilton Twp., Warren Co., Ohio.

10. **Charles Madison BOLLMAN**: born 15 Dec 1871 in Bedford Co., Pennsylvania; married 12 Apr 1891 in at J. W. Finks, Bedford Co., Pennsylvania; died 18 Sep 1960 in Bedford Co., Pennsylvania.

11. **Mary E FINK**: born 12 Jul 1873 in Bedford Co., Pennsylvania; died 7 Dec 1942 in Bedford Co., Pennsylvania.

12. **Alexander Henderson PIERCE**: born 22 Jun 1852 in Belmont Co., Ohio; married 7 Dec 1873 in Belmont Co., Ohio; died abt 1916 in Kanawha Co., West Virginia.

13. **Rebecca D. BROCK**: born 18 Jun 1853 in Belmont Co., Ohio; died 15 Jan 1921 in 616 Ann Street, Parkersburg, Wood Co., West Virginia.

14. **Charles K. MORRIS**: born Oct 1846; married 29 Mar 1874 in Jackson County, West Virginia.

15. **Eliza Jane BRITTON**: born Jun 1850 in Doddridge County, Virginia; died.

Generation 5

16. **Marsena Messer MURRAY**: born 12 Aug 1829 in Orwell, Vermont; married 4 Aug 1854 in Randolph, Vermont; died 10 Sep 1920 in Chattanooga, Hamilton Co., Tennessee.

17. **Emily P. PAINE**: born 10 Oct 1832 in Randolph, Vermont; died 24 Aug 1913 in Hamilton Township, Warren County, Ohio.

18. **William FREEZE**: born 3 Feb 1835 in Highland County, Ohio; married 22 Sep 1855 in Warren County, Ohio; died 25 Jul 1918 in National Military Home Hospital, Montgomery Co., Ohio.

19. **Mahalia SIGLER**: born Apr 1832 in Ohio; died 12 Jun 1913 in Warren County, Ohio.

20. **George Francis BOLLMAN**: born 18 Nov 1844 in Bedford Co, Pennsylvania; married 17 Mar 1870 in Hopewell Township, Bedford County, Pennsylvania; died 9 Mar 1929 in Nason Hospital, Roaring Spring, Blair Co, Pennsylvania.

21. **Elizabeth KELLY**: born 28 Dec 1844 in Hopewell, Bedford County, Pennsylvania; died 1933.

22. **John William FINK**: born 9 Dec 1847; married; died 24 Feb 1921.

23. **Lydia FLUKE**: born 1848; died 1933.

24. **William PIERCE**: born ca 1824 in Union Township, Belmont County, Ohio; married 16 Jul 1844 in Harrison, Ohio.

25. **Sarah Jane MANSFIELD**: born ca 1825 in Ohio.

26. **Robert BROCK**: born 13 Apr 1810 in Belmont Co, Ohio, United States; married 9 Mar 1831 in Stillwater Meeting House, Belmont County, Ohio; died 3 Oct 1855 in Belmont Co, Ohio, United States.

27. **Peninah DAWSON**: born 8 Mar 1812.

28. **Edwin MORRIS**: born 1824 in Ohio; married 28 May 1844 in Captina, Washington County, Ohio.

29. **Rachel HANSON**: born ca 1823 in Ohio.

30. **Gustavus S. BRITTON**: born abt 1818 in Monongalia Co., Virginia; married 14 Mar 1847 in Mount Morris, Pennsylvania; died 19 Mar 1904 in At home, Roane Co., West Virginia.

31. **Elizabeth MUSGRAVE**: born 27 Oct (?), 1826 in Monongalia Co., Virginia; died 15 Jun 1909 in at the old log cabin home place on the hill, Wirt Co., West Virginia.

Generation 6

32. **Orson Smith MURRAY**: born 23 Sep 1806 in Orwell, Addison, Vermont; married 2 Jun 1827; died 14 Jun 1885 in Warren Co, Ohio.

33. **Catherine Maria HIGGINS**: born 3 Jun 1805 in Benson, Rutland County, Vermont; died 18 May 1860 in Warren Co, Ohio.

34. **Albert Buckley PAINE**: born 18 Sep 1807 in Randolph, Vermont; married 19 May 1831 in Randolph, Vermont; died 1 May 1885 in Randolph, Vermont.

35. **Maria Lucy HALL**: born 6 Sep 1806 in Brookfield, Massachusetts; died 16 Nov 1853 in Vermont.

36. **John FREEZE Sr.**.

38. **Marcus SIGLER**: born abt 1795 in Virginia; married 1823 in Warren County, Ohio; died 23 Nov 1878 in Turtle Creek, Warren County, Ohio.

39. **Massie CHESTNUT**: born abt 1809 in Ohio.

40. **David Franklin BOLLMAN**: born 18 Dec 1820 in Snake Spring Township, Bedford County, Pennsylvania; died 8 Sep 1890 in at home, Hopewell, Bedford Co., Pennsylvania.

41. **Susanna FOREMAN**: born 1823; died 1855.

44. **James FINK**: born 13 Jan 1824; married; died 9 Mar 1872.

45. **Susannah FLUKE/FLUCK**.

46. **Henry Stover FLUKE**: married bef 1850; died 20 Apr 1893 in Bedford County, Pennsylvania.

47. **Mary A. RITCHEY**: born 1813; died 20 Mar 1893 in St. Paul's Cemetery, Yellow Creek, Bedford County, Pennsylvania.

52. **James BROCK**.

MOTHER NOTES: Catherine Maria HIGGINS
Birth (3 June 1805): Vermont birth record:
"Caty" Maria Higgins
Date of Birth: June 3, 1805
Mother: Caty Higgins
Father: Ichabod Higgins

Death (18 May 1860): The U.S. Federal Census Mortality Schedule shows her death in May of 1860. William Breed Murray's "Descendants of Jonathan Murray of East Guilford, Connecticut" shows 8 May. Her tombstone shows 18 May.

She died of "Bow Complaint" after 6 weeks.

Obituary, May 31, 1860: - At Yellow Springs, on the 18th inst., Mrs. Maria Murray, wife of O. S. Murray, of this county.

Headstone, Union Cemetery, Loveland, Ohio, established 1861. *Catherine, companion, Orsen S. Murray, died 5-18, 1860 in the fifty-fifth year of her age.*
General: From Ohio Biographical Sketches, 1876. The Biographical Encyclopaedia of Ohio of the Nineteenth Century. Written about Orson Smith Murray in his "seventieth year". "Mr. Murray married Catherine Maria Higgins, of the Baptist Society, in Orwell, where they both had grown up. They lived together thirty-three years, till her death in 1860. She was a woman of sterling qualities - of inherited and cultivated excellencies. They had nine children. Six - (Carlos Orson, Marsena Messer, Charles Burleigh, Rachel Robinson, Roselinda Bascom and Ichabod Higgins) - grew to maturity. All these, except Carlos, have married and are raising families of children.

NOTES

[1] Charles B. Murray, *Life Notes* (Cincinnati, OH, 1915): 17
[2] *Vermont Historical Gazetteer*, edited by Abby Maria Hemenway, Vol. I, 1867: 16.
[3] *Vermont Historical Gazetteer*, Vol. I: 73-74; *The Descendants of Jonathan Murray of East Guilford, Connecticut,* compiled by William B. Murray, 1956: 33.
[4] *U.S. Census, Vermont, 1810*.
[5] Ibid.
[6] Charles Morrissey, *Bicentennial History of Vermont* (New York: W.W. Norton, 1981): 107

---

[7] Abby Hemenway, *The History of Rutland County, Vermont* (White River Junction, VT, 1882): 499.

[8] Victor R. Rolando, "The Industrial Archaeology Study of Vermont: 1978-1993," *The Journal of Vermont Archaeology*, Vol. 1994: 143.

[9] *VHG*, Vol. 1: 74.

[10] *Vermont Gazetteer of 1849*: 95-96.

[11] C. B. Murray: 39.

[12] Moses Cheney, "Pioneer Abolitionist," *Vermont Watchman*, January 18, 1882.

[13] *The Biographical Encyclopedia of Ohio of the Nineteenth Century*. Cincinnati and Philadelphia: Galaxy Publishing Company, 1876; Wright was a college student in Vermont at the time

[14] Whitney Cross, *The Burned-over District: The Social and Intellectual History of Enthusiastic Religion in Western New York, 1800-1850* (New York: Harper & Row, 1950): 12.

[15] Charles Finney, *Oberlin Evangelist*, January 21, 1846: 11

[16] Bernard A. Weisberger, *They Gathered at the River* (Boston: Little, Brown & Co., 1958): 6

[17] Benjamin Brawley, "Lorenzo Dow," *The Journal of Negro History* 1, no. 3 (July 1916): 266

[18] "Lorenzo Dow," *North Star*, Danville, Vermont, May 12, 1834

[19] "Lorenzo Dow," *Charleston Daily Courier*, August 31.1820.

[20] "Lorenzo Dow," *Vermont Gazette*, January 21, 1823.

[21] Middlebury May 30, Vermont Journal (Windsor), June 5, 1820.

[22] *The Biographical Encyclopedia of Ohio of the Nineteenth Century*. Cincinnati And Philadelphia: Galaxy Publishing Company, 1876, 232; Charles B. Murray, "Death of Orson S. Murray," *Cincinnati Price Current* (from Valentine Nicholson Scrapbook, Indiana Historical Society).

[23] *Biographical Encyclopedia*: 232

[24] Ibid.

[25] Charles B. Murray, "Death of Orson S. Murray."

[26] https://tjrs.monticello.org/letter/1371

[27] Alice Dana Adams, *The Neglected Period of Anti-Slavery in America (1808-1831)* (Cambridge, MA: Radcliffe College, 1908): 199.

[28] "Forten Letter to Cuffe," http://www.pbs.org/wgbh/aia/part3/3h484.htm

[29] *First Annual Report of the New England Anti-Slavery Society* (Boston: Garrison and Knapp, 1833): 6

[30], Ibid, 36-39.

[31] "Why Abolition and Colonization Societies Cannot Coalesce," *The Liberator*, May 5, 1832.

[32] "To the Editor of the Vermont Telegraph," *Vermont Telegraph*, October 2, 1833.

[33] "Answer to 'C.W.'—No.1, " *Vermont Telegraph*, October 16, 1833.

[34] David Head, "Slave Smuggling by Foreign Privateers," *Journal of the Early Republic*, Fall 2013: 438; https://www.loc.gov/exhibits/african/afam002.html

[35] Head: 438.

[36] Oliver Johnson, *William Lloyd Garrison and His Times* (Boston: Houghton-Mifflin, 1881): 51-52

[37] Ibid: 26

[38] "Another Anti-Slavery Society," The Liberator, April 27, 1833.

[39] "The Colonization System," *Vermont Telegraph*, March 4, 1833

[40] https://westegg.com/inflation; "Agency in Vermont, *The Liberator,* May 4, 1833; John L. Myers, "The Beginnings of Antislavery Agencies in Vermont, 1832-1836," *Vermont History* (Summer 1968): 131.

[41] *Vermont Chronicle*, January 21, 1882.

[42] "For The Emancipator," *The Emancipator*, February 25, 1834

[43] "Abolition of Slavery," *Middlebury Argus*, November 4, 1833.

[44] *The Emancipator*, February 25, 1834

[45] Samuel J. May, *Some Recollections . . .* 82

[46] John Greenleaf Whittier, *The Writings of Whittier*, Vol. 7, "The Conflict with Slavery" (Boston: Houghton-Mifflin, 1892): 171-172

[47] Samuel J. May, *Some Recollections of Our Anti-Slavery Conflict* (Boston: Fields, Osgood & Co., 1869): 82

[48] "Letter from Orson S. Murray," *The Liberator*, December 18, 1863.

[49] Ibid: 81

[50] Whittier, "The Conflict with Slavery" : 176

[51] Ibid: 177

[52] May, *Some Recollections . . .* 86-88

[53] "Declaration of Sentiments," Preamble to the Constitution of the American Anti-Slavery Society (New York: American Anti-Slavery Society, 1835).

[54] "Proceedings of the Anti-Slavery Convention," New York, 1833; "Anti-Slavery Convention," *The Liberator*, December 21, 1833.

[55] May, *Some Recollections . . .* 96

[56] *Vermont Gazette*, December 31, 1833.

[57] "Outrage in Bennington," *The Liberator*, January 11, 1834.

[58] Whitney Cross, *The Burned-Over District* (Ithaca: Cornell University Press, 1950): 13.

[59] Emerson Klees, *The Crucible of Ferment*, Rochester: Friends of the Finger Lakes Press, 2001: 61-62.

[60] "Miller the Prophet," *St. Johnsbury Caledonian*, April, 27, 1841.

[61] Gordon: 29-33; "An Explanation of the 11th Chapter of Revelations," *Vermont Telegraph*, March 12, 1833.

[62] Sylvester Bliss, *Memoirs of William Miller* (Boston: Joshua V. Himes, 1853): 98

[63] Bliss: 98.

[64] "Personal Reign of Christ," *Vermont Telegraph*, October 30, 1832.

[65] "The Second and Personal Coming of Christ," *Vermont Telegraph*, November 6, 1832.

[66] "An explanation of the 11th Chapter of Revelation," *Vermont Telegraph*, March 12, 1833

[67] Clara Endicott Sears, *Days of Delusion* (Boston: Houghton-Mifflin, 1924): 41.

[68] Sears: 43.

[69] Ibid.

[70] "Splendid Meteor," *Vermont Courier*, November 15, 1833.

[71] Sears: 46.

[72] David L. Rowe, *Thunder and Trumpets* (School of Theology, Claremont CA: American Academy of Religion, 1983): 22

[73] "Mobocracy in Vermont," *The Liberator*, February 28, 1835

[74] 'Mobocracy in Vermont."

[75] "Pioneer Abolitionists," *Vermont Chronicle*, Jan 21, 1882.

[76] "Mobocracy in Vermont."

[77] "Pioneer Abolitionists."

[78] "Mobocracy in Vermont."

[79] *The Liberator*, October 18, 1834

[80] Wilbur Siebert, *Vermont's Anti-Slavery and Underground Railroad Record*, 1937: 26.

[81] "Vermont Anti-Slavery Convention," *The Liberator*, May 17, 1834.

[82] Susan Wyly-Jones, "The 1835 Anti-Abolition Meetings in the South," *Civil War History*, Vol XLVII: 295.

[83] "For the Free Press," *Middlebury Free Press*, May 5, 1835.

[84] "Annual Report of the American Anti-Slavery Society," New York: William S. Dorr, 1838.

[85] David Grimsted, *American Mobbing: 1828-1861* (New York: Oxford University Press, 1998): 4

[86] "Colored School at Canaan," *The Liberator,* September 5, 1835.

[87] Samuel J. May, *Some Recollections of Our Anti-Slavery Conflict* (Boston: Fields, Osgood & Co., 1869: 153

[88] May: 154

[89] May: 155

[90] Ibid.

[91] "Proceedings of the New York State Anti-Slavery Convention." Utica: *Standard and Democrat*, Oct. 1835: 48.

[92] [92] Alice H. Henderson, *The History of the New York State Anti-Slavery Society*, Diss. U. Michigan, 1963:61-62.

[93] Ibid: 63-64

[94] May, 163-165

[95] Octavius Brooks Frothingham, *Gerrit Smith: A Biography*. New York: G.P. Putnam's Sons, 1878: 165.

[96] Henderson, 65.

[97] Frothingham, 165.

[98] *Wiliam Lloyd Garrison: The Story of His Life Told By His Children*, Vol. 2, (Boston: Houghton-Mifflin, 1889): 4

[99] "The Boston Recorder Apologizing for Mobs," *The Liberator*, October 3, 1835.

[100] "Right and Wrong," Isaac Knapp: The Boston Female Anti-Slavery Society, 1836: 29; "Proceedings of the Case Against William Lloyd Garrison," reprinted from *Boston Atlas, Richmond Enquirer*, October 30, 1835.

[101] Oliver Johnson, *William Lloyd Garrison and His Times* (Boston: Houghton-Mifflin, 1881): 97

[102] "Right and Wrong"; Oliver Johnson: 133-136, 196-200. "Another Argument for Sir Robert Peel," *The Liberator*, October 24, 1835.

[103] "Responsibilities of an Editor," *Vermont Telegraph*, October 1, 1835.

[104] *Vermont Telegraph*, January 28, 1836.

[105] Josiah Morrow, "Further Recollections of a Radical, Social, and Religious Reformer of Warren County," *The Western Star*, April 9, 1914

[106] Steve Otfinoski, *Chester Arthur* (Tarrytown NY: Martin Cavendish Press., 2010): 14-15.

[107] Middlebury Free Press, May 5, 1835; "Vermont Telegraph," *The Liberator*, September 12, 1835.

[108] "Error of the Freedom Press," *Voice of Freedom*, August 12, 1847.

[109] "Agency in Vermont," *The Liberator,* May 4, 1833; Phone interview with Kevin P. Thornton, Brandon historian,
     April 1, 2022.

[110] Phone Interview with Thornton

[111] C.B. Murray:17; Orson S. Murray Deed Extracts, Brandon, Vermont Town Clerk's Office

[112] *Vermont Telegraph*, October 29, 1835.

[113] "Spirit of the Times—More Mobbing," Fort Ann, NY, November 19, 1834, reprinted *from Vermont Telegraph*, *The Liberato*r, January 1, 1836.

[114] Ibid.

[115] ibid.

[116] ibid.

[117] ibid.

[118] ibid.

[119] "Right and Wrong in Boston," *Boston Mercantile Journal* (Isaac Knapp: Boston, 1836): 62

[120] "The Baptist General Tract Society," *Vermont Telegraph*, January 7, 1836.

[121] See John R. McKivigan, *The War Against Pro-Slavery Religion* (Ithaca: Cornell University Press, 1984)

[122] "A Fugitive Slave," *Emancipator*, October 12, 1837: 94; Tom Calarco, *The Underground Railroad in the Adirondack Region* (Jefferson, NC: McFarland and Company, 2004): 52

[123] "The Spirit of Slavery," *Vermont Telegraph*, January 21, 1836.

[124] Ibid.

[125] ibid.

[126] Robert P. Ludlum, "The Anti-Slavery 'Gag Rule': History and Argument," *Journal of Negro History,* April 1941: 207

[127] Richard P. Kollen, "The House Gag Rule Debate," *OAH Magazine of History* , Summer, 1998: 55

[128] H. von Holst, *The Constitutional and Political History of the United States*, Vol. 2 (Chicago: Callaghan and Company, 1879): 245.

[129] William Birney, *James G. Birney and His Times*, New York: D. Appleton and Company, 1890: 240-248.

[130] "Anti-Abolition Riot in Cincinnati," *Vermont Telegraph*, August 18, 1838.

[131] Benjamin G. Merkel, "The Abolition Aspects of Missouri's Antislavery Controversy," *Missouri Historical Review*, April 1950: 239; Norman Dwight Harris, *History of Negro Slavery in Illinois and of the Slavery Agitation in that State* Diss. (University of Chicago, 1906): 68-73.

[132] "The St. Louis Observer," *Arkansas Times*, June 6, 1836.

[133] Ibid.

[134] Henry Tanner, *The Martyrdom of Lovejoy* (Chicago: Fergus Printing, 1881): 84-85.

[135] Owen Muelder, *Theodore Weld and the American Anti-Slavery Society* (Jefferson, NC: McFarland and Company, 2011): 58-59.

[136] "Report on Manual Labor Literary Institutions," *Vermont Telegraph*, Sept 28 through January 4, 1837.

[137] Norris F. Schneider, "Zanesville Rioters Attacked Putnam Conductors of the Underground Railroad," *The Zanesville News*, October 17, 1943, The Siebert Collection.

[138] "Letter from Theodore D. Weld, Jan. 26, 1836," *Vermont Telegraph*, April 28, 1836.

[139] John L. Meyers, "The Seventy," *Mid America: An Historical Review*, Vol. 1, 1966: 33-35;
Henry B. Stanton, *Random Recollections* (New York: Harper and Row, 1887): 56.

[140] "Letter from Mr. Weld, June 11, 1836," *The Liberator*, June 25, 1836.

[141] Myers: 43

[142] Ibid: 42

[143] "Well Done Burlington!" *Vermont Telegraph*, December 21, 1836.

[144] Ibid.

[145] "Revival in Ohio," *Vermont Telegraph*, January 31, 1838.

[146] Cross: 201-202.

[147] Footnote: Anne C. Loveland, "Evangelicalism and Immediate Emancipation in American Antislavery Thought," *Journal of Southern History*, May, 1966: 172.

[148] "Great Revival in Washington County, N.Y.," *Vermont Telegraph*, April 5, 1837.

[149] Ibid.

[150] "Prospectus—Volume X," Vermont Telegraph, September 23, 1837

[151] "Prospectus," September 23, 1837.

[152] Ibid.

[153] "Appeal of Clerical Abolitionists," "A Layman's Reply to a Clerical Appeal," *Vermont Telegraph*, October 4, 1837.

[154] "Reckless Definition of a Clerical Office, from *Friend of Man*," *Vermont Telegraph*, November 22, 1837.

[155] "Second Coming of Christ," *Vermont Telegraph*, October 25, 1837

[156] "Second Coming."

[157] "Brief Review," *Universalist Watchman*, January 7, 1837

[158] "Second Coming of Christ," *Vermont Telegraph*, December 27, 1837.

[159] "Second Coming of Christ," *Vermont Telegraph*, February 7, 1838

[160] "Second Coming of Christ," *Vermont Telegraph*, March 28, 1838.

[161] "War," *Vermont Telegraph,* February 11, 1836.

[162] "Lawfulness of War for Christians, Examined," *Vermont Telegraph*, November 2, 1836

[163] "The Herald of Peace," *Vermont Telegraph*, March 15, 1837

[164] Ibid.

[165] ibid.

[166] "The Object of Peace Societies Practicable," *Vermont Telegraph*, March 15, 1837

[167] "Constitution of the Vermont Peace Society," *Vermont Telegraph*, November 22, 1837.

[168] Rowland T. Robinson, "To the Editor of the Vermont Telegraph," Vermont Telegraph, August 30, 1837

[169] "Brooklyn, CT, August 11, 1837, Vermont Telegraph, August 30, 1837

[170] "War News," Vermont Telegraph, November 21, 1838.

[171] Fred Landon, "Canadian Negroes and the Rebellion of 1837," *Journal of Negro History*, 1922: 378.

[172] "The Editor of the New York Observer," *Vermont Telegraph*, October 31, 1838.

[173] "Anti-Slavery Society," *Vermont Chronicle,* March 21, 1838.

[174] "For the Vermont Telegraph," *Vermont Telegraph*, March 7, 1837.

[175] "Horse for Sale," *Vermont Telegraph*, April 12, 1837.

[176] 'Temperance," *Vermont Telegraph*, August 9, 1837

[177] "J. Holcomb's Address Concluded," Vermont *Telegraph*, August 16, 1837

[178] "Immediatism," *Vermont Telegraph*, May 9, 1838.

[179] "Influence Perverted," *Vermont Chronicle*, Sept 5, 1838; "For the Vermont Telegraph," *Vermont Telegraph*,
    September 26, 1838.

[180] "Patronage for the Telegraph," *Vermont Telegraph*, December 25,1839.

[181] "The Peace Declaration," *Vermont Telegraph*, October 10,1838

[182] "Truth is Great, and Will Prevail, *Vermont Telegraph*, March 15, 1837

[183] Hemenway, *Gazetteer*, Vol. 3: 435

[184] Ibid: 436

[185] "Hamilton Institution Again," *Vermont Telegraph,* April 3, 1837

[186] "A fugitive," *Vermont Telegraph*, April 11, 1838; The Address to The Slaves," *Vermont Telegraph*, March 30,
  1842.
[187] "Death of George G. Robinson," *The Enterprise and Vermonter*, November 9, 1894.
[188] Orson S. Murray to Rowland T. Robinson, Rokeby Collection, Nov. 21, 1875.
[189] "A Discussing People," *Vermont Telegraph,* August 30, 1837.
[190] "Praise for the Abolitionist Press," from the *Philanthropist,*" *Vermont Telegraph* January 4, 1837.
[191] "Resolutions," *Vermont Telegraph,* January 4, 1837.
[192] "Slave Labor Produce," *Vermont Telegraph,* January 4, 1837.
[193] "What the South Has Had," *People's Journal*, October 27, 1859.
[194] "Anti-Slavery," Rowland T. Robinson, *Vermont Telegraph*, January 25, 1837.
[195] "Vermont Anti-Slavery Society," *Vermont Telegraph*, March 1, 1837
[196] "Anti-Slavery Societies, *The Liberator*, August 4, 1837.
[197] "American Anti-Slavery Society," *Vermont Telegraph*, May 17, 1837
[198] "Further Proceedings of the American Anti-Slavery Society," *Vermont Telegraph*, May 24, 1837
[199] Ibid.
[200] Ibid.
[201] Ibid.
[202] Ibid.
[203] "Appeal of Clerical Abolitionists," *Vermont Telegraph*, October 4, 1837.
[204] See: John McKivigan, *The War Against Pro-slavery Religion* (Ithaca: Cornell University Press, 1974).
[205] *Manual of the Congregational Church in Union Village, Washington County, NY*. Albany: Munsell & Rowland, 1860: 9-10.
[206] Henry Tanner, *The Martyrdom of Lovejoy* (Chicago: Fergus Printing, 1881): 104.
[207] Tanner: 112.
[208] Tanner: 121.
[209] "Illinois is a Slave-Holding State"; "A number of gentlemen," *Alton Observer*, August 17, 1837.
[210] Tanner: 122.
[211] Tanner: 123-124.

[212] Norman Dwight Harris, *History of Negro Slavery in Illinois and of the Slavery Agitation in that State* Diss. (University of Chicago, 1906): 85-86.

[213] Joseph C. and Owen Lovejoy, *Memoir of Rev. Elijah P. Lovejoy*, New York: John S. Taylor, 1838: 252-256.

[214] Lovejoy: 277.

[215] Lovejoy: 280-281.

[216] Tanner 148-157; Lovejoy: 284-295.

[217] *"Owen Lovejoy: His Brother's Blood, Speeches and Writings, 1838-1864*, William and Jane Ann Moore, editors, (Champaign: University of Illinois Press, 2004): 24.

[218] Stephen B. Oates, *The Approaching Fury* (New York: HarperCollins, 1997): 172.

[219] "The Alton Murder," *Vermont Telegraph, December 6, 1837.*

[220] Murray to Rowland T. Robinson, Fosters Crossings, Ohio, November 21, 1875.

[221] *The Biographical Encyclopedia of Ohio of the Nineteenth Century* (Cincinnati and Philadelphia: Galaxy Publishing Company, 1876): 233

[222] *Vermont Telegraph*, January 11, April 19, June 14, July 12, December 27, 1837.

[223] "Letter from the Editor," *Vermont Telegraph*, April 29, 1838.

[224] Ibid.

[225] Ibid.

[226] Ibid.

[227] Ibid.

[228] Ibid.

[229] Ibid.

[230] Ibid.

[231] Ibid.

[232] "Mob Law Triumphant," *Vermont Telegraph*, May 23, 1838

[233] Ira V. Brown, "Racism and Sexism: The Case Against Pennsylvania Hall," *Phylon*, 2nd Qtr 1976: 127

[234] Brown: 128

[235] Brown: 129

[236] *History of Pennsylvania Hall Which Was Destroyed by a Mob* (Philadelphia: Merrihew and Gunn, 1838): 136, 143

[237] *History of Pennsylvania Hall*: 123

[238] *History of Pennsylvania Hall: 140*

[239] "Mob Law Triumphant."

[240] *History of Pennsylvania Hall: 140*

[241] Brown: 132

[242] Anna Davis Hallowell, *James and Lucretia Mott: Life and Letters* (Boston: Houghton-Mifflin, 1884): 128-129.

[243] "Postscript," reprinted from *Pennsylvania Freeman, Vermont Telegraph*, May 30, 1838.

[244] *Burning of Pennsylvania Hall*: 141.

[245] Brown, *Racism and Sexism*: 131

[246] "Pennsylvania Hall," *Philadelphia Inquirer*, June 15, 1838.

[247] "Attention Rangers," *Philadelphia Ledger*, March 26, 1842.

[248] "The Pro-Slavery Outrage," *Vermont Telegraph*, May 30, 1838.

[249] *Life Notes of Charles B. Murray*, Cincinnati, 1915: 37

[250] Ibid.

[251] "The Fugitive Safe," *Vermont Telegraph*, May 2, 1838.

[252] Oliver Johnson to Rowland T. Robinson, Jenner Township, Somerset County, PA, January 27, 1837, courtesy of   Rokeby Museum.

[253] Oliver Johnson to Rowland T. Robinson. Montpelier, VT, March 27, 1835.

[254] "Chittenden County, Vt.," *Friend of Man*, May 16, 1838

[255] "To the Editor of the Standard," Brandon, VT, *National Anti-Slavery Standard*, September 16, 1841.

[256] "A Touching Appeal," *Vermont Telegraph*, December 25, 1839.

[257] Ibid.

[258] "Such as you have, give," *Vermont Telegraph*, September 2, 1840; "Clothing for the Fugitives from Slavery," *Vermont Telegraph*, November 3, 1841

[259] "To the Address to the Slaves," *Vermont Telegraph*, April 13, 1842.

[260] "The Address To The Slaves," *Vermont Telegraph*, March 30, 1842.

[261] Rowland E. Robinson to Wilbur Siebert, Rokeby, VT, August 19, 1896.

[262] "Anti-Slavery Societies," *The Liberator,* August 4, 1837: 137 (47 of the 89 societies reported its member numbers that totaled 5957; there were no numbers reported for the remaining 42).

[263] See: Tom Calarco, The Truth About the Underground Railroad

[264] See: "Tom Calarco, The Fresh Air of Freedom," *Medium*: The Fresh Air of Freedom: Vermont's Disowned Underground Railroad | by Tom Calarco | Medium

[265] G.W. Sanborn to Wilbur Siebert, August 17, 1895; Aldis Brainerd to Wilbur Siebert, October 21, 1895

[266] Rowland E. Robinson to Wilbur Siebert, August 19, 1896.

[267] Letter from Chauncey Knapp to Mason Anthony. Montpelier, VT, August 20, 1838 (Vermont History Society).

[268] Rowland E. Robinson to Wilbur Siebert, August 19, 1896.

[269] *Green Mountain Freeman*, March 5, 1848; "Annual Report of the Albany Female A.S. Society," *Albany Patriot*, 5/10/1848.

[270] Owen Muelder, *Theodore Dwight Weld and the American Anti-Slavery Society*, McFarland and Company, Inc., 2011: 132-133.

[271] "August 19, 1839," *Vermont Telegraph*, August 21, 1840.

[272] *Vermont Telegraph,* August 21, 1839.

[273] "American and Foreign Bible Society," *The Vermont Telegraph*, September 4, 1839.

[274] Ibid.

[275] *The Code of Virginia* (Richmond: William F. Ritchie. 1849): 747.

[276] *Vermont Telegraph*, September 25, 1839

[277] "Died," *Vermont Telegraph*, January 29, 1840.

[278] Ibid.

[279] *Vermont Telegraph*, April 15, 1840.

[280] "The Rights of Women," *Vermont Telegraph*, August 5, 1840.

[281] Ibid.

[282] "The Rights of Women," *Vermont Telegraph*, November 11, 1840.

[283] Ibid.

[284] Oliver Johnson, *William Lloyd Garrison and His Times* (Boston: Houghton-Mifflin, 1882): 273.

[285] Collins: *Ibid*: 24

[286] "Annual Meeting of the American Anti-Slavery Society," *The Liberator*, May 17, 1839

[287] "Formation of the Massachusetts Abolition Society," Boston, 1839: 9

[288] Oliver Johnson, *William Lloyd Garrison and His Times* (Boston: Houghton-Mifflin, 1882): 271-285; Reinhard Johnson, *The Liberty Party, 1840-1848* (LSU Press, 2009): 5-21; John A. Collins, *Right and Wrong Amongst the Abolitionists in the United States* (Glasgow: Geo Gallie, 1840):12-40.

[289] Bertrand Wyatt-Brown, *Lewis Tappan and the Evangelical War Against Slavery* (Baton Rouge: LSU Press, 1969): 194-196.

[290] "The Albany Convention," *Vermont Telegraph*, April 22, 1840.

[291] "National Baptist Anti-Slavery Convention, *Vermont Telegraph*, May 6, 1840.

[292] Ibid.

[293] "Appeal to the Southern Baptists," *Vermont Telegraph*, May 27, 1840

[294] Oliver Johnson: 289.

[295] Dorothy Sterling, *Ahead of Her Time* (New York: W.W. Norton and Company, 1991): 104

296 Ibid.

297 Ibid: 105

298 "The Division in the Anti-Slavery Ranks," *Vermont Telegraph*, June 3, 1840.

299 Ibid.

300 "New England Anti-Slavery Convention," *Vermont Telegraph*, June 17 1840

301 "The Telegraph in Danger," *Vermont Telegraph*, January 25, 1837.

302 See McKivigan, *War Against Pro-Slavery Religion* (Ithaca: Cornell University Press, 1984).

303 "For the Free Press," *Middlebury Free Press*, February 17, 1835

304 "New England Anti-Slavery convention," Vermont Telegraph, June 16, 1836.

305 Ibid.

306 *Vermont Telegraph*, January 11, 1837.

307 "From the Friend of Man," *Vermont Telegraph*, January 25, 1837.

308 "News from Liberia, *Vermont Telegraph*, June 17, 1840.

309 Ibid.

310 "Non Resistance," *Vermont Telegraph*, June 24, 1840

311 "The Church and Slavery," *Vermont Telegraph*, August 12, 1840.

312 Geo. S. Brown, *Brown's Abridged Journal*, Troy, N.Y., 1849: 180-181

313 Geo. S. Brown: 181.

314 "Non Resistance," June 24,1840

315 Geo. S. Brown: 181.

316 "The Seventh Anniversary of the Vermont Anti-Slavery Society," *Vermont Telegraph*, January 20, 1841.

317 Ibid.

318 "Ultraism," *Vermont Telegraph*, June 16, 1841

319 "The Convention," *Vermont Telegraph*, October 6, 1841.

320 Ibid.

321 "Vermont Baptist Convention," *Vermont Telegraph*, October 20, 1841

322 "To the Baptist Churches of Vermont, "*Vermont Baptist Journal*, March 2, 1842

323 "Popular Religious Leaders and Reform," *Vermont Telegraph*, April 6, 1842.

324 "My Sabbath Practices," *Vermont Telegraph*, March 23, 1842

325 "Slavery As It Is," *Vermont Baptist Journal,* May 6, 1842.

326 "Slavery As It Is," *Vermont Telegraph,* May 25, 1842.

327 "Information," *Vermont Telegraph*, September 7, 1842; "From the Vermont Observer," "Remarks," *Vermont*

Telegraph, December 7, 1842.

[328] "Refuge of Oppression," The Liberator, October 21, 1842.

[329] John Mason Peck, _Forty years of pioneer life_ . . . (Philadelphia: American Baptist Publication Society, 1864): 276

[330] Rev. J.A. Smith, _Memoir of Rev. Nathaniel Colver_ (Boston: Lee and Shepard, 1873): 33.

[331] "Good Thoughts on Millerism," _Universalist Watchman,_ November 12, 1842.

[332] Sears: 117

[333] 54

[334] 57.

[335] 55-57

[336] Sylvester Bliss, _Memoirs of William Miller_ (Boston: Joshua Himes, 1853): 141

[337] Joshua V. Hines and Apollos Hale, _A Brief History of William Miller_ (Boston: Advent Christian Publication Society, 1915): 156.

[338] Sears: 133

[339] 91

[340] 110.

[341] "The Miller Camp Meeting at Newark--The Closing Scene," _New York Herald_, November 15.

[342] Ibid.

[343] Bliss: 327.

[344] "Synopsis of Miller's Views," _The Signs of the Times_, January 25, 1843; _Vermont Religious Observer_, January 10, 1843

[345] Sears: 86-90.

[346] "William Miller," _Burlington Weekly Press_, February 17, 1843

[347] "New Comet," _The Baltimore Sun,_ February 2, 1843.

[348] "The Noon-Day Comet," _Vermont Mercury_, March 3, 1843.

[349] Sylvester Bliss, _Memoirs of William Miller_, 228

[350] "Comet," _Rutland Weekly Herald_, March 28, 1843.

[351] Bliss: 228.

[352] Sears: 144.

[353] "The Second Advent," _Vermont Telegraph_, May 10, 1843

[354] "Various Views of the Telegraph," _Vermont Telegraph_, August 24, 1842.

[355] "My Late Tour," _Vermont Telegraph_, September 28, 1842

[356] Ibid.

[357] Ibid.

[358] "Sectarian Intolerance," _Vermont Telegraph_, October 5, 1842.

[359] Ibid.

[360] Ibid.

[361] "VT. Baptist Anti-Slavery Society," *Vermont Religious Observer*, November 1, 1842.

[362] "Vermont Observer – Imposition added to Fraud," *Vermont Telegraph*, November 23, 1842

[363] "For the Telegraph – Remarks," *Vermont Telegraph*, December 7, 1842

[364] "Tour on the East Side of the Mountain," *Vermont Telegraph*, December 21, 1842

[365] Ibid.

[366] Ibid.

[367] Ibid.

[368] "Editorial Correspondence," *Vermont Telegraph,* January 25, 1843.

[369] Ibid.

[370] "Eighth Anniversary of the Vermont Anti-Slavery Society," *Vermont Telegraph,* February 1, 1843.

[371] "Sanctuary Lynching," *Vermont Telegraph*, January 25, 1843.

[372] Ibid.

[373] "O.S. Murray in Whiting," *Vermont Religious Observer*, March 21, 1843; CB Murray: 39.

[374] Charles Burleigh to RT Robinson, Montpelier, March 11, 1843.

[375] "My Pecuniary Affairs," *Vermont Telegraph*, March 29, 1843

[376] Ibid.

[377] Ibid.

[378] Ibid.

[379] Ibid.

[380] Ibid.

[381] "Editorial Correspondence, *Vermont Telegraph*, May 24, 1843

[382] Ibid.

[383] Ibid.

[384] "Social Reform and Human Progress," *Vermont Telegraph*, February 8, 1843.

[385] "Universal Inquiry and Reform," *Vermont Telegraph*, May 24, 1843.

[386] Ibid.

[387] "Spirit of Western Abolitionists," *The National Anti-Slavery Standard*, May 18, 1843

[388] "At Home Again," *Vermont Telegraph*, September 6, 1843.

[389] "Error of the Freedom Press," *Voice of Freedom*, August 12, 1847

[390] Charles B. Murray, *Life Notes*: 19

[391] Kevin Thornton, Brandon, Vermont, to Tom Calarco, May 5, 2022.

[392] The Regenerator," *Vermont Telegraph*, June 28, 1843.

[393] "At Home Again," *Vermont Telegraph*, September 6, 1843.

[394] Charles B. Murray, *Life Notes* (Cincinnati Price Current, 1915): 19

[395] "Prospectus," *Regenerator*, January 1, 1844.

[396] "Reply to I. Newton Peirce," The Regenerator," April 25, 1848.

[397] "Orson S. Murray," *New York Tribune*, December 30, 1843.

[398] Charles B. Murray: 32.

[399] "Editorial Correspondence," *Vermont Telegraph*, August 30, 1843.

[400] "Orson S. Murray," *New York Tribune*, December 30, 1843; "The Regenerator," *New York Tribune*, January 4, 1844.

[401] "New York Tribune," *The Regenerator*, February 19, 1844

[402] *The Regenerator*, January 22, 1844.

[403] "Disorganizations," *The Regenerator*, April 29, 1844.

[404] "The Sabbath," *The Regenerator*, June 15, 1844

[405] "Report from Brother Wattles," *The Regenerator*, April 4, 1844.

[406] 'Diet—My Own Practice," *The Regenerator*, April !852.

[407] *The Regenerator*, March 4, April 8, May 25, June 8, 1844.

[408] "From all the evidence . . ." *The Regenerator*, June 8, 1844

[409] Charles B. Murray: 19

[410] John Humphrey Noyes, *American Socialisms* (Philadelphia: J. P. Lippincott, 1869): 316.

[411] Noyes: 320-321.

[412] Thomas D. Hamm, *God's Government Begun* (Bloomington, IN: Indiana University Press, 1995): 113.

[413] "Some Account of the Man Who Was Wiser than His Grandfather," *The Middlebury Galaxy, Middlebury Register*, September 25, 1844

[414] Emerson Klees, *The Crucible of Ferment* (Rochester: Cameo Press, 2001): 71

[415] "Terrible Gale," *Buffalo Daily Gazette,* October 21, 1844.

[416] "Orson S. Murray," *Vermont Union Whig*, November 7, 1844.

[417] "Orson S. Murray: Storm on the Lake," *Voice of Freedom*, Nov. 14, 1844; "Terrible Gale," *Buffalo Evening News*, Oct. 19, 1844; "The Gale—Further Particulars," *Buffalo Evening News,* October 21, 1844; *The Buffalo History Gazette,* https://www.buffalohistorygazette.net/2010/09/the-lake-erie-seiche-disaster-of-1844.html

[418] *Regenerator Extra*, January 1, 1845

[419] Papers of Valentine Nicholson, 1843-1844 (accessed at the Indiana History Center).

[420] Charles B. Murray: 17; Hamm: 113; Nicholson papers, 1843-1844.

[421] A.J. MacDonald, as quoted in John Humphrey Noyes, *American Socialisms* (Philadelphia: J. P. Lippincott, 1869): 314.

[422] *Ibid*: 315

[423] Valentine Nicholson, Indianapolis, to Wilbur Siebert, September 10, 1892.

[424] "Memoirs of Long Ago," J.F. Nicholson, *The Western Star,* December 10, 1885.

[425] Valentine Nicholson to daughter Libbie," Fountain City, Indiana, July 4, 1881 (Indiana Historical Society).

[426] "Economy and Industry in whom?" *The Regenerator*, January 1, 1845.

[427] "To the Friends of a Free Press," *The Regenerator*, January 1, 1845.

[428] *Ibid.*

[429] *Ibid.*

[430] *Ibid.*

[431] "I believe I can't Spare the Money"; "Economy and Industry – in whom?"; "A Dangerous Paper," *The Regenerator*, January 1, 1845.

[432] "Prospectus," *The Regenerator*, January 1, 1845.

[433] *Ibid.*

[434] *Ibid.*

[435] *Ibid*

[436] *Ibid.*

[437] "Introductory," *The Regenerator*, January 1, 1845.

[438] "Thoughts on Community," *The Regenerator*, J.R. Smith, March 25, 1844

[439] "The Products of the Soil," *The Regenerator*, April 15, 1844

[440] "Quite a Coincidence," *The Regenerator,* Apr. 14, 1845.

[441] "To the Friends of a Free Press," *The Regenerator*, Jan. 1, 1845.

[442] *Ibid.*

[443] *Ibid.*

[444] *History of Warren County, Ohio* (Beers: Chicago, 1882): 290.

[445] *Ibid.*

[446] *Ibid.*

[447] "The Regenerator," *The Regenerator*, April 14, 1845.

[448] John Noyes, *History of American Socialism*, (Philadelphia: J.P. Lippincott, 1870): 327

[449] Charles B. Murray, *Life Notes* (Cincinnati, OH: 1915): 20

[450] *Ibid*: 55

[451] "Receipts," *The Regenerator*, April 28, July 21, 1845.

[452] "A Philosophical Life—Or the Life of a Philosopher," Robert Cheyne, *The Regenerator*, August, 1849

[453] "Letter from Brother Walbridge," *The Regenerator*, January 25, 1846

[454] John Wattles letter, *The Regenerator*, April 14, 1845.

[455] "Indicatory," *The Regenerator,* August 4, 1845.

[456] "Fruit Hills," *The Regenerator*, John White, September 7, 1846

[457] "Fruit Hills," Joseph Gregory, Fruit Hills, *The Regenerator*, August 18, 1845

[458] "Further About Our Community Matters," *The Regenerator*, C.D. Lewis, Dayton, Ohio, July 1852

[459] *The Regenerator*, April 14, 1845.

[460] Orson S. Murray, *The Regenerator*, April 14, 1845.

[461] Joel P. Davis, Des Moines, Iowa, to Wilbur Siebert, August 28, September 10, 1892

[462] Henry T. Butterworth to Wilbur Siebert, June 9, 1892

[463] Robert W. Carroll, "An Underground Railway: Fugitive Slaves and the Butterworths," *Cincinnati Times-Star*, August 19, 1896.

[464] John Janney Interview, Wilbur Siebert, March 24, 1892.

[465] George Dakin, La Porte, Indiana to Wilbur Siebert, August 24, 1894.

[466] R.G. Corwin, Lebanon, to Wilbur Siebert, September 11, 1895.

[467] "Fruit Hills," *The Regenerator*, Joseph Gregory, August 18, 1845

[468] "Help Wanted for the Regenerator," *The Regenerator*, Oct 15, 29, 1846.

[469] "Died," *The Regenerator*, June 1, 1846.

[470] *Beer's History of Clinton County*, 1882: 266

[471] "Men and Other Animals," S. Whipple, Utica, NY, *The Regenerator*, November 16, 1846

[472] *Ibid.*

[473] Short Notice to Subscribers," *The Regenerator,* December 14, 1846.

[474] "I will make no apologies," *The Regenerator*, February 8, 1847.

[475] Fruit Hills," September 7, 1846.

[476] *Handbook of Hydropathy*, Heman Morgan, *The Regenerator*, April 15, 1844.

[477] "Lung Disease," *The Regenerator*, March 9, 1846.

[478] "Two Theories: Or the Infidel's Mistake," *New Republic*, September 13, 1862

[479] "Mr. Garrison," *The Regenerator,* January 25, 1847.

[480] "Extracts from a Letter," *The Regenerator*, February 22, 1847.

[481] "Letter from Thos E. Longshore, *Murray's Review*, October 1854

[482] "Letter from Henry Soffe," *The Regenerator*, July 27, 1846

[483] "Communication from Jacob Lybrand," *The Regenerator*, July 27, 1846.

[484] "Letter from Robert Cheyne," *The Regenerator*, November 16, 1846.

[485] "The Regenerator," comments to letter from I. Newton Peirce, *The Regenerator*, March 3, 1848.

[486] "Poetry," *The Regenerator*, March 22, 1847.

[487] "Animal Relations," *The Regenerator*, July 26, 1847.

[488] "Congenial Neighborhoods," *The Regenerator*, November 15, 1847

[489] "Connection with the Soil," *The Regenerator*, November 1, 1847

[490] "The City," *The Regenerator*, April 5, 1848

[491] "Extracts from a Letter," *The Regenerator*, April 5, 1848.

[492] Private Matters Made Public, *The Regenerator,* February 8, 1848

[493] The Green Mountain Gem, January 1, 1848

[494] "Godology—Idolatry," *The Regenerator*, September 15, 1848

[495] Josiah Morrow, *The Life and Speeches of Thomas Corwin* (Cincinnati: W.H. Anderson, 1896): 29

[496] "Law," *The Regenerator*, September 6, 1847, October 18, 1847; "Mind, *The Regenerator*, January 12, 1846.

[497] "Mind," *The Regenerator*, January 12, 1846

[498] "A Broken Arm," *The Regenerator*, September 20, 1847

[499] *The Regenerator*, October 18, 1847

[500] *Ibid.*

[501] Morrow: 89

[502] "Dues for the Regenerator, *The Regenerator*, February 15, 1849

[503] "Letter from Dr. Shew," *The Regenerator*, February 9, 1846

[504] "Obituary," *The Regenerator Extra*, May 20, 1849.

[505] "Dr. Charles Jewett," *The Regenerator*, April 1, 1849.

[506] *The Regenerator Extra*, May 20, 1849

[507] *Ibid.*

[508] *Ibid.*

[509] "Quaker Quiet. Refinement of Violence," *The Regenerator*, June 1, 1844.

[510] "Obituary," *The Regenerator*, December, 1849

[511] "Condolence," includes letter from John C. Ferguson, *The Regenerator*, June, 1849

[512] *Ibid.*

[513] *Ibid.*

[514] *Ibid.*

[515] "The Lamented Philosopher and Philanthropist," *The Regenerator Extra,* May 20, 1849

[516] Thomas MacKellar, Ph.D., *American Printer: A Manual of Typography* (Mackellar, Smith & Jordan, 1885): 127.

[517] Pennock Pusey, Eaton, Md, May 6, 1849, *The Regenerator*, June 1, 1849

[518] "A Philosophical Life—Or the Life of a Philosopher," Robert Cheyne, *The Regenerator*, September, 1849

[519] "The Lamented Philosopher . . ." May 20, 1849.

[520] *The Regenerator Extra*, May 20, 1849.

[521] *Ibid;* "A Philosophical Life . . ." September 1849.

[522] *The Regenerator Extra*, May 20, 1849.

[523] "Obituary," *The Regenerator*, December 1849

[524] *Ibid*.

[525] *Ibid*.

[526] *Ibid*.

[527] "Died," *The Regenerator*, March 15, 1849

[528] "Obituary," December 1849

[529] *Ibid*.

[530] "Communication from Christian Burghalder," *The Regenerator*, March 15, 1849

[531] "The Regenerator," *The Regenerator,* September 1849 (Murray states that an arrangement is being made with a printer to help with production but doesn't give his name. It may be Cheyne who listed his address as Fruit Hills in the next issue).

[532] Geneanet Family Tree, Ancestry.com

[533] "Spirits," *The Regenerator*, February 1850

[534] "James and Lucretia Mott," reprinted from *The Liberator*, *The Regenerator,* December 1849

[535] "The Liberator and Quackery," "John Conant and the Rev. Lawrence Conant," *The Regenerator*, March 1850; "The Jewish and Christian Religions," *The Regenerator*, December 1849

[536] "Bible Teaching—Bible Influence," *The Regenerator,* March 1850

[537] "Bible Teaching—Bible Influence," *The Regenerator,* April 1850

[538] *The Regenerator Extra,* June 1852.

[539] "The Consumption Of Dead Animals," *The Regenerator,* April 1850

[540] "Spirits and Their Doings in Western New York," *The Regenerator*, March 1850.

[541] *The Regenerator Extra*, June 1852.

[542] "Diet—My Own Practice," *The Regenerator*, April 1852

[543] "More About the Mysterious Noises," *The Regenerator*, July 1850.

[544] "The Mysterious Noises—otherwise Spiritual Knockings, *The Regenerator*, August 1850

[545] "Religion and Government," *The Regenerator*, September 1850

[546] 'Extracts from a Letter, To a Friend in Vermont," *The Regenerator*, March 1851.

[547] "Spiritual Manifestations," *The Regenerator,* May 1851.

[548] "Mysterious Communications," *The Regenerator*, February 1851

[549] "Mysterious Manifestations," *The Regenerator*, June 1851

[550] *Ibid.*

[551] "The Mysterious Manifestations—Extracts from a Letter," *The Regenerator*, August 1851

[552] *Ibid.*

[553] "The Rappings," *The Regenerator*, September 1851

[554] "Rainy Day Sketches," Marsena account of trip and mention of encounter with spirit of Carlos, *The Regenerator*, November 1851

[555] "Not a Rainy Day Sketch," *The Regenerator,"* January 1852

[556] "The Mysterious Manifestations—Extracts from Letters," *The Regenerator*, January 1852

[557] "Lights from the Spirit World," *The Regenerator*, April 1852

[558] "Spiritual Manifestations," *The Regenerator*, July 1852

[559] "Death of a Good Man," The Regenerator, April 1852

[560] "The Denouement," *The Regenerator Extra*, June 1852

[561] "Further About Community Matters," *The Regenerator,* July 1852

[562] "My Sickness," *The Regenerator*, December 1852

[563] "Orson S. Murray," *Middlebury Register, Green Mountain Herald, St. Albans Weekly Messenger,* February 2, 9, 17, 1853.

[564] "To My Friends," *The Regenerator,* January 1853.

[565] *Memoirs of the Miami Valley* (Chicago: Robert O. Law, 1919): 419-420

[566] *Vermont Journal*, May 4, 1855

[567] "Slavery," *Murray's Review,* June 1855

[568] "Cincinnati Anti-Slavery Convention," *Anti-Slavery Bugle*, May 5, 1855.

[569] "Slavery."

[570] "Cincinnati Anti-Slavery Convention."

[571] "Spiritual Manifestation," *The Regenerator,* March 1853, April 1853, "Table Turnings," September 1853; "Spiritualism," *Murray's Review*, November 1854, October 1855, December 1855, February 1856, "Doubts of Immortality by a Clergyman, "December 1855, "Mysterious Manifestations—Some Things in my own Experience," January 1856, "More Spiritualism," February 1856, "Spiritual Investigation," March 1856.

[572] "Mysterious Manifestations—Some Things in my own Experience," *Murray's Review*, January 1856

[573] "Vacation," *Murray's Review*, March 1856.

[574] *Life Notes*: 51

[575] "Johnny Appleseed," (Hovey's Magazine of Horticulture, Coshocton, Ohio, 1846), *The Regenerator*, September 21, 1846.

[576] *Life Notes*: 51, 299.

[577] *Western Star*, September 25, 1919

[578] "Small Potatoes for Planting," *The Regenerator*, October 1850

[579] *Life Notes*: 51

[580] "Large Trees in the State of New York," *The Regenerator*, August 1852.

[581] George Morris, "Woodman Spare that Tree," *The Regenerator*, February 1850.

[582] *Life Notes*: 51

[583] "Deaths," *The Western Star*, May 31, 1860.

[584] *Life Notes, 22*

[585] *Ibid*, 51.

[586] *Ibid*, 23.

[587] "The Infidels in Convention," *New York Daily Herald,* October 12, 1860.

[588] "The Struggle of the Hour," A Discourse Delivered at the Paine Celebration in Cincinnati by Orson S. Murray, January 29, 1861.

[589] "The Struggle of the Hour," *The Liberator,* April 19, 1861.

[590] "Be Not Deceived"—Be Not Mocked," *The Liberator*, May 31, 1861.

[591] Life Notes, 33-34.

[592] Lorenzo Sears, *Wendell Phillips, Orator and Agitator*, (New York: Doubleday, Page & Co, 1909): 234

[593] *Ibid.*

[594] "The Lecture of Wendell Phillips – the Disgraceful Mob Violence," *The Cincinnati Enquirer*, March 25, 1862

[595] *Ibid.*

[596] "Wendell Phillip's Lecture," *The Chicago Tribune*, March 27, 1862

[597] "The Lecture of Wendell Phillips."

[598] "The President Insults The People," *The Liberator*, July 25, 1862

[599] William Kashatus, *Just Over the Line*, (West Chester PA: Chester County Historical Society, 2002): 72-73

[600] James A. McGowan, *Station Master of the Underground Railroad* (Jefferson, NC: McFarland & Company, Inc., 2004): 127-128.

[601] David H. Goldfield, *The American Journey*. (New York: Pearson, 2011): 424–426

[602] Kashatus: 74

[603] "A Card," *The New Republic*, September 6, 1862

[604] "An Independent Marriage," *Monmouth Democrat*, November 6, 1862

[605] Conversation with Karen Dinsmore, Mason, Ohio.

[606] Robert C. Smedley, *History of the Underground Railroad in Chester and the Neighboring Counties of Pennsylvania* (Lancaster, PA, 1883, reprinted by Stackpole Books with an Introduction by Christopher Densmore, 2005).

[607] Kashatus, 60-61.

[608] Smedley: 264-265

[609] *Ibid*: 266, 269.

[610] *The Liberator*: "The President's Proclamation," January 23, 1863; "The Arch Traitors—The Betrayers and Murderers," February 27, 1863; "The Fugitive Slave Law," May 1, 1863; "The Fugitive Slave Law and the Republican Congress," July 31, 1863.

[611] "Letter from Orson S. Murray – Reminiscences — A Heretic Put on the Pillory and Properly Punished," *The Liberator*, December 18, 1863

[612] "Anniversary of the Third Decade of the American Anti-Slavery Society," Chicago Tribune, December 8, 1863; "Third Decade of the American Anti-Slavery Society. Celebration in Philadelphia," *National Anti-Slavery Standard,* December 9, 1863.

[613] "Anniversary of the Third Decade . . ."

[614] "Proceedings of the American Anti - Slavery Society, at Its Third Decade , Held In The City Of Philadelphia, Dec . 3d And 4th, 1863," American Anti-Slavery Society , New York, No. 48 Beekman Street, 1864: 22

[615] *Ibid*: 7

[616] John Greenleaf Whittier, "The Anti-Slavery Convention of 1833, The Atlantic Monthly, February, 1874: 168

[617] "Proceedings . . .": 40

[618] *Ibid*: 56

[619] *Ibid*: 118

[620] "Letter — A Heretic Put on the Pillory and Properly Punished."

[621] "The Anti-Slavery and the Future," The Buffalo Daily Republic, December 8, 1863; "William Lloyd Garrison," *Coshocton Democrat* (OH), December 9, 1863.

[622] "Decade Meeting Reminiscences," *The Liberator*, January 22, 1864.

[623] Beers, *History of Warren County, Ohio*, 1058

[624] "American Women's Emancipation Society," *Woodhull and Claflins Weekly*, December 27, 1873: 5-6.

[625] "Letter from Orson S. Murray, Fruit Hills, Ohio, to Rowland T. Robinson, Rokeby, Vermont, November 21, 1875.

[626] C.B Murray, *Notes*, 39

[627] "A Man Who Wrote His Own Funeral Address," *Cincinnati Enquirer*, June 18, 1885

[628] *Ibid.*

[629] "Orson S. Murray," *Lebanon Gazette,* June 24, 1885.

[630] "A Man Who Wrote His Own Funeral Address."

[631] *Ibid.*

[632] *Ibid.*

[633] *Ibid*

[634] "Another Landmark Gone," *Lebanon Gazette*, June 24, 1885

[635] *Ibid.*

[636] *Ibid*: 36

[637] "The Higher Law*," The Regenerator*, August 1851

[638] "Modern Cremation Should Replace Earth-Burial: An expose of the dangers caused by inhumation and an explanation of the superior merits of incineration upon new and scientific principles," compiled by Max Lew, 1885.

[639] The description of the cremation that follows is taken from the following publications: "Reduced to White Dust," *Elyria (Ohio) Weekly Republican*, July 16, 1885; "The Cremation of One of the Earliest Abolitionists," *Lancaster Intelligencer*, June 25, 1885; "An Atheist Cremated," *Lancaster Examiner*, June 24, 1885

[640] "Reduced to White Dust," *Elyria (Ohio) Weekly Republican*, July 16, 1885.